THE PLACE DE LA BASTILLE

Contents

Acknowledgements

I SHOULD LIKE to thank Glasgow University, and in particular the School of Modern Languages and Cultures, for granting me two periods of study leave, one in 2007 to research this book, the other in 2010 to write it, as well as financial support for several research visits to Paris. Staff in the Bibliothèque nationale de France, the Bibliothèque historique de la Ville de Paris, the Forum des images and the Bibliothèque du film were extremely helpful. Hugues Azérad, Philippe and Laurence Binet, Caecilia Pieri and Marion Schmid provided accommodation in Paris at different times. Members of the Francofil web-list offered valuable help with various queries. Lucille Cairns, Évelyne Cohen, Olivier Dortu, David Drake, Katie Durand, Éric Hazan, Eleonore Kofman and Joachim Pflieger were sources of (very different kinds of) help and support. Finally, Anthony Cond at Liverpool University Press was a most patient and user-friendly series editor.

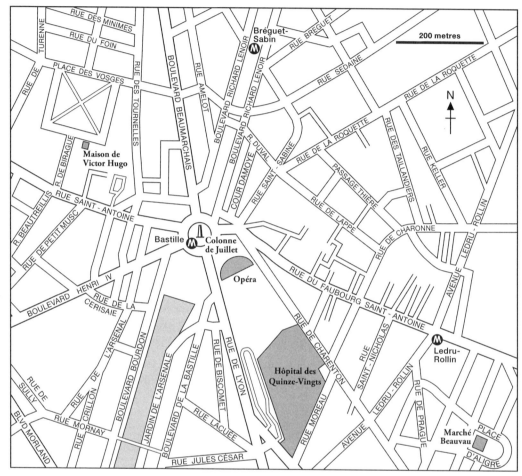

Map by Stephen Ramsay Cartography

Introduction:
The Place de la Bastille

A MONG the many Parisian squares which may form part of the visitor's itinerary, the Place de la Bastille is among the least inviting – a whirligig of fairly characterless late nineteenth-century buildings, with on one side the glassy modernity of the controversial 1989 opera house. At its centre stands the 1840 Colonne de Juillet, erected in homage to those killed in the 1830 July Revolution, many of whom are buried in its base. Lacking the monumental elegance of (in very different ways) the nearby Place des Vosges or the Place de la Concorde, or the imposing perspective down the Champs-Élysées afforded by the Place de l'Étoile (officially now known as the Place Charles de Gaulle), the Place de la Bastille is primarily seen as an interchange, the nexus of three Métro lines and a number of bus routes.

Why, then, choose this *quartier* for a detailed cultural and historical survey? Other areas have more evident appeal – artistically (Montparnasse), intellectually (Saint-Germain-des-Prés and the Latin Quarter), hedonistically (Montmartre) or architecturally (the Champs-Élysées). The adjacent Marais – successively a popular Jewish *quartier*, the showpiece of the renovation of Paris undertaken in the 1960s under André Malraux and the major gay area of the capital – would generally be thought to possess greater ethnocentric interest. Bastille, unlike the areas just mentioned, would not figure on most tourists' lists of *quartiers* to be visited. The exceptions to this rule will probably be, on the one hand culture vultures drawn not only by the Opéra but also by the nine art-cinema screens nearby, on the other history buffs eager to visit the spot where the eponymous fortress was stormed, and thus the French Revolution, and today's nation-state, began.

It is this interstice between contemporary culture and the dawn of modern history that is fundamental to an understanding of why the area nowadays known simply as 'Bastille' is among the most important of Paris's *lieux de mémoire* / 'sites of memory'. That term, coined by Pierre Nora, denotes a historical site perceived in its 'lien vécu au présent éternel' / 'lived

1

connection with the eternal present'. For Nora, 'Les lieux de mémoire naissent et vivent du sentiment qu'il n'y a pas de mémoire spontanée'[1] / 'Sites of memory stem from and are sustained by the sense that there is no such thing as spontaneous memory'. Memory, individual or collective, is often constructed by and dependent on the places with which it is associated, and the Bastille area is among the most significant of these in the whole of Paris.

That memory subtends the *quartier*'s evolution from bastion of working-class militancy to newly fashionable bourgeois-bohemian area, epitomized by the opening of the Opera two hundred years after the storming of the eponymous fortress. Paris as the world capital of the street riot and civic unrest is to be found here side-by-side with Paris as centre of entertainment and culture. The juxtaposition of the July column and the Opera (as in our jacket photograph) incarnates this dual and often overlapping identity more dramatically than anywhere else in the city, making the area an architectural palimpsest in which different, often divergent tendencies in the evolution of Paris as a whole may be read.

The *quartier* was known from its foundation in the late fifteenth century through to a hundred or so years ago as the Faubourg-Saint-Antoine, sometimes abbreviated when the context made it sufficiently clear to the Faubourg.* Its reputation was a fiery one, exemplified by Georges Touchard-Lafosse who in 1844 opined that the Faubourg and the main street running through it, the rue du Faubourg-Saint-Antoine, 'furent le cratère d'où s'échappa le plus souvent la lave révolutionnaire'[2] / 'were the crater from which the lava of revolution most often escaped'. That revolutionary enthusiasm, most strikingly visible in 1789, was also in evidence in 1830, when the restored Bourbon Monarchy was overthrown, in 1848 during the February revolution that deposed Louis-Philippe and again in the June Days and their unsuccessful attempt to radicalize the nascent Second Republic, and to a lesser extent in December 1851, with the protests against Louis-Napoloon's coup that was to make him Emperor. In the most tumultuous 'long half-century' of France's political history, the Faubourg played a consistently active part – the result in large measure of the skilled labourers, employed above all in the furniture and metal industries, that formed the backbone of its population. The great social historian of Paris Louis Chevalier describes the Faubourg as 'le lieu privilégié pour la célébration de ce culte que le peuple se rend surtout à lui-même'[3]

---

* I shall use Faubourg with a capital letter when I am referring specifically to the Faubourg Saint-Antoine, reserving the lower case for the term in a more general sense, though I shall respect original usage in quotations.

/ 'the privileged place for the celebration of the people's cult of itself' – an indication of how entrenched the folk-memory of the *quartier*'s reputation remained more than a century after its basis in historical reality had all but disappeared. There was euphoria, albeit short-lived, in 1936 with the election of the left-wing Popular Front government, but the events of May 1968 passed the area by, centring initially on the Left Bank and its student population and spreading to the more modern industrial working-class bastions in suburbs such as Boulogne-Billancourt and further afield from Paris, in cities such as Caen and Nantes. The Faubourg-Saint-Antoine as revolutionary epicentre had a short life in narrowly historical terms, but a rich and abiding one as a *lieu de mémoire*. It thus figures prominently in Éric Hazan's *L'Invention de Paris* (2002), a splendidly erudite and politically committed overview of the city's political and cultural history to which reference will often made in the pages that follow. Hazan begins his work with an evocation of the different *quartiers* or 'villages' that make up Paris and the 'précision chirurgicale' / 'surgical precision' that often characterizes their boundaries. His opening sentence gives as an example: 'Celui qui traverse le boulevard Beaumarchais et descend vers la rue Amelot sait qu'il quitte le Marais pour le quartier de la Bastille'[4] / 'Anybody who crosses the boulevard Beaumarchais and walks down the rue Amelot knows that he is leaving the Marais for the Bastille area.'

It is of course the Place de la Bastille that most vividly carries the charge of historical memory, named as it is after the fortress and prison whose destruction on 14 July 1789 triggered the French Revolution, and some of whose stones, uncovered in 1899 during the building of a Métro tunnel, are still to be found in a park near the station. The symbolic resonance of the Place along with its sheer size have made it, ever since the 1790 Fête de la Fédération celebrating the (short-lived) establishment of a constitutional monarchy in France, an important rallying-point for the Left. Daniel Stern – the pseudonym of Marie d'Agoult, a French countess who became the lover of Franz Liszt and the mother of Cosima, subsequently to marry Richard Wagner – declares in her *Histoire de la Révolution de 1848* that on 25 June of that year '[l]a place de la Bastille présente un spectacle effrayant. Une immense barricade crénelée en ceint tout un côté, depuis la rue Bourdon jusqu'à la rue Jean Beausire, et se relie aux barricades du grand boulevard et à celles // qui ferment l'entrée des rues de la Roquette, du Faubourg-Saint-Antoine et de Charenton. Le drapeau rouge flotte sur la colonne de Juillet'[5] I / 'The Place de la Bastille was a terrifying sight. A vast crenellated barricade lined one whole side of it, from the rue Bourdon to the rue Jean Beausire, and linked up with the barricades on the main boulevard and with those that closed off the rue de la Roquette, the rue du Faubourg Saint-Antoine and the rue de Charenton. The red flag flew from the July Column.' In torrential rain on the evening of 10 May 1981, the Place was filled with jubilant crowds celebrating the election of François Mitterrand as the Fifth Republic's first (and thus far only) Socialist President, and it has served as the focus for numerous less spectacular rallies and demonstrations over the years, most recently against the 2006 proposals to introduce new employment legislation which would have made it easier to dismiss workers under the age of twenty-six. Situated on the edge of the *quartier* which nowadays bears its name, the Place de la Bastille is nevertheless that area's mythical epicentre. This 'espace fonctionnel, sans qualités exceptionnelles'[6] / 'functional space, with no exceptional qualities' (Blais, *A la Bastille* (2004), p. 10) derives its resonance from the memory of the events to which it played host – not only those of 14 July, but the 1830 and 1848 revolts. Fernand Braudel, among the most prominent historians of the *Annales* school, drew the distinction between what he termed *histoire événementielle* – the 'names-and-dates' approach characteristic of most political history – and the *longue durée*, which concerns itself with longer-term underlying shifts and structures. Mapping this onto the area which is to be our object of study, it might be possible to say that the Place de la Bastille is the focus of its *histoire événementielle*, from 1789 through to 1981, while the surrounding area represents the *longue durée* – the social, economic and political subsoil from which many of the major events of history sprang.

The history of the *quartier* has been largely, as I have already suggested, a working-class one. The furniture industry, so long its backbone and still visible in a number of shops and businesses in and close to the rue du Faubourg-Saint-Antoine, was facilitated by the presence nearby of the Canal Saint-Martin, making it possible for barges to bring wood to the area. First Louis XI in 1471, then Louis XIV in 1657 enacted decrees to grant the *quartier* special status as a species of free-trade zone, exempt from regulation by the guilds that dominated manufacturing in France – an immense boost to its economic activity. Workers from the Auvergne area of central France were to form the mainstay of this, reinforced by incomers from eastern France and what is now Germany. Nowadays, like many another inner-city area, the *quartier* is a shadow of its erstwhile industrial self, though Chinese textile merchants have since the mid-1990s established an important presence around the rue Sedaine and the rue Popincourt. That deindustralization is perhaps figured in the effective replacement of its old name, the Faubourg, with its strong proletarian connotations, by that of Bastille, or even in Parisian slang by Bastoche. Michel Pinçon and Monique Pinçon-Charlot state that: 'Selon que l'on accorde plus d'importance au passé ouvrier ou au contraire au présent d'un quartier à la mode, on parlera de faubourg Saint-Antoine ou de Bastille'[7] / 'Depending on whether we are focusing more on the working-class past or on today's fashionable area, we shall use Faubourg Saint-Antoine or Bastille' – a usage that will frequently be followed in these pages. 'Faubourg' with a capital letter will often be used as shorthand for the Faubourg Saint-Antoine.

Even in its 'Faubourg' days, all work and no play was never the *quartier*'s watchword; the rue de Lappe was from the end of the nineteenth century renowned for its nightlife, often animated by Auvergnats whose bagpipe- and later accordion-playing provided dance music, and cafés, restaurants and night-clubs have always been an integral part of life in the area. Nowadays, it plays host to a number of artists' and architects' workshops, often occupying premises vacated by the furniture industry. The opening of the Opéra in 1989 catalysed immense changes in what had already begun to become a gentrified area; cafés, restaurants, night-clubs have proliferated, though the eastern end, centred on the Aligre market which has been there since 1781, bears more traces of the *quartier*'s working-class past, with a fairly high north African and increasingly Eastern European population. The opening of the Centre Georges Pompidou (popularly known as Beaubourg) in 1977 marked a major shift in the cultural focus of Paris away from the traditional purlieus of the Left Bank towards the Right Bank and the east – a move accentuated by the opening of the Parc de la Villette in 1982 and more recently by that of the Opéra. Bastille (a term I shall use without the definite article to obviate confusion with the fortress) has played a key part in that shift. The adjacent Marais area, to the west, may have more bourgeois cachet, but its denizens are still largely dependent on Bastille for their cultural consumption, as the aforementioned presence of nine cinema-screens to the Marais's two makes clear.

The *quartier*'s evolution from revolutionary proletarian hive through to radical-chic residential and cultural centre is scarcely a uniquely Parisian phenomenon. The London area of Clerkenwell, whose watch- and clockmakers were the equivalent of the Faubourg's furniture-makers and which still plays host to the Marx Memorial Library, has undergone a not dissimilar evolution. Paris in this respect is, as so often, an exemplar of the modern and post-modern city, to be studied at once in its typicality and in its distinctiveness.

The Bastille *quartier* spans two Paris *arrondissements*, the 11th and the 12th, divided by its main thoroughfare, the rue du Faubourg-Saint-Antoine, linking the Place de la Bastille and the Place de la Nation. Pinçon and

Pinçon-Charlot assert that '[l]es habitants vivent la rue du Faubourg-Saint-Antoine comme une véritable ligne de fracture'[8] / 'the inhabitants experience the rue du Faubourg-Saint-Antoine as a real dividing-line' between the bourgeois 11th to the north and the popular 12th to the south. Like all such divisions this is not a hard-and-fast one, but captures the relative heterogeneity that imparts to the *quartier* much of its flavour. It is bounded to the west by the Marais, to the east by Nation, to the south by the area around the Gare de Lyon and to the north by Popincourt and République. My peregrinations may periodically stray slightly outside these strict limits, especially in the direction of Popincourt which merges into Bastille rather than being clearly separated from it as is for instance the Marais – an errancy for which I unblushingly claim *droit de flâneur*. Off the main thoroughfare run the transversal arteries of the rue de la Roquette and the rue de Charonne along with the boulevard Richard-Lenoir, site of one of Paris's best street markets. Among the area's most distinctive features is its wealth of courtyards and passages, survivals of its manufacturing heyday which nowadays offer enticing terrain for that most Parisian of phenomena, the *flâneur*. This book ends with a suggested walking-tour of the area, which will draw upon the historical, literary, artistic, cinematic and anecdotal material to be presented in the intervening pages. Limits of time and space mean that I shall be confining myself by and large to work originally written and published in French, with a very few exceptions such as (in the opening chapter) Walter Benjamin's *Passagenwerk / The Arcades Project*. Before embarking upon this rich mass of detail, however, I want first to address the vast but inescapable question of what it means to write (about) the city in general and Paris in particular.

What does it mean to write about a city? The question has been posed by a variety of writers in the modern era, not only in a Parisian context. Julien Gracq's *La Forme d'une ville* – its title derived from Baudelaire, one of the most significant of writers about Paris – evokes the western French city of Nantes in a series of personal reminiscences, while in a totally different vein Italo Calvino describes a succession of *Invisible Cities* which are so many different avatars of that quintessentially poetic city Venice. More recently, and in more academic vein, Andrew Webber's *Berlin in the Twentieth Century: A Cultural Topography* constructs its city – for long Paris's only rival as the major metropolis of continental Europe – as 'a city of plural identifications, a territory of transition, of departures and arrivals both internal and external'.[9] The efflorescence of such writing stems perhaps in part from the fact that the very concept of what a city is has undergone immense changes in recent years. The idea of a long-standing built-up urban area with a clearly defined centre has been eroded by the rise of more scattered conurbations such as Los Angeles or Houston, to say nothing of 'purpose-built' capitals such as Canberra or Brasilia. With the onset of globalization came the concept of the 'world city' – a concept used by the sociologist Saskia Sassen to denote conurbations fundamental to the newly integrated world economy. New York, London and Tokyo were the examples chosen by Sassen, though Paris is frequently cited as the fourth-ranking example. The criteria for acceptance as a world city are primarily economic rather than historical or cultural; thus, Milan would rank higher than Rome despite the latter's greater artistic and historical importance. More generally, the European model of what constitutes a city has been undercut by the more diffuse structure and layout of Asian, American or Australasian metropolises. What might this mean for writing about Paris, in so many ways the archetypal European city, in the early twenty-first century?

The dominant view of Paris, certainly from an Anglophone standpoint, has been as *la ville lumière*, the City of Light – European if not global headquarters of style, architectural, sartorial, gastronomic, cinematic and conceptual. Henry James's American visitors (it would be demeaning to call them 'tourists') may serve as an example of how revered the city has been in this regard. Latterly, however, a different perspective has come to the fore – one in which Paris's vaunted architectural elegance appears, from Haussmann's boulevards through to Mitterrand's *grands projets*, as the concretisation of an overweeningly centralized and inflexible state, while its dominance of the worlds of fashion and cuisine has been seriously challenged by Italy and Spain respectively. Almost all the Parisian intellectual gurus of the post-war years are dead, their work widely if inaccurately seen as *passé* or even discredited; French feminism is viewed as having suffocated in an intellectual ghetto while having had precious little impact on what remains a resolutely sexist society; and the failure of that society to address adequately the concerns of its ethnic minorities, exemplified in the 2005 *banlieue* riots, testifies to the arthritic outmodedness of the Republican model. Paris, on this view, would figure on a continuum of twenty-first-century European cities closer to Rome – the Eternal City whose very eternity has enabled Milan to become the real nerve-centre of contemporary Italy – or the ossified elegance of Vienna than to those more dynamic capitals that are post-Franco Madrid, post-unification Berlin or even post-imperial, post-Big Bang London. Andrew Hussey in *Paris: The Secret History* says that 'one former lover of Paris, the English artist Ralph Rumney, has likened the city to "the corpse of an old whore"'[10] – a volte-face that distils in concentrated form the polarized responses the city has provoked over time.

What both narratives of Paris tend to do is to postulate it – the hagiographers would probably prefer to speak of 'her' – as for better or worse immutable, yet one of the city's most distinctive characteristics throughout its existence has been its role as fomenter of revolution and harbinger of upheaval. The horizon of political revolution – a fundamental factor in Parisian identity from the wars of religion through 1789 and until as recently as 1968 – now seems to put it mildly a distant one, but other, less seismic forms of social change have to a degree picked up where it left off. Paris's erstwhile ethnic homogeneity is a thing of the past, for it is now among the largest African cities in the world – something to which the Aligre market bears eloquent witness. Its reputation as erotic epicentre may have dwindled into the catchpenny squalor of Pigalle and the rue Saint-Denis, but the redevelopment of the Marais and the 1982 lowering of the male homosexual age of consent have between them given a new resonance to the term 'gay Paree'. Finally, the city has been significantly affected by decentralization – on a national scale, instanced by the setting-up of local and regional assemblies, but more importantly in this context internally, by way of the institution of an elected mayor, followed by the revival of the *conseil municipal*. For centuries cultural and intellectual power were the province of the Left Bank, particularly the 5th and 6th *arrondissements*, but they too have been more widely distributed, particularly towards the north and east of the city. The Bastille Opera is among the most significant recent examples of this.

My choice of the Bastille area as an object of study is thus in part motivated by shifts in the image, identity and topography of Paris which go some way towards undercutting the sharply opposed views of the city just evoked. At once deeply rooted in French history, which in its modern avatar began in the Place de la Bastille on 14 July 1789, and emblematic of the ethnic, economic and cultural developments that have characterized latter-day Paris, the *quartier* provides a prism through which changes in the city as a whole can be viewed and analysed.

Writing about Paris is a phenomenon almost as old as the city itself – which is to say one that goes back to the Middle Ages and beyond. The rapscallion fifteenth-century poet François Villon – the Bob Dylan *de ses jours?* – has a good claim to be the first major writer of the city, above all the Latin Quarter in which he conspicuously misspent his youth. The kind of writing that interests me in this chapter, however, is the attempt not just to evoke an urban setting but to survey and in a sense construct it, to produce a cultural topography – to address the question posed earlier of what it means to write (about) a city. Such writing seems, not coincidentally, to be coincident with the dawn of the modern* era, its two heralds Louis-Sébastien Mercier and Restif de la Bretonne. Mercier's *Le Tableau de Paris*, completed in 1788, is a comprehensive survey of the mores and ethnology of the pre-revolutionary city, conspicuously less dry than it may sound. 'Il y a de l'esprit dans les voitures; mais le génie est a pied'[11] / 'Wit rides in carriages, but genius goes on foot.' Mercier here foreshadows the nineteenth-century flâneur – the urban stroller who walks the streets of his, or sometimes her, city not to get from A to B but to savour its ambiance and perhaps even to experience its essence. It was in 1786 that Restif, social realist and erotic fantasist rolled into one, began writing *Les Nuits de Paris*, an at once prurient and scrupulously documented account of his scriptorial alter ego's nocturnal promenades, which end with suspicious frequency in the rescue of a damsel in distress. The Faubourg Saint-Antoine, we shall see, makes fleeting appearances in both works as an enticing but not entirely reputable area.

In a modern, or even post-modern, context the paradigmatic text for writing about Paris remains Walter Benjamin's *Passagenwerk*, rendered into English as *The Arcades Project*. When Benjamin committed suicide while attempting to escape the Nazis in 1940, this vast work – a study of the nineteenth-century Paris arcades, for him the most significant architectural form of their time – remained largely in note form; it was not to appear in book form until the 1980s. Partly because it was never completed, and partly because of Benjamin's fragmentary and citational mode of writing (often compared to a collage or palimpsest), *The Arcades Project* reads like a work oddly in advance of its time, a montage of observations, quotations – above all from Baudelaire, for Benjamin the quintessential writer of nineteenth-century Parisian modernity – and aphorisms to which keywords such as 'flâneur', 'fashion', 'decline' are periodically appended. The flâneur – sometimes a flâneuse – has since Baudelaire been fundamental to writing about Paris in particular, a world city before ever the term was coined and far more pedestrian-friendly because of its relatively small scale than New York or London. For Benjamin the flâneur 'was a figure of the modern artist-poet, a figure keenly aware of the bustle of modern life, an amateur detective and investigator of the city, but also a sign of the alienation of the city and of capitalism'.[12] Benjamin's own mode of writing is a form of flânerie in which the appended keywords often resemble cyberlinks, and in its amalgam of

* I use this term, here and hereinafter, in its generally accepted French sense to refer to the history of France since the 1789 Revolution.

order and aleatoriness provides a powerful pre-text for subsequent writing of and about the city. 'The street conducts the flâneur into a vanished time.'[13] Our exploration of the Bastille / Faubourg Saint-Antoine area, on an incomparably more modest scale, will among other things aim to do likewise.

For Benjamin that area is at once typical of the Paris of its time and separate from it. Typical, in that it bears the imprint of Napoleon III's prefect of the Paris area Baron Haussmann, who laid out the boulevard city we know today with a view at once to improving public hygiene and to making popular revolts of the kind that have characterized the city's history easier to contain and suppress ('Construction in the Faubourg Saint-Antoine: Boulevard Prince Eugène, Boulevard Mazas,* and Boulevard Richard Lenoir, as strategic axes').[14] Separate, and recalling the fact that the area lay on the very edge of Paris until the city's incorporation of outlying communes in 1860, in that as Benjamin says, quoting the revolutionary Austrian writer and journalist Sigmund Engländer:

> Two steps from the Place de la Bastille to the Faubourg Saint-Antoine, people still say, 'I am going to Paris'. ... This suburb has its own mores and customs, even its own language. The municipality has numbered the houses here, as in all other parts of Paris; but if you ask one of the inhabitants of this suburb for his address, he will always give you the name his house bears and not the cold, official number. ... This house is known by the name 'To the King of Siam', that by 'Star of Gold'; this house is called 'Court of the Two Sisters', and that one is called 'Name of Jesus'; others carry the name 'Basket of Flowers', or 'Saint Esprit', or 'Bel Air', or 'Hunting Box', or 'The Good Seed'. (Sigmund Engländer, *Geschichte des französischen Arbeiterassociationen* (Hamburg, 1864), vol. 3, p. 126.)[15]

The sheer anthropological strangeness of this extract would alone make its inclusion here worthwhile; but beyond that what is most striking is perhaps the stress it places on the Faubourg's liminality, its status as a place apart, in Paris but in some sense not altogether of it. Benjamin reminds us, this time drawing on Dubech and d'Espezel's *Histoire de Paris*, that the first Paris omnibus, on 30 January 1828, ran the length of the boulevards between the Bastille and Madeleine, linking one of the capital's most fashionable districts

---

* The first two boulevards are now known as the boulevard Voltaire and the boulevard Diderot respectively.

with one that was only just part of it. Linkages – topographical, historical and textual alike – are fundamental to *The Arcades Project*, which in its plurality and non-linearity has exercised an immense influence on subsequent writing of the city in general and Paris in particular.

The Arcades Project, while it draws extensively upon canonical French writing of the nineteenth century – Baudelaire, as already mentioned, but also Balzac and Hugo whose work evoking the Faubourg Saint-Antoine will be surveyed in a later chapter – also has important early twentieth-century pre-texts, some of which I shall now mention even though they may not make explicit allusion to the *quartier* because their effect on how Paris has been and can be written about has been considerable. The Surrealist Louis Aragon's 1926 *Le Paysan de Paris* prefigures, in far more florid and oneiric mode, Benjamin – who makes a number of allusions to it – in its first section, devoted to the passage de l'Opéra. Here Aragon speaks of 'le fleuve humain qui transporte journellement de la Bastille à la Madeleine d'incroyables flots de rêverie et de langueur' / 'the human river that each day transports from Bastille to Madeleine unbelievable tides of reverie and langour' – a river whose course may soon be diverted by the widening of the boulevard Haussmann, thereby modifying 'tout le cours des pensées d'un quartier, et peut-être d'un monde'[16] / 'the whole course of the thoughts of a *quartier*, and perhaps of a world'. The city not only bears the imprint of its inhabitants' deeds and thoughts, it moulds and conditions them – a *lieu de mémoire* in an active as well as a passive sense.

Aragon's text is quite deliberately echoed by the title of Léon-Paul Fargue's *Le Piéton de Paris* (1939), though the transition from peasant to pedestrian suggests a more familiar, less alien approach to the city. Both are founding texts of flânerie, Fargue's racier and more anecdotal than Aragon's, with which it nevertheless has a good deal in common. He begins with a reflection on his method of working which at first appears to cast doubt on the existence of any such thing:

> Ma méthode de travail? Quelle serait-elle? Et d'abord, en aurais-je une? Serais-je l'esclave de quelque discipline régulière? […] La question me redescend vers le rêve. Je comprends qu'elle contienne, pour *certains*, *certaines* doses d'intérêt.[17]

> My working method? What might that be? And first of all, do I even have such a thing? Am I the slave of any regular discipline? […] That question brings me back down to dreaming, which I understand may, for *some*, have *some* degree of interest.

The central importance of dreaming for the Surrealists in general and, in this context, Aragon in particular is at once evoked and, by way of the italicized words, elided here. Aragon chooses to explore areas of Paris off the beaten track – the passage de l'Opéra and the Buttes-Chaumont park, in what was then the working-class north-east of the city – while Fargue's wanderings encompass more widely explored areas such as Montmartre, Montparnasse and Bastille's westerly neighbour the Marais. In a series of short chapters – it might be more apposite to speak of vignettes – Fargue renders the distinctiveness of the *quartiers* he explores, their otherness to the Paris of which they nevertheless form part. Thus, beneath the multi-ethnic touristic display of Montparnasse he detects 'le vrai Montparnasse, celui qui n'a ni murs ni portes et qui, plus que tout autre sanctuaire, pourrait revendiquer le célèbre mot de passe [...] "Nul n'entre ici s'il n'est artiste"' [18] / 'the real Montparnasse, the one with neither walls nor gates which, more than any other sanctuary, could lay claim to the celebrated pass word: "No admission if you are not an artist".'

Fargue's city, like in different ways Aragon's and Benjamin's, is a hidden one, an edifice of dream (three of his chapters bear the title 'rêve' or 'rêverie'), whose mysterious essence eludes definition and can best be captured, albeit fleetingly, in the form of the passage – a key word in both its topographical and its metaphorical sense – from one fragment or shard of textuality to another.

This may all seem a very long way from the kind of cultural history being attempted here, but the method I am adopting – if indeed, like Fargue's, it can be described as such – will, given the vast amount of material and the finite space at my disposal, inevitably involve a good deal of movement, of passage, between types and genres of texts, from *longue durée* history to literary and cinematic reproduction by way of personal observation and interviews. 'Flânerie at a computer' might not be a bad description of what *The Arcades Project, avant la lettre* to be sure, undertakes, thereby exercising an immense influence over how cities, above all Paris, have been written about ever since.

Indissociable from such writing, and from any consideration of modern Paris, is the component of myth, analysed by Roger Caillois in his highly influential 1938 essay 'Paris, mythe moderne'. For Caillois 'le mythe [...] appartient par définition au *collectif*' [19] / 'The myth, by definition, partakes of the *collective*' and is thus a highly apposite category for thinking about that quintessential form of collectivity that is the modern-day city. Caillois dates the 'promotion du décor urbain à la qualité épique' [20] / 'promotion of the city's décor to epic quality' to the early nineteenth century, the period at which 'le monde des suprêmes grandeurs et des inexpiables déchéances, des violences et des mystères ininterrompus […] le monde où, à tout instant, tout est partout possible, ce monde n'est plus lointain, inaccessible et autonome; c'est celui où chacun passe sa vie'[21] / 'the world of supreme greatness and irreversible downfall, of continual violence and mystery […] the world where everything is always possible at any time, this world is no longer distant, inaccessible and autonomous; it is the world in which everybody spends their life.' This is the Parisian world of Hugo and Balzac, but also of the detective novel instanced by Caillois, and we shall see that Bastille has provided the setting for a number of twentieth-century *romans noirs*, or *polars* as the French call them.

This universe in which 'le mythique a partout contaminé le réel'[22] / 'the mythical has everywhere contaminated the real' bears striking similarities to the Parisian microcosms of Benjamin, Aragon and Fargue. Guy Debord, one of the most significant left-wing thinkers and activists of the 1960s and 1970s, and a founder of the Situationist International whose critique of society drew on variants of surrealism and Marxism, annexed this view of the city to explicitly political ends by way of his conception of the *dérive* (literally, 'drift'). The *dérive* sought to uncover the unrealized revolutionary potential of the everyday by way of a politicized avatar of flânerie:

> Entre les divers procédés situationnistes, la dérive se définit comme une technique du passage hâtif à travers des ambiances variées. Le concept de dérive est indissolublement lié à la reconnaissance d'effets de nature psychogéographique, et à l'affirmation d'un comportement ludique-constructif, ce qui l'oppose en tous points aux notions classiques de voyage et de promenade.[23]

> The *dérive*, one of a variety of Situationist procedures, can be defined as a technique of rapid passage through different types of atmosphere. The concept of *dérive* is indissolubly linked to the recognition of psycho-geographical effects, and to the affirmation of a kind of conduct that is at once playful and constructive, which makes it the polar opposite of the classic notions of the journey or the promenade.

'Sous les pavés, la plage' ('Beneath the cobblestones, the beach'): one of May 1968's most evocative – as well as least conventionally political – watchwords, echoes the dream-in-action that was the Situationist *dérive*. Flânerie in the Faubourg Saint-Antoine, if only because of the political connotations with which the *quartier* is saturated, is likely to partake in some measure of the *dérive*, however distant the revolutionary ambitions of that latter may now appear.

Flânerie, of a markedly less politicized kind than the *dérive*, is what might oxymoronically be described as a guiding principle in the work of authors such as Jacques Réda and Marc Augé. Réda tells us in *Les Ruines de Paris* that '[j]'ai découvert un square inattendu près de la rue Desnouettes. Ma première intention était d'aller au Sacré-Coeur, enfin je veux dire à Montmartre. Et puis me voilà parti du côté de la place Balard'[24] / 'I have discovered an unexpected garden-square near the rue Desnouettes. My original intention was to go to the Sacré-Coeur, or rather Montmartre. And then there I was setting off towards the place Balard' – a classic piece of flânerie, veering on a whim from the north of Paris to its 'deep south' in the 15th *arrondissement*. Augé's *Un ethnologue dans le métro* would seem at first glance to choose the most unpropitious terrain possible for the flâneur's avocation, for 'la caractère codé et ordonné de la circulation métropolitaine impose à tout un chacun des comportements dont il ne saurait s'écarter qu'en s'exposant à être sanctionné'[25] / 'the coded, ordered quality of travel on the Métro forces each of its users to behave in set ways or run the risk of disapproval or worse'. Yet even in this most task-orientated of urban environments, consecrated as it is to the quotidian business of getting from A to B, 'un même individu peut être alternativement considéré ou non comme un autre: il y a de l'autre dans le même, et la part de même qui est dans l'autre est indispensable à la définition du moi social, le seul qui soit formulable et pensable'[26] / 'the same individual can be considered as being or not being another: there is otherness in the same, and the part of the same that is in the other is indispensable to the definition of the social self, the only articulable, even thinkable kind.'

'There is otherness in the same': Augé's phrase could stand as an epigraph for the kind of writing-the-city with which I am concerned here. It thus seems appropriate here to invoke three works by Anglophone writers, foreigners at large in Paris, which in different ways have inflected my own view of what it means to write about the city in general and Paris in particular. Edmund White's *The Flâneur* gives its strolls through Paris an erotic slant by way of the author's searches for gay sexual pleasure, in the 1920s at least to be found on the rue de Lappe where 'large gay balls were frequently given',[27] and instances the Bastille as one of the four boundary points – along with the Arc de Triomphe, the Eiffel Tower and the Panthéon – of 'the classic Paris'.[28] Bastille figures both topographically and culturally as liminal area in a text whose succinctness acts as a counterweight to its romanticism and which shows that even after the decades of mass tourism Paris remains a magnificently secret city. Michael Sheringham in *Everyday Life:*

Theories and Practices from Surrealism to the Present (whose cover shows the rue de la Roquette) offers a genealogy, going back to Benjamin and beyond, for the intense interest shown in the everyday since the 1980s. The explorer of the everyday is for Sheringham, following Jean-Didier Urbain, a 'proximate ethnographer: someone who makes the familiar strange by pretending he is a stranger to it'.[29] Sometimes such pretence is unnecessary, as Sheringham illustrates when he recounts the difficulty that quintessentially Left Bank denizen the novelist Georges Perec encountered when asked to participate in an architectural research study of part of the 11th *arrondissement*, not far from Bastille ('On the first of his two sorties the place seemed impenetrable: he didn't "see" anything').[30] The everyday, paradoxically considering its *a priori* evanescent quality, partakes of the *longue durée*, with its foregrounding of the seemingly non-eventful, rather than of the *histoire événementielle* with which it is nevertheless deeply imbricated. The everyday necessarily forms part of any attempt to write (about) a *quartier*, so redolent is the term itself of the comings and goings of daily life. Finally, Andrew Hussey's magisterial – the wrong word for a systematically irreverent work, but precisely because of that an irresistible one – *Paris: The Secret History* recounts the, or better a, history of Paris as 'a carnival of light and terror',[31] a *ville lumière* of a very different kind from that beloved by Paris-by-night tourists. In Hussey's account – itself influenced by Peter Ackroyd's *London: The Biography* – *histoire événementielle* and the *longue durée* flow into and out of each other, yielding a polymorphous view of, among other things, 'the city where, after centuries of bloody conflict, the people's revolution was invented'[32] cheek-by-jowl with 'the biggest African city in the world'.[33] These two Parises, as the page references make clear, bookend Hussey's history, and both have evident relevance to the Bastille / Faubourg Saint-Antoine *quartier*.

The 'terror' and 'bloody conflict' to which Hussey refers do not exactly loom large in most contemporary visitors' view of Paris, yet they form an abiding part of the city's history, and even more so its mythology. Louis Chevalier's *Classes laborieuses et classes dangereuses* traces the development of this view in the first half of the nineteenth century, a period characterized by 'la marque du crime sur l'ensemble du paysage urbain'[34] / 'the mark of crime on the whole urban landscape'. That nascent industrial working class which had been in the forefront of the 1789 Revolution appears in nineteenth-century history, journalism and literature as potentially sinister and threatening. Key authors here are Victor Hugo, whose *Les Misérables* will occupy an important place in Chapter Three, and Eugène Sue, author of *Les Mystères de*

Paris which appeared in serial form in 1842–43. Sue's hero, Rodolphe, is a nobleman who penetrates the lower orders – what Marx and Engels were at the same time calling the lumpenproletariat – in disguise to understand their problems and right the injustices they suffer. *Les Mystères de Paris* was wildly popular when it was published, readers even writing to the author to demand (successfully) that he reinstate a character who had been written out of the dizzyingly implausible narrative. Much as was to happen later, with the gangster / private-eye novel or the *film noir*, aficionados of Sue were doubtless attracted by the prospect of 'vicarious participation in a turbulent saturnalia of lawlessness and transgression'.[35]

This view, in more light-hearted fashion, is exemplified in Claude Dubois's *La Bastoche: bal-musette, plaisir et crime, 1750–1939*. Dubois gives a racy account of this aspect of the *quartier*, epitomized by the nickname 'Bastoche', which became particularly popular during the Belle Époque, between 1871 and 1914, thanks to a song 'A la Bastoche' by the cabaret artist Aristide Bruant. Bruant sings of a young inhabitant of the area who 'n'faisait pas sa société / Du génie de la liberté / I'n'était pas républicain' ('didn't hang out with the genius of freedom, and was no republican'),* and meets his nemesis robbing a bus-driver on a day when he has had nothing to eat. The Faubourg Saint-Antoine – along with its opposite number the Faubourg Saint-Marceau, also known as Saint-Marcel, on the left bank – was for a very long time the poorest area of Paris, so that its reputation was by definition not an entirely savoury one. Pierre-Joseph-Spiridion Dufey, in his 1821 *Mémorial d'un Parisien*, may purvey a somewhat sanitized view of the area when he writes that '[t]out y annonce le calme heureux de l'industrieuse médiocrité: moeurs regulières, amour du travail et de la paix, vêtements simples et propres, union dans les ménages'[36] / 'Everything there speaks of calm, happy, industrious mediocrity: conventional morality, a love of peaceful work, simple but clean clothing, unified households', but the political volatility of the *quartier* is illustrated by Chevalier's assertion that '[r]edouté, surveillé de près, le faubourg Saint-Antoine est pourvu de patrouilles et de soupes populaires'[37] / 'feared and under close surveillance, the faubourg Saint-Antoine was equipped with police patrols and soup kitchens' – the latter perhaps stemming from the same altruistic motives that were to inspire Sue's Rodolphe. Auguste Luchet encapsulates the contradictory – or complementary – qualities of the area in saying that its inhabitants were 'la population la plus laborieuse, la plus robuste, mais aussi la plus turbulente et la plus terrible quand elle est excitée'[38] / 'the hardest-working and most robust, but also the most turbulent and the

---

* The 'génie de la liberté' refers to the statue atop the Bastille column.

most terrifying when their blood was up'. The industrial expansion of the time, with its concomitant over-population, and the preponderance of skilled workers between them do much to account for this seemingly contradictory perception of the *quartier*. The Faubourg Saint-Antoine in this respect stands as a microcosm of how the urban masses of Paris were widely perceived and represented. For the historians Jean-Louis Robert and Danielle Tartakowsky:

> Le peuple de Paris, c'est donc d'abord le faubourg. En 1830, c'était d'abord le faubourg Saint-Antoine. Sans exagérer les choses, on pourrait dire que de la fin du dix-neuvième siècle et du début du vingtième siècle ce fut Belleville, puis au vingtième siècle, autre construction politique, Saint-Denis et la banlieue rouge. Mais la mémoire des lieux ne s'effaçant pas de la Ville-capitale, les faubourgs courent toujours de la République à la Bastille, de la Bastille à la Nation, de la Nation à Belleville, de Belleville à Saint-Denis ...[39]

> The people of Paris means first and foremost the faubourg. In 1830, that meant first of all the Faubourg Saint-Antoine. Without any exaggeration we can say that from the end of the nineteenth and beginning of the twentieth century it was Belleville, then during the twentieth century another political construction, Saint-Denis and the *banlieue rouge*.* But since the capital city has not lost its local memories, the faubourgs are still alive and kicking, from République to Bastille, from Bastille to Nation, from Nation to Belleville, from Belleville to Saint-Denis ...

This emphasizes the changing morphology of Paris and its region – one of the major narrative strands in what follows – and the manner in which different areas, progressively further from the centre, have successively embodied something like an essence of the faubourg† as potential hotbed of social and political upheaval – the place where the *classes laborieuses* have been liable to become *classes dangereuses* at moments of crisis.‡

---

* This expression refers to the working-class suburbs immediately outside Paris which have a long left-wing, especially Communist, tradition, and of which Saint-Denis, to the north, is the archetype.

† I use lower case here to differentiate the faubourg as type of urban space from the Faubourg Saint-Antoine.

‡ I shall hereinafter use these terms in the original French, so closely connected are they with the Paris about which I shall be writing.

The danger they posed, however, was not solely a political one; criminality formed an important part of it. For Chevalier, Mercier and Restif – here as often the 'conjoined twins' of early writing about Paris – foreshadow the perception of the urban masses as potentially dangerous. I say 'potentially' because in Mercier at least criminality is a marginal phenomenon; what he evokes is 'un Paris malsain, brutal, habité dans ses faubourgs par une population primitive, mais non pas un Paris menacé par le crime et hanté par la peur; encombré de malheureux, mais non de criminels'[40] / 'an unhealthy and brutal Paris the population of whose faubourgs is primitive, but not a Paris threatened by crime and haunted by fear; a city burdened with unfortunates but not with criminals'. By the time *Les Misérables* was published, seventy-four years later, the boundary between the 'malheureux' and the 'criminels' had become eroded – something perhaps suggested by the work's very title, encompassing as it does the materially and the morally wretched. This forms part of what Karlheinz Stierle has called 'le sublime de la ville' / 'the sublime aspect of the city' – 'sublime' here to be understood in a Kantian sense as an amalgam of delight and fear – which came to the fore 'dans le Paris des années 1830 et 1840, époque où la ville semblait donner à l'esprit du temps une forme lisible'[41] / 'in the Paris of the 1830s and 1840s, a period at which the city seemed to give visible form to the *Zeitgeist*'.

That Paris may be no more, but its representations abide, and with them the notion that there is an intimate connection between the city and the different *Zeitgeists* through which it passes. 'As the familiar becomes unfamiliar, the new and old meanings of buildings, roads, street signs, squares and open spaces are revealed.'[42] That might serve as a working definition of the common thread of the otherwise highly divergent readings and writings of Paris, and the modern city in general, I have, with what seems almost insulting brevity, alluded to here. What I am attempting is thus a simultaneous work of familiarization and defamiliarization, sketching a view of how 'my' *quartier* came to be what it is today through its representations in an intimidatingly wide range of texts. My approach will be a deliberately if not defiantly eclectic one, bringing together canonical literature, works of political, social and cultural history, autobiography, journalism, films, paintings, strip cartoons and any other textual reproductions that appear relevant. The inscription of place rather than period or genre as the prime focus of my work owes much – paradoxically it might seem for a project dealing with the epicentre of mainland France – to post-colonialism and

Francophone studies. These areas have brought into the hitherto *hexagonal** domain of French studies texts from other French-speaking communities, from Quebec to Polynesia by way of the Maghreb and even Walloon Belgium, and in so doing loosened the grip of a France itself dominated by Paris. That enterprise of decentring informs, in however indirect a way, my choice to write about Bastille / Faubourg Saint-Antoine rather than a more geographically and culturally central area such as the Marais or the Latin Quarter. More ethnically heterogeneous than these *quartiers*, more socially mutable too, more liminal in every sense for all its current gentrified reality, the area, as well as being of great interest in its own right, may serve as well as any other as a prism through which changes in Paris, and hence in France as a microcosm of Europe, can be refracted.

Let's see.

---

* This epithet, derived from the territory's supposedly hexagonal shape, is a popular term for mainland France.

Chapter One

'What's that poor creature doing here?': the area and the fortress before the Revolution of 1789

THE TWO BUILDINGS that gave the *quartier* its names represented, unsurprisingly, the two major repositories of power in pre-modern France: the (Roman Catholic) Church and the State. The area was, as its neighbour the Marais had been until cleared by the Knights Templar in the eleventh century, for long a marshy wasteland, traversed by an old Roman road leading eastwards out of the city. It was in 1198 that the Crusades preacher Foulques de Neuilly established a residence for repentant prostitutes on the site of what is now the Hôpital Saint-Antoine, at 184 rue du Faubourg-Saint-Antoine. This became a Cistercian abbey in 1204, whose abbess bore the title 'La Dame du Faubourg'. In 1229 Louis IX bestowed upon it the title of Abbaye Royale, which was to foster considerable economic activity in the area; the marshes were drained, and the closeness of the Seine facilitated the arrival by water of building materials, including the wood which was to form the basis of the furniture industry. Louis VI's son and heir, Philippe, had been killed in 1131 when his horse was startled by a stray pig, since when pigs had been banned from the streets of Paris. Louis XI instituted an exemption from this prohibition for the abbey's pigs on condition that they wore a bell marked with a cross – an illustration of the prestige the monastery was beginning to enjoy, and a privilege which lingered on in the form of the gingerbread pigs it produced in memory of its patron saint's largely honey-based diet in the wilderness. These were characteristic snacks sold at the local fair, the Foire du Trône – in the eighteenth century held near the abbey, but moving to the Place de la Nation in 1841 – though by all accounts they tasted execrable.

With the privileges conferred upon the area by first Louis XI, then Louis XIV, workmen flocked there, encouraged by the absence of taxation, and the furniture industry expanded substantially. Market-gardening was also significant in the early economic activity of the area, though obviously driven out by industrialization. The importance of the Abbaye for the surrounding area is clearly demonstrated in *Les Dames du faubourg* (1984), by Jean Diwo, who took up writing historical novels on his retirement from *Paris-Match*, for which he had long worked as a journalist. *Les Dames du faubourg* is the first of, and gives its name to, a trilogy of novels (the others are *Le Lit d'acajou / The Mahogany Bed* – and *Le Génie de la Bastille / The Genius of the Bastille*, in reference to the statue of the Genius of Liberty that crowns the column). The first novel begins just after Louis XI has signed the decree giving the Faubourg fiscal independence – 'l'acte de naissance du faubourg Saint-Antoine, patrie du meuble, royaume du bois, État souverain de la scie et du rabot'[1] / 'the birth certificate of the Faubourg Saint-Antoine, the homeland of furniture, the kingdom of wood, the sovereign state of the saw and the plane'. The somewhat heavy tone of the phrase just quoted is not untypical of the novel-cycle as a whole, lightened perhaps by the fact that Diwo's nuns occasionally adopt a fairly latitudinarian attitude towards their vows. Before the end of the first chapter the abbess – the 'Dame du Faubourg' herself – is in the grip of a culpable attraction for the young carpenter Jean Cottion, newly arrived from Lyon to become 'le premier ouvrier libre de Saint-Antoine'[2] / 'the first free workman of Saint-Antoine'. This she sublimates by way of a liaison she engineers between Jean and her cousin Élisabeth, boarding in the monastery while waiting to be married off to a wealthy older man. The young couple's 'voyage au "royaume des choses charnelles"'[3] / 'journey to the "kingdom of carnal matters"' is but the first of a number of illicit love-affairs with which the text is spiced.

To reduce *Les Dames du faubourg* to what used to be known as a 'bodice-ripper' would, however, be to do the work, for all its middlebrow stylistic longueurs, an injustice. Diwo's novel-cycle is of interest because of its interweaving of three types of story: the family saga, the historical novel and a narrative of technical progress. The lives of Cottion's descendants form the backbone of *Les Dames du faubourg*, which makes copious allusion to historical events, often featuring real-life characters such as the libertine François I who 'ne faisait rien pour endiguer un courant de débauche qui scandalisait beaucoup le population ouvrière puritaine de Saint-Antoine'[4] / 'made no attempt to stem a tide of debauchery which greatly scandalized the puritanical working-class population of Saint-Antoine' or later Louis XIV's cousin the Duchess of Montpensier, known as La Grande Mademoiselle. In 1652, during the Fronde – the effective civil war which during Louis's childhood pitted partisans of the Vicomte de Turenne against those of the Duc de Condé – there was a pitched battle in the Faubourg between the two sides, in which La Grande Mademoiselle – the cousin of Condé, whom she supposedly dreamt of marrying – opened the gates under her control and turned the Bastille cannon against Turenne's royalists. Diwo's fictionalized account has the chief minister, Cardinal Mazarin, saying to the king as a cannonball landed at their feet: "'Ce boulet a tué le mari de Mademoiselle!'" [5] / "'That cannonball has killed Mademoiselle's husband!'" – and indeed La Grande Mademoiselle was exiled from court for five years and was to marry only secretly and belatedly.

As important as the personal or political histories in the work, however, is the closely documented attention it pays to developments in the furniture industry. Thus, the invention of the chest of drawers by André-Charles Boulle – the pre-eminent cabinet-maker of late seventeenth- and early eighteenth-century France, who gave his name to the École Boulle, founded in 1886 and still the country's major school of furniture and interior design – is given prominence on a par with the more historically significant or emotionally resonant events that make up the narrative. The sense of place that characterises all three volumes of Diwo's trilogy is closely connected with the industry which gave the *quartier* its identity and, as the beginning of the first volume shows, was intimately linked with the presence of the abbey.

Diwo's first volume ends on 13 July 1789; its successors will be dealt with in subsequent chapters. The abbey became a hospital in 1795 after the revolutionary confiscation of Church property and has remained one ever since, though only its old cloister remains of the original buildings. This is one of two major hospitals in the *quartier*, the other being the Hôpital des Quinze-Vingts, in the rue de Charenton. This was founded by Louis IX in 1260 to lodge three hundred – whence its name – blind people, and moved to its present location in 1780.

Despite its erstwhile pomp and prestige, I have not located any literary or cinematic reconstructions of the area apart from Diwo's in which the abbey figures prominently – something which can certainly not be said of its other most celebrated, indeed notorious, building, the Bastille itself, built in the early fourteenth century as a bastion but enlarged between 1370 and 1383 into a fortress to defend eastern Paris. It became a prison in 1403, and in the almost four hundred years between then and its fall played host to some 6000 inmates. It has come to stand since, and because of, its fall for the repressiveness and brutality of the Ancien Régime; de Gaulle, in an Algiers speech of 1943, said: "'Quand la lutte s'engage entre le peuple et la Bastille, c'est toujours la Bastille qui finit par avoir tort'" [6] / "'When there is a struggle between the people and the Bastille, it's always the Bastille that turns out to be wrong.'" Louis-Sébastien Mercier in *L'An 2440*, written nineteen years before the Revolution, imagines the fortress razed to the ground and replaced by a temple to mercy – an astute if not entirely accurate prediction.

Yet the Bastille was far from the worst of the Ancien Régime's prisons. Indeed, it had a somewhat up-market reputation, exemplified by its roster of celebrated inhabitants. The celebrated potter Bernard Palissy died there in 1590, probably imprisoned because of his Protestantism, and after becoming a state prison in the seventeenth century it was to play host to such luminaries as Voltaire and, just before its fall, the Marquis de Sade. Conditions for prisoners were often described as surprisingly good, with an extensive library and a wide choice of food. The prison's symbolic reputation sprang, paradoxically, in part from the type of inmates it housed, who were frequently there because they had in one way or other crossed the monarch or the State. Louis XIV's Superintendent of Finances, Nicolas Fouquet, was imprisoned there for excessive ambition, exemplified by his having the temerity to build a magnificent château at Vaux-le-Vicomte, outside Paris. No such fripperies as prosecution or trial were necessary for such incarceration, which generally took place by the simple device of the *lettre de cachet*. These letters signed by the King were effectively private arrest warrants, which needed to give no reason for their execution and were often used in pursuit of private or ideological vendettas. Thus, Richelieu briefly had the cynical aphorist La Rochefoucauld detained in the Bastille, while Voltaire was twice imprisoned there. It was in reference to this that the procession transporting his remains to the Pantheon briefly stopped there on 12 July 1791. Along with political and religious prisoners it sometimes housed – often at the request of their families – libertines whose impulses had got the better of them, such as Cyrano de Bergerac's nephew who served a spell there in 1707 for masturbating in Notre-Dame. Mercier, writing immediately before the Revolution, recounts an anecdote which exemplifies the Bastille's reputation for detention motivated by political intrigue:

> Deux prisonniers d'État admis à prendre l'air ensemble dans la cour aperçurent un chien qui faisait autour d'eux maints et maints sauts. Pourquoi ce pauvre animal est-il ici, dit l'un d'eux? que fait-il dans ce château royal? à sa place j'en sortirais bien. Oh! dit l'autre, il est sans doute retenu de force. – Qu'aurait-il fait pour cela? – Il aura mordu le chien du ministre; – ou du sous-ministre, bien plus redoutable que le premier.[7]

Two State prisoners allowed to walk together in the courtyard noticed a dog gambolling around them. What's that poor creature doing here?

asked one of them. What's he doing in this royal château? In his place I'd be well out of here. Oh! said the other one, he's probably being held by force. – What can he have done to deserve that? – He must have bitten the minister's dog; – or even the junior minister's, who is more fearsome still.

Among the fortress's most noteworthy guests were the Duc de Biron, a senior general and Marshal of France beheaded for conspiracy with Spain and Savoy in 1602 – the only prisoner to have been executed within the prison, in order to avoid possible protests – and François de Bassompierre, likewise a Marshal of France. De Bassompierre spent thirteen years there for conspiracy against Richelieu, whose liberal dispatching of his enemies to the Bastille reinforced its image as a state and political prison. Specifically political skulduggery, however, was not a necessary condition for incarceration; the memorialist Bussy-Rabutin served more than a year in 1665 for writing *Histoire amoureuse des Gaules*, a witty but scurrilous account of amorous intrigues among ladies at court. Voltaire earned his two sojourns first, in 1717, by publishing an indecent satire on the Duc d'Orléans, Regent of France, and his daughter and then, in 1725, by insulting a young nobleman, the Chevalier de Rohan. The polemicist Simon-Nicholas Henri de Linguet enjoyed nearly two years from 1780 for a broadside directed against the general and diplomat the Duc de Duras; this sentence inspired his *Mémoires sur la Bastille*, which bemoan in probably exaggerated, and certainly highly seasoned, tones the conditions of his confinement. Linguet – clearly not among the more privileged prisoners – says that the prison regime 'ne ressemble à rien de ce qui s'est jamais pratiqué, ou se pratique aujourd'hui, dans le monde'[8] / 'is like nothing that has ever been practised, or is practised today, anywhere in the world' – a plaint surely grounded as much in the arbitrariness of his and others' detention as in conditions within the prison.

The two Bastille inmates whose stories yield the richest harvest, however, are Jean Henri Latude and the still unidentified figure known for two hundred years and more as the Man in the Iron Mask. Latude was initially imprisoned in 1749 for sending a box of ostensibly poisoned chocolates to Madame de Pompadour, in the hope of currying favour and possible financial reward. He was transferred to the Château de Vincennes, three miles to the east, whence he succeeded in escaping in 1750; recaptured, he was returned to the Bastille, where he defaced library books with insulting poems about Pompadour, and remained there until a second escape in 1756, with the aid of an impromptu ladder fashioned out of scraps of wood and material. Back in Vincennes, he escaped yet once more in 1764, to be promptly recaptured. In 1775 he was sent to the asylum at Charenton where the Marquis de Sade was to die almost forty years later, and in 1777 finally granted his freedom on condition that he remained away from Paris an injunction of which he took no notice. In 1784 he was finally given permission to reside in the capital, and after the fall of the fortress reinvented himself as a revolutionary *avant la lettre*. His *Mémoires authenthiques* in all probability do little to justify their epithet; Latude was unquestionably a mythomaniac, albeit an uncommonly sympathetic and ingenious one, whose status as a revolutionary icon stemmed from the fact that he 'semble avoir résumé dans sa vie de souffrances toutes les iniquités d'un gouvernement arbitraire'[9] / 'seems to have summed up in his life of suffering all the iniquities of an arbitrary government'. After the Revolution he obtained compensation from Pompadour's estate, despite which he died poor in 1805 at the impressive age of eighty. He makes an appearance, played by Robert Lamoureux, in Sacha Guitry's 1955 'historical' film *Si Paris nous était conté*, which also features an episode devoted to the much better-known Man in the Iron Mask.

The Man in the Iron Mask – according to some sources in fact a velvet one – ranks among the best-known prisoners of all time, largely thanks to Alexandre Dumas's fictionalized treatment of his story in the last of the three volumes of *Les Trois Mousquetaires*, *Le Vicomte de Bragelonne*, filmed by Randall Wallace as *The Man in the Iron Mask* with Leonardo DiCaprio. Dumas's hypothesis is that the mysterious captive, supposedly held in the Bastille from the late 1680s (or perhaps 1698) until his death in 1703, was Louis XIV's identical twin brother Philippe – an idea first mooted by Voltaire in *Le Siècle de Louis XV*, and echoed in Victor Hugo's unfinished 1839 play *Les Jumeaux*. Marcel Pagnol's *Le Secret du masque de fer* floats a similar hypothesis, though his twin brother bears the name James.

This illustrious literary pedigree does not, alas, make the theory its advocates advance any more credible. Jean-Christian Petitfils in *Le Masque de fer: entre histoire et légende* lists no fewer than fifty-two hypotheses about the prisoner's true identity, which have inspired more than a thousand books about him as well as three international conferences. As with the far more sinister Jack the Ripper, the very fecundity of speculation has rendered any definitive resolution of the mystery impossible.

One prominent contender was the Italian diplomat Ercole Mattioli, secretary to the Duke of Mantua, who had been involved in a maladroit double-crossing attempt to sell a fortified city near Turin to Louis XIV. The king supposedly avenged – and quite literally masked – the embarrassment this caused him by imprisoning Mattioli first in Piedmont and subsequently in the Bastille. There is, however, countervailing evidence to suggest that Mattioli died in captivity near Cannes in 1694. Another often-mentioned name is that of Eustache Danger (less evocatively sometimes given as Dauger), a prisoner who had served as domestic to Fouquet during his incarceration and might therefore have been privy to compromising secrets. The accounts given by Petitfils and Funck-Brentano (*La Bastille et ses secrets*) of the intrigues that may have underlain the detention of these suspects are tortuous rather than persuasive, but perhaps that is precisely their point; it is the game of disguise itself that is the point rather than a now impossible identification of the 'Mask''s identity. Along with Louis XIV's twin, other candidates have included Fouquet, whose death in captivity in 1680 would then have been a false rumour concocted by his bitter rival Colbert to forestall his rumoured liberation, Molière, d'Artagnan (the real-life original of Dumas's musketeer), and perhaps most appealingly through its sheer implausibility a black slave of restricted growth who had fathered a love-child with Louis XIV's queen.

It is through Dumas's work above all that the Man in the Iron Mask has become an archetypal figure, albeit nowadays a somewhat forgotten one. Dumas's rollicking cloak-and-dagger adventures, like the historical novel more generally, have fallen into comparative neglect of late, upstaged by more recent modes of popular fiction and lacking the high-cultural prestige of a Balzac or even a Hugo to sustain academic interest. It is perhaps significant that the format in which the Iron Mask sections of *Le Vicomte de Bragelonne* – a dauntingly lengthy work, occupying 1710 pages in one paperback edition – were most readily available when I sought the work out in Paris was a Livre de Poche 'Jeunesse' edition, recommended for those of twelve and upwards. Yet Dumas's work can be argued to have a serious historical and political agenda, for it represents the most extended literary treatment of a theme impossible for writers of the time to tackle directly – the conquest of personal power by Louis XIV, who in the 1660s established himself as the undisputed ruler of France he was to remain until his death in 1715.

The historical accuracy of Dumas's account is already called into question by the fact that his novel takes place some twenty years before the 'historical' Iron Mask – if that is not an oxymoron – supposedly entered the Bastille. Dumas stated, however, that if he chose to present the Mask as Louis XIV's brother this was on literary rather than historical grounds; his Iron Mask is explicitly constructed as myth rather than as plausible hypothesis.

Aramis, one of his three musketeers and bishop of the Breton city of Vannes, seeks with the aid of the disgraced Fouquet to install Louis XIV's twin brother Philippe, whose existence he is one of the few to suspect, on the throne, and become the new king's prime minister as a stepping-stone to the papacy. In a thoroughly preposterous imbroglio, Aramis succeeds in kidnapping the king and exchanging him with Philippe, but his scheme is derailed by Fouquet's unwillingness to play along. Perversely loyal to his monarch, Fouquet springs Louis XIV from the Bastille and brings the twins face to face in the Louvre palace. Philippe is taken off to the Ile Saint-Marguerite wearing an iron mask which he is never to remove on pain of death, and where he will presumably spend the remainder of his days. Dumas was to adapt the Iron Mask section of his novel into a stage play, *Le Prisonnier de la Bastille*, which ends with Aramis and Porthos taking refuge in the Breton island of Belle-Ile-en-Mer after their plot is discovered and Porthos's being blown up by a barrel of gunpowder.

It is not fanciful to see Dumas's story as a Freudian tale *avant la lettre*, bearing as it does clear traces of the family romance – the fantasy in which a child imagines that it is not really the offspring of its parents, but of different, generally more lofty birth. One of Dumas's most striking passages occurs when Aramis asks Philippe whether there were any mirrors in the house where he passed his early years. Philippe has never heard the words 'glace' or 'miroir', not been allowed access to any documents that might give a clue to his true identity. Aramis shows Philippe a likeness of Louis XIV and then, for the first time (he is twenty-three years old), his own reflection in a mirror – the moment at which according to the psychoanalyst Jacques Lacan the young child gains access to its own subjectivity. The 'real' king, asleep as Fouquet's guest at Vaux-le-Vicomte, has a dream in which he sees a man's face identical to his own, so that when the twins finally come face to face the moment has been prepared by an artful series of reflections and mirrorings which bid fair to make us forget the rank implausibility of the scenario.

Pagnol, for his part, reviews the various possible identities of the prisoner, dismissing the widespread Mattioli hypothesis after lengthy discussion and opting instead for Eustache Dauger, himself but an alias for James, Louis XIV's identical twin. More prosaic though Pagnol's approach certainly is it is scarcely more persuasive than Dumas's, as might befit a writer celebrated for the *galéjades* or Provençal tall tales that stud his work. Henri Decoin, in the best-known cinematic adaptation of the myth, *Le Masque de fer* (1962), likewise opts for the 'twin brother' solution. Decoin's film, in the same somewhat dated cloak-and-dagger vein as Christian-Jaque's *Fanfan la tulipe* of ten years before, stars Jean Marais buckling his swash as d'Artagnan along with Claudine Auger as the jailer's daughter Isabelle, coveted by Louis but faithfully smitten with his twin, here called Henri. A slightly more novel spin is provided by Patrick Cothias and Marc Rénier's strip-cartoon version of 1991, drawn like a colourful TV costume-drama or even a heritage film, which reveals the prisoner, through the agency of a talking and eavesdropping owl, as none other than Molière – in reality the rightful king of France since Louis XIV is the offspring of Richelieu and Anne of Austria.

Royalty as soap opera is not, clearly, a twentieth-century invention. As with the far more sinister Jack the Ripper, the very fecundity of speculation surrounding the Mask's identity – even conceivably his existence – has made it impossible to establish, and the myth is nowhere near so culturally prominent as it was a century ago. Yet the mysterious captive remains the most celebrated of all the inmates of the Bastille in French culture at least, though the Marquis de Sade (transferred to an asylum in early July 1789, and forced to abandon fifteen volumes of manuscripts) nowadays received more attention, and Dr Marnette in Dickens's unquestionably fictional *A Tale of Two Cities* is probably better known to an English-speaking audience. By the time the fortress fell, it housed only seven prisoners, one at least of whom was mad. It owed its reputation as the incarnation of all that was most odious about the *Ancien Régime* to the secrecy that surrounded many of its captives, which prompted Constantin de Renneville to entitle his 1715 history of the prison *L'Inquisition francaise*. Renneville's reliability, however, may be felt to be called into question by the fact that according to Monique Cottret in *La Bastille à prendre* he was mentally disturbed enough to mix his excrement into the other prisoners' soup. The Bastille, organized on the principle of the dungeon and its emphasis on secrecy, was to be, at least in France and perhaps in Western Europe, among the last jails of its kind; the modern prison identified by Michel Foucault in *Surveiller et punir*, with its stress on surveillance and visibility, perhaps owes its coming into being to the revolutionary social changes triggered by the storming of the fortress in 1789.

What of the area surrounding the Bastille, to which the monastery had given its name, and which was incorporated into Paris in 1702? It was the base and home not only of Boulle, but of other celebrated furniture-makers such as the mid-eighteenth-century Germans Oeden and Riesener – evidence of how early the industry opened itself to workers from outside France. Craftsmanship, however, sat cheek-by-jowl with less savoury goings-on; thus Restif de la Bretonne recounts a nocturnal promenade there during which he became lost in the rue de la Roquette, and encountered a distressed young woman, pregnant by her lover and fleeing an arranged marriage. Prompt as ever to save damsels in distress, he confides her to ' la garde d'une dame de grande qualité' [10] / 'the care of a lady of high station', living

in the neighbouring, but more salubrious, *quartier* of the Marais. The rue
de la Roquette, then as thereafter, appears to have had a less diligent and
serious reputation than the rest of the area, described by Alain Thillay as
'une ruche ouvrière'[11] / 'a workers' beehive' in which proletarian unrest was
already a constant fear of the regime. There had been riots protesting against
overcharging for bread in 1725; two rioters were hanged. It thus seems
appropriate that the dramatist Beaumarchais, whose 1784 *Le Mariage de Figaro*
was described by Napoleon as 'the Revolution in action', and who oversaw
the demolition of the fortress in August 1789, should have lived towards
the end of his life in a luxurious mansion complete with an English-style
landscaped garden covering 4000 square metres, and adorned with the
inscription: 'Ce petit jardin fut planté / L'an premier de la Liberté' / 'This
little garden was planted / In the first year of Liberty'), on the boulevard
that now bears his name. This alas was pulled down in 1818.

Yet only part of the area – the western side, close to the fortress –
was in actual fact densely populated, though the expansion of the Aligre
market in 1781 doubtless contributed to the growth of the eastern part.
Alain Thillay speaks of the *quartier*'s 'faux ouvriers', whom he defines as
'tous ceux qui travaillent sans répondre aux conditions statutaires fixées
par les communautés de métier, ou corporations, chargées de la police
économique par la monarchie'[12] / 'all those who worked without abiding by
the statutory conditions laid down by the guilds and corporations entrusted
by the monarchy with policing the economy'. This somewhat anarchistic
vision is tempered by Thillay's description of 'un quartier ouvrier et
populaire pour lequel la liberté du travail ne conduit pas inéluctablement
au libéralisme économique tel que nous l'entendons à partie du XIXe
siècle'[13] / 'a popular, working-class area in which freedom to work did
not inevitably lead to the kind of free-market economy that was to prevail
from the nineteenth century on' (366). For Thillay nineteenth-century
writers such as Hugo and Jules Vallès, overstated in hindsight the political
and revolutionary consciousness of the *quartier*, while 'l'idée d'un "contre-
modèle" à l'organisation corporative, antérieur à la Révolution française et
fondé sur la liberté du travail, s'avère probablement trop schématique'[14]
/ 'the idea of an alternative model to guild organization, predating the
Revolution and founded on the freedom to work, is in all probably too
schematic'.

However rose-tinted the view undermined by Thillay may be, it
unquestionably played, and continues to play, a fundamental part in the
image and resonance of the area. The proximity of a largely self-regulating
community of skilled workers, often living in conditions of crowding and

deprivation, to the emblem of the *Ancien Régime*'s arbitrary repressiveness can be seen, if not as a powder-keg, then certainly as a fuse ready to be lit. Louis XVI famously wrote in his diary for 14 July 1789: 'Rien' / 'Nothing' (though this may well have been a reference to his returning empty-handed from the day's hunting). That that entry, even if misinterpreted, should turn out to have been one of the most celebrated wrong calls in history owed, we shall see in the next chapter, much to the Faubourg Saint-Antoine.

Chapter Two

'Thought blew the Bastille apart': the fall of the fortress and the revolutionary years, 1789–1815

B Y THE LATE 1780s the Bastille had become so unpopular, and so costly to maintain, that plans were afoot to transfer all its inmates to Vincennes. Flysheets were circulating demanding its closure, along with attacks on the *lettre de cachet*. The country was deep in an economic crisis whose details were exposed in 1781 by the director-general of finances, Jacques Necker, in his *Compte rendu au roi* – an act of open government which earned him great popularity but also contributed to his dismissal later that year. Brought back amid worsening financial turmoil in 1788, he helped to convene the Estates-General – an assembly of representatives of the nobility, the Church and the *tiers état* or common people – in an attempt to stave off growing popular discontent. It was to be too little, too late; in June 1789 the *tiers état* representatives transformed themselves into the National Assembly. The beginnings of a parliamentary democratic structure were in place. Necker's dismissal, for a second time, on 11 July was received with fury by the majority of the population. The unpopularity of the fortress was increasingly mirrored by that of the regime it represented – nowhere more so than in the Faubourg, which before the revolution represented some ten per cent of the total area of Paris. Louis-Sébastien Mercier's observation, only a few years before the Bastille was to fall, now reads ironically:

La Bastille [...] a l'air de tenir bon, de vouloir épouvanter sans cesse nos regards de son hideuse figure. Sur ces fossés, témoins des jeux sanglants de la Fronde, s'élèvent des bâtiments qui feront douter s'il y eût jamais là des remparts que le boulet a frappés.[1]

The Bastille seems to hold its ground, as if wanting always to shock our gaze with its hideous form. Above these ditches, which witnessed the bloodthirsty games of the Fronde, rise buildings which give leave to doubt whether there were really once there ramparts struck by cannonballs.

More than a century earlier the satirical free-thinking poet Claude Le Petit – a kind of latter-day Villon who was burnt to death in 1662 for his scurrilous writings about Mazarin – had offered a more accurate prognosis when he wrote about the fortress, in typically salty fashion:

> Est-ce une tour? En est-ce quatre?
> Et qui seroit le cul foireux
> Qui n'eust la force de l'abattre
> D'une pétarade ou de deux?' [2]

> Is it one tower? Is it four?
> And who would the shitarse be
> Who didn't have the strength to knock it down
> With one or two volleys of farts?

There had been riots in the Faubourg a few months before, in April, when Jean-Baptiste Réveillon, owner of a wallpaper factory there, proposed to lower the salaries of his workforce, followed in this by the saltpetre manufacturer Hanriot. On 28 April the National Guard fired on demonstrators who had burnt the two men in effigy, killing some three hundred. Claude Quétel avers that '[c]'est le 28 avril 1789, sous les murs de la Bastille, que la Révolution a vraiment commencé, entendons au sens de la violence révolutionnaire' / 'It was on 28 April 1789, below the walls of the Bastille, that the Revolution, or at least revolutionary violence, really began'.[3] Réveillon, by a bizarre coincidence, found himself obliged to seek refuge in the fortress, on the auspicious date of 1 May; he was not to feel it safe to emerge until the very end of the month.

On the morning of 14 July a large crowd went to the Hôtel des Invalides and helped themselves to the 30 000 guns or so stored there before marching on the Bastille in search of ammunition. The governor of the fortress, de Launay (sometimes spelt de Launey), initially received successive deputations courteously, but in the early afternoon the guards opened fire. Republican myth has it that de Launay inveigled the crowd into the fortress the better to pick them off, though there is evidence to suggest that in fact the initial broadside was intended to deter rather than to kill. It did not succeed; by the middle of the afternoon de Launay was ready to surrender, reputedly using his own handkerchief in lieu of a white flag. He was seized by the crowd and beheaded, while the seven remaining prisoners were freed. Popular joy was unconfined, in Paris and the provinces alike. The *Ancien Régime* was not long to survive the collapse of one of the most hated symbols of its arbitrary power.

Pierre Citron lists a number of works – poems, short plays and parodies – produced in the immediate aftermath of the storming, including one in which the unfortunate fortress bemoans its destruction in verse. The hegemonic view of 14 July, however, is that articulated by the great historian Jules Michelet, who for ten years lived in the rue de la Roquette. Michelet's *Histoire de la révolution française* views the fall of the fortress as a quasi-religious event, analogous to Joshua's destruction of the walls of Jericho. For Michelet:

> Une idée se leva sur Paris avec le jour, et tous virent la même lumière. Une lumière dans les esprits, et dans chaque coeur une voix: Va, et tu prendras la Bastille! [...] L'attaque de la Bastille ne fut nullement raisonnable. Ce fut un acte de foi.

> One idea rose over Paris with the day, and everybody saw the same light. One light in people's minds, and in each heart one voice: Go ahead, and you will take the Bastille! [...] The attack on the Bastille was in no way reasonable. It was an act of faith.[4]

Christopher Prendergast observes that 'for Michelet the storming of the Bastille is represented as grand *archè*, the founding moment of a world-historical event, the pure embodiment of a world-shattering and world-creating inauguration'.[5] In a manuscript to be found in the Bibliothèque historique de la Ville de Paris, Michelet writes of the Faubourg as a 'triple serpent artériel et chaque allée une veine; triple croissant, triple serpent (faubourgs de Charenton, de Charonne; Roquette non ouverte) dont la bouche double aboutit à la porte Saint-Antoine' / 'threefold arterial serpent each of whose throughways is a vein; a threefold crescent, a threefold snake (the faubourgs de Charenton and de Charonne with the closed-off rue de Roquette) whose double mouth leads to the porte Saint-Antoine'[6] – a perception, like that of the fall of the fortress, eminently in accord with the mythopoeic populism that characterizes his writing of history, and has done much to shape subsequent views of 14 July and of the Faubourg's role in it.

Such a view is already present, in attenuated form, in Pierre-Mathieu

Parein's *La Prise de la Bastille*, a musical comedy written in 1791. Parein had participated in the storming of the fortress and was to become an important polemicist and later general in the revolutionary army. His dramatic skills, alas, were less impressive, and the play on its rare performances was poorly received in France at least, though it was staged in three London theatres. It speaks, approvingly, of the people as 'un hydre à cent têtes' / 'a hundred-headed hydra',[7] ending on a note of what might be called 'revolution lite' as the people in chorus sing a hymn to freedom and call for mercy to the vanquished. Georges Lecocq in 1881 was to refer to the Faubourg as 'cet antre de la Révolution, dont le nom seul fait pâlir certaines gens' / 'that cavern of Revolution whose mere name causes some to turn pale',[8] reinforcing the sense of an almost organic link between the *quartier* and the momentous event that had taken place there.

Among fictional representations of the storming, Alexandre Dumas's *Ange Pitou* – one of his 'Marie-Antoinette' cycle of romances – partakes of a similar heady rhetoric. *Ange Pitou* was published in 1853, the same year as the final volume of Michelet's history, and emphasises the role of the Faubourg in the events of 14 July, using the same corporeal metaphor as Michelet's manuscript ('toutes les artères du faubourg Saint-Antoine lui envoyèrent, chemin faisant, ce qu'elles avaient de plus chaud et de plus vif en sang populaire' / 'Every artery of the faubourg Saint-Antoine sent it [the revolutionary army] their hottest and liveliest popular blood').[9] The revolutionary general Billot has an exchange with de Launay, whom he insists on calling 'citizen' whereas de Launay proclaims himself to be a French gentleman – a curious preecho of the scene in Renoir's 1938 film *La Marseillaise* in which Louis Jouvet as Roederer expresses his surprise at hearing the term 'citoyen' for the first time. Dumas's revolution is not merely popular and visceral, but intellectual and ideological. 'C'est que depuis cent ans ce n'est plus seulement la matière inerte qu'on enferme dans la forteresse royale: c'est la pensée. Le pensée a fait éclater la Bastille, et le peuple est entré par la brèche' / 'for a hundred years it's not just inert matter that has been locked up in the royal fortress: it is thought. Thought blew the Bastille apart, and the people rushed in through the breach'[10] – a probable reference to the imprisonment there of Voltaire and Sade, and beyond that to the role of Enlightenment ideas in fomenting the climate of revolution.

Romain Rolland – largely forgotten nowadays, though in 1915 he was awarded the Nobel Prize for Literature – likewise places the local population at the centre of his dithyrambic stage-play *Le 14 Juillet: action populaire*. De Launay is here shown breaking things in his room and crying like a child (as he might well have done considering what was to befall him), while the innocent young Julie, who lives with her mother in the rue Saint-Antoine and takes pity on the prisoners she sees passing, is hailed as the incarnation of liberty by a jubilant crowd at the end, who sing: 'O notre liberté, notre lumière, notre amour! Que tu es petite encore, délicate et fragile!' / 'O our liberty, our light, our love! How small you still are, delicate and fragile!'[11]

Mythologization of the storming, then, began early, as did its commercialization. A builder named Pierre-François Palloy won the contract to demolish the fortress and made miniature Bastilles out of the ruins, sending some to revolutionary sections and the newly organized *départements* but selling many more. He became known as *le patriote*, but changed sides with suspicious rapidity each time a new regime came to power in the succeeding years, and died ruined in 1835.

Palloy is one of the historical characters to figure in the second volume of Jean Diwo's trilogy, *Le Lit d'acajou*, along with such as Mercier and Riesner, who brings back a key as a souvenir of the fortress. Diwo takes what might be described as a moderate view of the revolution, largely through one of his central characters, Bertrand de Valfroy, married to the niece of Réveillon. The latter is presented as not hostile to republican values but fearful of the disorderly mob. The *classes dangereuses* discourse here trumps the headier view taken by Michelet; among the most notorious propagators of this view were Hippolyte Taine in the late nineteenth century and Frantz Funck-Brentano in the 1930s, both of whom refer to the assailants as 'lie' / 'scum'. Funck-Brentano opined in his 1925 book on the area that its revolutionary temperament was to be traced back to the overthrowing of the elsewhere strict corporation rules in 1471, while asserting paradoxically that it remained 'le quartier de Paris d'où l'air de la vieille France se dégage avec le plus d'intensité' / 'the Paris *quartier* which most powerfully exudes the atmosphere of old France'.[12] Even in the rhetoric of a nationalist monarchist such as Funck-Brentano's rhetoric '*classes laborieuses*' and '*classes dangereuses*' sit uneasily side by side as they do in so many representations of the Parisian proletariat.

First prize for lurid depiction of the aftermath of the fortress's capture, however, incontestably goes to the right-wing nationalist historian – later to become a campaigner for Marshal Pétain's release – Louis Madelin:

> On a dit assez les scènes de cannibalisme qui suivirent: sachant de quels éléments se mêlait cette foule dite parisienne, nous ne saurions d'ailleurs nous en étonner. Mais la foule parisienne elle-même se sentait maintenant prise de cette fièvre de sang si horriblement contagieuse. Tandis qu'on portait en triomphe les quelques prisonniers délivrés

(quatre faussaires, deux fous et un débauché sadique), les défenseurs, traînés dehors, étaient accueillis par des cris d'anthropophages. Et tout à coup Paris, dans la terreur, vit refluer le foule hurlante au-dessus de laquelle, au bout des piques, des têtes éclaboussées de sang, les yeux mi-clos, oscillaient. La foule acclamait les brigands, leur donnant pour des années droit de cité – et déjà droit de domination.[13]

Enough has been said about the scenes of cannibalism that ensued: knowing what elements went to make up this so-called Parisian crowd, there is no reason for surprise at this. But the Parisian crowd itself was now in the grip of a horribly contagious blood-lust. While the few freed prisoners (four forgers, two madmen and a sadistic debauchee) were being carried along in triumph, the defenders, dragged outside, were greeted by cannibalistic shrieks. And all at once Paris, in the grip of terror, saw the screaming crowd come surging back, and above it, on pikes, blood-spattered heads with half-closed eyes swaying to and fro. The crowd greeted the brigands, giving them citizenship rights for years to come – and already the right to dominate.

Madelin's moral panic and fear of the mob takes to an almost self-parodic extreme the discourse on the *'classes dangereuses'* which has been such an important feature of writing about Paris, and in particular the Faubourg, since the Revolution. More sober and better-documented views, however, are not far to seek. Raymond Monnier paints a vivid picture of the Faubourg in the revolutionary years as an area whose inhabitants came from all over the country – notably the north, Normandy and above all Auvergne in central France – and beyond, particularly Germany. For Chevalier, '[c]e sont des gens de l'est et du Nord qui ont fait la Révolution française à Paris, ainsi que les Révolutions de 1830 et de 1848; ils appartenaient à des régions plus profondément urbaines que les autres régions de France et conservant des traditions de vie municipale active, tourmentée et souvent sanglante' / 'it was people from eastern and northern France who were largely responsible for the French revolution in Paris, as well as the 1830 and 1848 revolutions; they came from more highly urbanized regions than elsewhere in France and retained active, turbulent and often bloody traditions of city life.'[14] Two-thirds of the Faubourg's 43 000 inhabitants – and all its female ones – were ineligible to vote under the largely property-based franchise established in 1789, but class consciousness was strong, and Monnier estimates that seventy per cent of those who took part in the assault on the fortress lived in the *quartier*. Economic conditions were poor, with much unemployment in the winter of 1788–89, and the combination of hardship and social unrest was to be marked for many years afterwards. The Convention, with secularizing fervour, removed the word 'saint' from the principal thoroughfare, which was briefly known as simply the rue du Faubourg Antoine.

The revolutionary years are described, in very different ways, by Diwo in *Le Lit d'acajou* and Tony Révillon in his novel *Le Faubourg Saint-Antoine*. Diwo's narrative is liberally spiked with local colour, as when he cites a 'vieux proverbe d'atelier' / 'old workshop proverb' 'Qui traverse un passage du faubourg, de sa belle est amoureuse toujours' / 'Anybody who walks through a passage of the Faubourg will remain forever in love with his sweetheart'[15] – a reference to the numerous pedestrian passages in the *quartier*, characteristic of other urban industrial areas too such as the Croix-Rousse in Lyon. Diwo describes the Terror, in almost Dickensian terms, as 'entraînant dans ses engrenages affolés tous ceux qui tentaient de lui résister' / 'dragging into its maddened mechanisms all who tried to resist it'[16] – indicative of the ideologically dulcet tone of his three-volume historical soap opera, in which politics functions as backcloth to the evocation of life in a working-class 'urban village' with its succession of generations, romantic intrigues and increasing pace of technical innovation, leaving the Faubourg's artisans sometimes feeling 'un peu orphelins' / 'slightly orphaned'.[17]

Révillon's text, by contrast, is a full-blooded example of committed proletarian literature. Révillon, a left-wing journalist, served as member of parliament for the working-class Paris district of Belleville between 1881 and 1893, and *Le Faubourg Saint-Antoine* was published in the year in which he was elected. His story opens with a clear homage to Dickens – as in *A Tale of Two Cities*, an aristocrat knocks over a young child in his carriage and disdainfully offers financial compensation, which is thrown angrily back at him. As in *Les Dames du faubourg*, the amorous, the economic (here incorporating the nascent textile industry) and the historical intertwine, though it is difficult to imagine any of Diwo's characters speaking in such impeccably Marxist terms as Révillon's Henri when he says in 1792: 'La bourgeoisie a fait sa révolution; le peuple prépare la sienne' / 'The bourgeoisie has made its revolution, the people are preparing theirs.'[18]

Ariane Mnouchkine's 1970 play *1789*, written in conjunction with her Théâtre du Soleil theatre company, was made into a film in 1974. In keeping with the dominant political aesthetic of the time, both play and film draw upon the Bakhtinian carnival and the Brechtian alienation effect to present a vision of 14 July and its aftermath as at once jubilant popular festival and propaedeutic for the kind of people's revolution portended by Révillon, which, at any rate at the time the play was first produced, seemed to many in France to be imminent. Mnouchkine's euphoric tone captures the effervescence of May 1968 while remaining faithful to a historical context related by the characters in small whispering groups to the audience. I saw the play shortly after it opened in France and still remember vividly the excitement these scenes caused me, with their recounting of popular anger at Necker's dismissal and the search for ammunition which led inexorably to the Bastille. The Faubourg does not figure explicitly in Mnouchkine's text, but her actors clearly represent, at least in large part, its denizens.

The pictorial arts and music have also evoked the fall of the fortress. Contemporary paintings, such as those by Jean-Pierre Houël and Hubert Robert, depict the Bastille as a lowering monster overshadowing any human presence, though Charles Thévenin's 1793 representation focuses more on the assailants in bitter combat. Marcel Poëte, the great early twentieth-century historian of Paris, describes Jean-Louis Prieur's drawing of the storming in archetypally mythopoeic tones:

> Un dessin contemporain, de Prieur, représente la rue envahie par la foule devant la massive prison; d'une terrasse voisine et des fenêtres des maisons, des gens regardent ou manifestent; il s' en trouve même juchés sur les toits du Petit-Marché; les gardes françaises sont portées en triomphe; il semble que l'on entende les cris poussés par les manifestants et le sourd grondement du peuple en marche, spectacle tant de fois renouvelé depuis et trait de physionomie inséparable de Paris révolutionnaire.[19]

> A contemporary drawing, by Prieur, represents the street invaded by the crowd in front of the massive prison; from a nearby terrace and from the windows of houses, people are watching or showing their support; some are even perched on the roofs of the Petit-Marché. The French Guards* are borne along in triumph; it is as if we could hear the shouts of the demonstrators and the muffled rumble of the people on the march, a sight seen so many times since and a characteristic inseparable from revolutionary Paris.

Paul-Georges Sansonetti, in a doctoral thesis, stresses the realistic quality of most engravings representing the storming, in which 'l'on voit essentiellement le peuple de Paris en action' / 'what we basically see is the

---

* This regiment, whose mission was to protect the monarchy and maintain order in Paris, defected virtually en bloc to the revolutionary cause on 14 July.

people of Paris in action'.[20] Sansonetti offers detailed analysis of individual texts and images, presenting them as *bande dessinée avant la lettre*. There are also some schoolbook depictions in *bande dessinée* style, but more celebrated and interesting than these by far is Man Ray's 1938 *Portrait imaginaire de D. A. F. de Sade*, housed in the Menil collection in Houston. This foregrounds a bust of the portly Sade of the later years, fashioned from stones from the Bastille which, in a species of *mise en abyme*, is visible in the background, almost as though Sade had recycled his prison into his work. *Bande dessinée* reproductions include that by Patrick Cothias and Hadi Temglit, who glory in de Launay's head on a pike, accompanied by approving commentary by 'Mariane' (*sic*) despite 'quelques excès bien excusables' / 'a few quite excusable excesses',[21] while Daniel Bardet and Dominique Hé in *La Révolution enfin!* – a less pictorially rich work than Cothias's – accord an important place to 'le patriote Palloy'. Among the numerous songs written to celebrate the great day was one by Sylvain Maréchal, an associate of the utopian pre-communist Gracchus Babeuf who published it in his clandestine paper *L'Éclaireur du peuple*. The words proudly proclaim: 'Le peuple et le Soldat unis / Ont bien su réduire en débris / Le Trône et la Bastille' ('The people and the Soldier united / Were able to reduce to rubble / The Throne and the Bastille')[22] – sentiments clearly likely to be shared by the inhabitants of the *quartier*, as the song's title, *Chanson nouvelle à l'usage des faubourgs*, suggests. More than two hundred years later, no less a figure than Roger Waters – best known as a member of the progressive rock group Pink Floyd – was to include a scene devoted to the fall of the Bastille in his opera *Ça ira*, named after one of the best-known French revolutionary songs. Waters's work, with a French libretto, was originally intended by François Mitterrand to be staged by the Paris Opera – situated of course in the Place de la Bastille – to celebrate the bicentennial, but the conservatism of the Opera's directors prevailed, and it was not performed, in a revised version, until 2004, in Malta. Although a recording of it, with Bryn Terfel, has sold well internationally, it would seem that to date *Ça ira* has still to be performed in France.

There were many ambitious plans for the site of the fortress after its demolition. Anne-Josèphe Théroigne de Méricourt, a flamboyant supporter of the Girondin tendency, advocated the building of a grandiose palace to house the new legislative assembly, while a 1791 proposal recommended an allegorical column representing Liberty, the Motherland, Concord and Law, to be crowned with a statue of Louis XVI. A less infelicitious suggestion reads like a theme-park *avant la lettre*, suggesting a harmonious landscaping of the remaining ruins. More modestly, in 1792, the site was turned into a square to celebrate liberty, and there seems to have been broad agreement on the construction of a column, though this was not to come to fruition until the reign of Louis-Philippe. The first anniversary of the storming – the first 'Bastille Day', as it is often known in English – was marked by the Fête de la Fédération, a vast popular celebration attended by Louis XVI, but this was held at the other end of Paris, on the Champ de Mars, now the site of the Eiffel Tower. It was to mark the apogee of the brief period of constitutional monarchy; two years later Louis was to be deposed, and he was guillotined in 1793.

The increasing unrest of these years, needless to say, was marked in the Faubourg Saint-Antoine. The abolition of the monastery was part of the process of secularization that led to the renaming of the principal thoroughfare, which was briefly known as simply the rue du Faubourg Antoine. The abbey's disappearance was not, however, entirely beneficial to the Faubourg, for along with it went 'le centre symbolique de juridiction protectionniste' / 'the symbolic centre of protectionist jurisdiction',[23] and hence much of the social cohesion of the area. Poverty was rife; the average worker earned in a day less than the price of two loaves of bread, and it was not surprising that the *quartier*'s inhabitants led the 1792 assault on the Tuileries that brought about the deposition of Louis XVI. Prominent among them was Antoine Santerre, subsequently to be the king's jailer and alleged to have told the drummers to drown out his would-be final speech before his execution. Santerre owned a brewery at 232 rue du Faubourg Saint-Antoine, which prompts the reflection that Dickens – who never actually set foot in the Faubourg – may have chosen the wrong, though culturally more plausible, type of alcohol when he made the Defarge couple in *A Tale of Two Cities* owners of a wine-shop. They were scarcely unique in this respect, for in 1807 there were 200 outlets for the sale of alcohol in the Faubourg. Santerre's propertied status indicates that the area housed a diverse middle-class population, described by Sophie Fagay as including 'toutes les catégories socio-politiques de la classe bourgeoise victorieuse' / 'every socio-politiocal category of the victorious bourgeois class'.[24] But the dominant social group remained working-class. The overthrow of the Girondins in May 1793 is often seen as marking the entry onto the political scene of the *sans-culottes* – the poorest members of the *tiers état* – many of whom lived in the Faubourg. Their political tenor can be gauged from Gérard Moreau's remark that Jacques Hébert's extreme radical newspaper *Le Père Duchesne*, perhaps best known nowadays through its invocation by Roland Barthes at the opening of *Le Degré zéro de l'écriture*, 'dans un langage populaire et cru se fait le porte-parole des faubourgs Saint-Antoine et Saint-Marcel' / 'in popular, indeed vulgar language made itself the voice of the Faubourgs Saint-Antoine and Saint-Marceau'.[25] Those two faubourgs presented a joint address to the Convention in 1793 in the name of their *sans-culottes*, demanding the formation of a revolutionary battalion to fight in the Rhineland. It was the Faubourg Saint-Antoine that was the first Parisian *quartier* to advocate putting the king on trial, and the June 1794 decree that instituted the Terror was seemingly greeted there with jubilation.

Thermidor (the 1794 coup that overthrew Robespierre), with its apparent attempt to put back the revolutionary clock, was predictably less well received, and the Faubourg was again prominent in the Prairial pro-Jacobin insurrection of 1795, in which a Girondin deputy was assassinated. This was harshly put down, and the Directoire was to find few friends in the *quartier*, which accounts for the enthusiasm with which it embraced Napoleon Bonaparte. The years of his rule, successively as First Consul and as Emperor, were marked by great poverty; many workers lived from hand to mouth, traditional industrial sectors such as shoemaking and metalworking were in decline and the financial situation of single women in particular was likely to be catastrophic. Yet in a shrewd building of class alliances, Napoleon 'réussit à rallier les catégories populaires et la petite bourgeoisie du Faubourg' / 'managed to rally the working classes and the petite bourgeoisie of the Faubourg'[26] – largely thanks to a combination of post-revolutionary exhaustion, national enthusiasm for Bonaparte's military successes and gratitude for the various commissions his regime gave the local workshops. It was Napoleon too who ordered the construction of the Canal Saint-Martin (1802–25) – still a working canal though much given over to tourist traffic – which flows into the Seine via the Bassin de l'Arsenal, nowadays an urban marina. This waterway axis greatly facilitated the movement of goods into and out of the *quartier*.

It was in 1805 that the 'sections' into which Paris had been divided – a term uncomfortably resonant of the Revolution – were replaced by *arrondissements*; the Faubourg, along with its northern neighbour Popincourt, formed part of the eighth. Its economic activity was undergoing a major change at this time with the rise of the textile industry, though the furniture trade remained active in and around the courtyards which still form one of the area's distinctive features. Two Norman businessmen, François Richard and Joseph Lenoir-Dufresne, opened Paris's first cotton mill in an abandoned convent in the rue de Charonne; encouraged by Napoleon, their activity prospered, and more mills were set up in Picardy and Normandy. Lenoir-Dufresne died aged thirty-seven in 1806, supposedly so beloved by his employees that their sobs drowned out the priest's address at his funeral. It was in response to his deathbed request Richard adopted his name, being known henceforth as Richard-Lenoir. Richard-Lenoir, who had been imprisoned for debt in 1789 and escaped during the anti-Réveillon riots of that year, rapidly became one of the richest men in France, though by 1813 competition from imports and the country's deteriorating financial and military situation had all but ruined him. The reign of 'King Cotton', important in the economy of the Faubourg under Napoleon, was to be a brief one, but its trace lives on in the name of the Boulevard Richard-Lenoir, just to the east of the Marais, which houses one of Paris's largest street markets.

Heads of state have since Napoleon's time often nurtured, and sometimes even put into practice, grandiose plans to leave their mark on Paris; the Bastille Opera was one of the last of François Mitterrand's *grands projets*, while the square itself formed an important part of the Napoleonic design that found its most magniloquent expression in the Arc de Triomphe. Napoleon initially intended to link the Place de la Bastille to the Louvre by way of a 'rue Impériale', but like his plans for a lavish circular square (an oxymoron in English but not in French) this was judged too costly and came to nothing. The square was laid out in 1803, but was not to be developed in something like its present form until Baron Haussmann undertook his massive transformation of Paris under the Second Empire.

Napoleon's major – and in hindsight at least most quirkily appealing – contribution to the Place de la Bastille, for a brief period at least, was his plan for the construction of an immense statue in the form of an elephant. He had invaded Egypt in 1798, hoping to use it as a bridgehead for a campaign against British trade interests in India, and taking with him a large number of assorted scientists to explore the country's natural and cultural resources and bring to it the supposed benefits of Western civilization. Edward Said has described Napoleon's campaign as a form of cultural colonization, seeking not only to dominate Egypt politically but 'to render it completely open, to make it totally accessible to European scrutiny'.[27] For Said, the campaign was important in engendering that Orientalism which Said sees as a means of recuperating the otherness of the Orient and submitting it to Western symbolic power, often constructing the 'mysterious East' as a series of 'highly stylized simulacra, elaborately wrought imitations of what a live Orient might be thought to look like'.[28]

Said's thesis is borne out by the fact that there are no elephants to be found in the wild in Egypt, nor have there been for literally millennia. The elephant is an ideal 'Orientalist' animal given that it is indigenous to both Africa and Asia, so can do duty as an imitation of 'what a live Orient' – a term which of course encompasses, and even conveniently blurs, the two continents – 'might be thought to look like'. Napoleon's statue was sculpted in 1813 by Pierre-Charles Bridan, who took as his model an African elephant in the Jardin des Plantes zoo. The original plan was for a bronze effigy, to be constructed from cannons seized from the Spanish, whose trunk would have served as a fountain, but only a plaster one, by way of a 'trial run', was ever built. Its keeper, Levasseur, received an honorarium of 800 francs per year plus free accommodation in one of its legs.

What, if anything, the elephant was supposed to represent was never clear. Was it an Orientalist fantasy, an allegory of wisdom and strength – qualities traditionally associated with the animal – or a not-so-subtle allegory of the reach of France's imperial power? The latter hypothesis seems to be borne out by the fact that when the monarchy was restored, in 1815, plans for the bronze effigy were promptly dropped. The condition of the plaster one deteriorated to such a point that when it was demolished in 1846 a horde of rats poured out to infest the *quartier*. By that time the July Column, built in 1839, dominated the square as it has done ever since, and the elephant cut a shabby figure beside it. It supposedly impressed provincials visiting the capital, but the local inhabitants complained that it acted as a lair for thieves. Michelet comments in his *Journal* on the '[é]chafaudage du monument de juillet à côté de l'éléphant de plâtre qui fond à la pluie: caducité précoce du grand empire' / 'scaffolding of the July monument next to the plaster elephant dissolving in the rain: the premature expiry of the great empire' – tome 1 116).[29] The best-known literary allusion to the elephant is to be found in Victor Hugo's *Les Misérables*, to be discussed in the next chapter; the mid-nineteenth-century caricaturist Paul Gavarni alludes to it in a drawing depicting a young lad opening the door to an amply proportioned female visitor and calling out to his mother: 'Maman, c'est cette grosse dame dont papa dit toujours que c'est l'éléphant de la Bastille!' / 'Mum, here's that fat lady Dad always calls the Bastille elephant!'[30] There is still, at 40 boulevard Beaumarchais, a café called L'Éléphant Noctambule, frequented by Henry Miller in the 1930s because it was the haunt of his favourite prostitute, Germaine Deaugard. More edifyingly, in 1989 a polyester and metal replica toured France as part of the bicentennial celebrations, housing an audio-visual montage on the subject of liberty. Elephants evidently never forget.

Chapter Three

'The strategy of the generals of Africa shattered': the Restoration, Orleanist and Second Republic Years, 1815–1851

THE JULY COLUMN which now stands in the centre of the Place de la Bastille was a long time in the planning. The foundation-stone of a column, which was to sit atop a scale model of the fortress, had been laid on 14 July 1792, but the Convention abandoned the project. Jacques-Louis David, foreshadowing the Egyptophilia of Napoleon's elephant, built a large plaster fountain in 1793 in the form of the goddess Isis, but this was a transitory phenomenon. Not until Louis-Philippe had taken power, in 1830, was it decided to erect a monument not only to 1789 but also to the July Days that had brought him to power. For the revolutionary Faubourg this was a dubious tribute; to quote Jean-Paul Blais:

> Marquer dans ce quartier la naissance de la monarchie parlementaire est une récupération affichée de la colère des faubourgs. N'est-ce pas une manière d'affirmer que la liberté et l'ordre appartiennent d'abord au pouvoir dominant?[1]

> To mark in this *quartier* the birth of parliamentary monarchy was a clear-cut recuperation of the anger of the faubourgs. Was it not a way of affirming that liberty and order belong above all to the dominant regime?

Hugo, for his part, was to describe the column as 'le monument manqué d'une révolution avortée' / 'the failed monument of an abortive revolution',[2] all but disregarding its homage to 1789 and perceiving it, with a measure of accuracy, as a eulogy to the Orleanist monarchy. Louis-Philippe laid the foundation stone on 28 July 1831, though the monument was not to be completed for nine years. Its most striking feature is the figure of liberty that crowns it, often known as 'Le Génie de la Bastille', which has given its name to a contemporary association for the propagation of artistic activity in the *quartier*. The 'Génie', four metres high (the column measures just over forty-six), was the work of Auguste Dumont, and depicts a clearly male figure holding broken chains in one hand and the torch of freedom in the other. The female republican icon Marianne might have been thought a better choice, but Adolphe Thiers, doyen of conservative republicanism for many years and Prime Minister at the time the monument was being planned, was determined to avoid so potentially incendiary a symbol. Opinions on the statue have varied considerably; for Armand Lanoux it is a 'grand phallus faubourien' / 'large Faubourg phallus',[3] whereas the novelist Huysmans wrote slightingly of it and the Japanese singer Yumi Nara expressed herself fascinated by its changing hues as the day wore on. Théophile Gautier made the column the subject of a ludicrously pompous eulogy, *Le 28 Juillet 1840*, while its inauguration on that date was accompanied by Berlioz's somewhat more successfully elevated *Symphonie funèbre et triomphale*, conducted by the composer. The symphony closes, in a probable homage to Beethoven's Ninth, with a choral movement, whose words (by Antony Deschamps) are of a distinctly unrevolutionary tenor ('Changez, nobles guerriers, / tous vos lauriers / pour des palmes immortelles! / 'Change, o noble warriors, / all your laurels / for immortal palms!).[4] Louis-Philippe, fearing for his life after an attempted assassination in the nearby boulevard du Temple five years earlier, was absent from the ceremony, which was attended by a large crowd. The first suicide from the top of the column occurred the following year; it has long been closed to the public for safety reasons.

The column was also a tomb, for in its base were interred the remains of combatants killed during the July Days and the 1848 revolution that overthrew Louis-Philippe. These were joined by mummies brought back from Egypt by Bonaparte, and previously stored in the Bibliothèque Nationale, where their condition was deteriorating fast. All these remains were destroyed by a fire started during the Commune in 1871. The names of 615 July dead are embossed in gold letters around the base of the monument, which while it scarcely ranks among Paris's major attractions is the most instantly recognizable symbol of the *quartier* and figures in numerous films, such as Cédric Klapisch's *Paris* (2008), by way of an establishing shot. June 1848 saw the burning at the foot of the column of Louis-Philippe's throne, dragged there all the way from the Tuileries, as well as the transfer of 196 bodies of those killed in the February fighting. A 200 000-strong cortege accompanied the remains from the Madeleine to the square.

What of the Faubourg during this turbulent period in France's history? Unsurprisingly it was active in both 1830 and 1848, while the 1832 funeral of the Napoleonic general Lamarque – a stalwart opponent of the Bourbons – sparked off two days of rioting when it passed through the area. This, we shall see, plays an important part in Victor Hugo's *Les Misérables*. Life in the area continued to be harsh for many, with low wages and infrequent but sometimes violent strikes. Two prisons in the rue de la Roquette were opened in 1830, remaining in service until 1974. The Grande Roquette was the main prison for those under sentence of death, and between 1851 and 1899 was the site of the guillotine, whose former site is now marked by five stones and which claimed sixty-nine victims – including one woman – during this period. Most notorious of these was probably Jean-Baptiste Troppmann, who murdered a family of eight in the suburb of Pantin to get his hands on their fortune and was publicly guillotined on 18 January 1870. His execution attracted a huge crowd and was given grisly coverage in the nascent tabloid press, as well as a horrified report by the Russian writer Ivan Turgenev who was present but turned away in revulsion as the blade fell and became a strong opponent of capital punishment. The Petite Roquette was primarily for young offenders, often imprisoned on flimsy criteria; thus, an eleven-year-old boy was sent there at the request of his aunt and mother because, finding himself too hot at home, he had set out towards Père-Lachaise without their permission. Gabriel Delessert, the Prefect of Police, humanized the conditions for these young detainees in 1838, allocating them teachers and providing them with individual cells, which led to a marked reduction in recidivism. The rue de la Roquette was described as being between 1840 and 1890 the most gloomy and sinister street in Paris, while Hippolyte Meynadier in his 1843 *Paris sous le point de vue pittoresque et monumental*, which in pre-Hausmannian fashion advocated the building of six large new boulevards, wrote of the rue Saint-Antoine as the capital's grimiest road; it is difficult to imagine its Faubourg prolongation in any better state.

More jovially, the second half of the July Monarchy has been described as the peak period of the Parisian ball, and the Faubourg boasted two dance halls, each covering 200 square metres. The precarious conditions of life in the *quartier*, however, made it unsurprising that its inhabitants were leading figures in the 1830 revolution, described by Pierre Citron as 'le mythe révolutionnaire parisien dans sa forme la plus douce' / 'the Parisian revolutionary myth in its gentlest form'[5] – presumably because it lasted only three days, though some 1000 were killed during that time. Delacroix's celebrated painting *La Liberté guidant le peuple* remains the emblematic representation of the final downfall of the Bourbons, and more generally of the romanticized myth of revolution invoked by Citron. Diwo in the final volume of his triptych, *Le Génie de la Bastille*, has one of his characters wonder: '[P]enses-tu que le Faubourg va, comme en 89, marcher comme un seul homme?' / 'Do you think that as in 1789 the Faubourg will act as one man?'[6] It does, of course, with the sacrifice of the young Faubourg apprentice locksmith Arcole – clearly named after one of Napoleon's most famous victories – killed on a barricade at fourteen as he cries: '"Je vais vous montrer comment on sait mourir!"' / 'I'll show you that we know how to die!"'[7]

Of more local significance than 1830 to the Faubourg, however, was the scarcely less bloody rioting (800 dead) of June 1832, following the death of Lamarque. This general had been a left-wing member of parliament since 1828 and was given responsibility for suppressing legitimist revolts against the July Monarchy when Louis-Philippe came to power. The cholera epidemic which claimed him caused some 20 000 deaths in Paris. His funeral procession was watched, among a host of other mourners, by Alexandre Dumas, himself suffering from cholera, whose *Mémoires* speak of the rising tide of discontent in Paris. George Sand's novel *Horace* (1842), set largely in a student milieu, features scenes set during the rioting, in which two important characters nearly lose their lives. The militant republican Antoine-François-Marius Rey-Dussueil gives it a prominent place in his *Le Faubourg Saint-Merri* (1832) – glutinous to the point of unreadability, but of passing interest because of its observation that 'de la Bastille à la place du Châtelet, il y a mieux qu'une course; c'est presque un voyage' / 'from the Bastille to the place du Châtelet, there is more than a short distance; it's almost a journey.'[8] The journey referred to here is clearly a social and economic as much as a geographical one – further proof of the gulf between the poorer and the wealthier areas of Paris.

The 1832 riots would, however, be an all-but-forgotten moment of Parisian history were it not for their importance in Victor Hugo's *Les Misérables*. This extraordinary novel is probably best known nowadays through the Boublil / Schönberg musical, as I write in its twenty-fifth year on the London stage. It has been filmed, at the last count, twenty-six times, including one Egyptian and two Japanese adaptations, yet is rarely to be found on the university syllabus – partly the result of its length (1507 pages in my three-volume paperback edition), but also because Hugo is frequently perceived as too popular a writer, too lacking in what the sociologist Pierre Bourdieu calls 'distinction'. His image as demotic *monstre sacré*, epitomized by the two million mourners who joined his funeral procession in 1885, has almost certainly worked against what I believe to be the due recognition of his work as one of the very greatest of novels, foreshadowing many later avant-garde developments in for instance its use of digression and its treatment and deployment of slang. Hugo, to quote Frédéric Sayer, 'fait de Paris l'archétype de toutes les villes et de la civilisation elle-même'⁹ / 'makes Paris the archetype of all cities and of civilization itself' – nowhere more markedly than in the Parisian sections of *Les Misérables*. In what follows I shall confine myself to the role played by the Faubourg and its denizens in Hugo's narrative, where they can be said to represent, metonymically, the working classes of Paris – and thus perhaps, to follow Sayer, of the whole of nineteenth-century humanity.

Much of the novel's fourth part takes place during the 1832 uprising. Hugo describes the gathering tension in the capital from April of that year in terms that situate the Faubourg as the epicentre of revolutionary tendencies not only in Paris, but throughout the country:

> Quelque chose de terrible couvait. On entrevoyait les linéaments encore peu distincts et mal éclairés d'une révolution possible. La France regardait Paris; Paris regardait le faubourg Saint-Antoine.
>
> Le faubourg Saint-Antoine, sourdement chauffé, entrait en ébullition.[10]

> Something terrible was brewing. One could make out the still indistinct and ill-lit features of a possible revolution. France looked to Paris; Paris looked to the Faubourg Saint-Antoine.
>
> The Faubourg Saint-Antoine, muted but heated, was coming to the boil.

Lamarque's funeral is to be the catalyst of what Hugo describes as an insurrection (distinguished from the more random and less progressive 'émeute' or riot)[11] prepared by the woodworkers of the *quartier*, which swiftly spreads throughout the capital. The sonorous description of this 'vaste tumulte, comme une foule d'éclairs dans un seul roulement de tonnerre' / 'vast tumult, like a host of lightning-flashes amid a single thunderclap'[12] – revolution as force of nature, in keeping with the pantheistic lyricism that pervades his work – might have become fatiguing if it had not been succeeded by a narrative focus on Hugo's clearest embodiment of the people of Paris, the street-urchin Gavroche. Gavroche has gone on to give his name to such diverse institutions as a community newspaper published in the Aligre area between 1956 and 1962, a quarterly left-wing Paris journal of popular history and, less appositely, one of

London's most expensive restaurants. In so far as he has a home, it is the Place de la Bastille itself, inside the Napoleonic elephant best known for its role in Hugo's novel. Here he offers a night's shelter to two waifs, who unbeknown to him are in fact his younger brothers. Hugo's description of the elephant is intriguingly ambiguous; initially he sees it as 'une sorte de symbole de la force populaire' / 'a kind of symbol of the people's strength', a view strengthened by its proximity to the 'spectre invisible de la Bastille', but in the next paragraph it is assimilated in its decayed state to the old order in decline ('Il avait quelque chose d'une ordure qu'on va balayer et quelque chose d'une majesté qu'on va décapiter' / 'It resembled both a pile of rubbish about to be swept away and a monarch who is going to be decapitated').[13] For Jacques Seebacher Gavroche succeeds in appropriating the elephant, which he describes as the 'expansion historiquement avortée du génie napoléonien, sommation de l'encyclopédisme des lumières' / 'the historically frustrated expansion of Napoleonic genius, the summation of Enlightenment Encyclopedism',[14] at once to the neo-biblical mythical agenda so characteristic of Hugo and to his own need for the home denied him elsewhere:

> Gavroche le petit retourne 'l'idée' de Napoléon le Grand en un 'ventre biblique de la baleine', l'impossibilité des matériaux nobles en carcasse de gravois, le symbole titanique du peuple en caverne de titi, le plein jour en rat de cave, les ressources du Jardin des Plantes en chaleur et en sécurité d'alcove.[15]

> Little Gavroche turns the great Napoleon's 'idea' into a 'biblical belly of the whale', the impossibility of noble material into a carcass made of debris, the titanic symbol of the people into a street urchin's den, the bright light of day into a cellar rat, the resources of the Jardin des Plantes into the warmth and security of an alcove.

Gavroche dies, shot on a barricade near what is now the Forum des Halles, as he sings the song 'C'est la faute à Voltaire' – probably Hugo's own composition, though the satirist Béranger had written a similar ditty some years before, and well known now through Alain Boublil's musical setting of it. Gavroche has punctuated his participation in the insurrection, almost in the manner of a Brechtian commentary, with a series of songs – one of which includes the words 'Mais il reste encore des bastilles [sic] ' / 'But there are still some Bastilles left' [16] – which Hugo suggests are of his own composition ('Gavroche était un gamin de lettres' / 'Gavroche was a literary urchin').[17]

Stierle operates a kind of identification between novelist and character in saying of Hugo:

> A l'instar de son héros Gavroche, il vit dans le langage, langage plein de vie et étrange, et sait en disposer à son gré. Il cherche le jeu de mots ou avec les mots, la parodie, le langage populaire in épuisable dans sa diversité et sa couleur, et la langue lyrique du poète romantique.[18]

> Like his hero Gavroche, he dwells in language, a language that is strange and full of life, and knows how to deploy it as he wishes. He seeks plays on or with words, parody, the language of the people, inexhaustible in its diversity and colour, and the lyrical language of the Romantic poet.

But Gavroche is not only a surrogate for Hugo, though that is certainly one of his roles; he plays a similar role for the Faubourg Saint-Antoine, and thus for Paris in revolt. For Claudette Combes 'Gavroche est un héros comme Paris est un héros. La transfiguration du gamin n'est qu'un symbole de la transfiguration de la cité'[19] / 'Gavroche is a hero as Paris is a hero. The transfiguration of the urchin is but a symbol of the transformation of the city' – a transformation in which as we have seen the Faubourg and its denizens played a vital part. Working-class self-education was to make an important contribution to the life of the Faubourg from the end of the nineteenth century, with the foundation of the Université populaire in 1898, and Gavroche's lyrical and satirical inventiveness can certainly be seen as a precursor of that. Technically homeless Gavroche may be, but in our context it would be no exaggeration to describe him as at home, physically and linguistically, on the streets of Paris and, thanks to the shelter afforded by the elephant, in the Faubourg in particular.

The Paris of *Les Misérables* has come to be regarded as shorthand for the capital as working-class and revolutionary city. Thus, Émile Tersen draws a comparison with the Liberation in averring that 'le Paris populaire [...] sait s'il le faut, soulever ses pavés; on l'a vu en août 1944. Il reste, en dépit des apparences et des faux semblants, malgré le "gay Paris" qui masque la vérité, le Paris des *Misérables*'[20] / 'the people's Paris [...] knows, if need be, how to prise up its cobblestones, as we saw in August 1944. It remains, notwithstanding contradictory appearances, despite the "gay Paris" that masks the truth, the Paris of *Les Misérables*.' ('Gay' is, of course, here used in its original sense; we are not in the Marais ...) Such a view, historical and mythopoeic at once, is crystallized in the figure of the barricade, from

1789 to 1968 the defining emblem of Parisian social upheaval. Hugo devotes an entire chapter to the barricades constructed in 1848, contrasting the 'Scylla' of the Faubourg du Temple (near the Place de la République) with the 'Charybdis' of the Faubourg Saint-Antoine. The latter – one 'mother' barricade backed up by nineteen smaller ones – is described in lavishly epic terms, as 'l'acropole des va-nu-pieds […] digne d'apparaître à l'endroit même où la Bastille avait disparu'[21] / 'the Acropolis of the penniless […] worthy of appearing in the very spot from which the Bastille had disappeared'. It stems directly from the poverty of the *quartier* ('[o]n eût dit […] que le faubourg Saint-Antoine l'avait poussé là à sa porte d'un colossal coup de balai, faisant de sa misère sa barricade'[22] / 'it was as if […] the Faubourg Saint-Antoine had driven it to its gate with one colossal sweep, turning its wretchedness into its barricade'). Hugo's grandiosity, indeed his 'colossal sweep', here as so often elsewhere is thrown into relief and complemented by the historical and material grounding of his account.

Hugo is, we should recall, describing not the overthrow of Louis-Philippe in February 1848, but the June Days that followed – an uprising sparked off by the decision of the newly constituted Assemblée Nationale to close the *ateliers nationaux*, publicly funded to provide work and an income for the unemployed. His account of the barricades is 'totalement étrangère au reste du livre'[23] / 'totally foreign to the rest of the book', whose narrative closes with Jean Valjean's death in 1833; Éric Hazan argues that the only reason for the inclusion of this chapter – apart, we may think, from Hugo's inveterate penchant for the digression, of which he is a past master – is the homage it pays to the June insurgents. This seems all the more plausible since if their insurrection had been successful it would have prevented the coming to power of Louis Napoloon, whose self-proclamation as Emperor in 1851 drove Hugo into the Guernsey exile in which *Les Misérables* was written. If I deal with this section of the novel here rather than later in this chapter, along with other accounts of 1848, I am thus doing no more than following Hugo's own asynchronous example. The barricade is presented as a synecdoche for the Faubourg that built it, which 'faisait arme de tout; tout ce que la guerre civile peut jeter à la tête de la société sortait de là' / 'turned everything into a weapon; everything civil war can throw at society flew from it' – up to and including impromptu missiles such as clothes-buttons and scraps of pottery. 'C'était un tas d'ordures et c'était le Sinaï'[24] / 'It was a rubbish-heap and it was Mount Sinai' – the latter in reference to he spot where God allegedly gave the Ten Commandments to Moses. Hugo asserts that the June Days were 'la Carmagnole défiant la Marseillaise' – the 'Marseillaise' representing the fledgling Second Republic, while the 'Carmagnole' – a revolutionary song dating from 1792, which gloats over the imprisonment of Louis XVI and Marie-Antoinette – represents those who rose up in June demanding the maintenance of the *ateliers* and a 'democratic and social republic'. The Faubourg is identified with the Carmagnole when Hugo goes on to describe the uprising as a '[d]éfi insensé, mais héroïque, car ce vieux faubourg est un héros' / 'senseless but heroic act of defiance, for this old faubourg is a hero'. The paragraph that follows merits quotation in full for its identification of the barricade with the Faubourg and the manner in which one is described through the other:

> Le faubourg et sa redoute se prêtaient main-forte. Le faubourg s'épaulait à la redoute, la redoute s'acculait au faubourg. La vaste barricade s'étalait comme une falaise où venait se briser la stratégie des généraux d'Afrique. Ses cavernes, ses excroissances, ses verrues, ses gibbosités, grimaçaient, pour ainsi dire, et ricanaient sous la fumée. La mitraille s'y évanouissait dans l'informe; les obus s'y enfonçaient, s'y engloutissaient, s'y engouffraient; les boulets n'y réussissaient qu'à trouer des trous; à quoi bon canonner le chaos? Et les régiments, accoutumés aux plus farouches visions de la guerre, regardaient d'un oeil inquiet cette espèce de redoute bête fauve, par le hérissement sanglier, et par l'énormité montagne.[25]

> The Faubourg and the redoubt lent each other help. The Faubourg supported itself on the redoubt, the redoubt leant on the Faubourg. The vast barricade spread out like a cliff against which the strategy of the generals of Africa shattered. Its caverns, its excrescences, its warts, its bulges were so to speak grimacing and sniggering in the smoke. The bullets disappeared into shapelessness; the shells buried themselves, were swallowed up and engulfed; the cannonballs merely made holes; what's the use of firing cannon at chaos? And the regiments, accustomed to the wildest visions of war, looked anxiously at this redoubt as if it were a savage beast – wild-boar-like in its bristling, mountainous in its immensity.

If ever a writer can be said to have performed the oxymoronic task of articulating chaos, it was Hugo. Here that articulation has a specific topographical and symbolic resonance which draws upon the Faubourg's sulphurous reputation, more perilous even than the 'dark continent' for those who sought to quell it. For Karen Masters-Wicks Hugo's barricades function as 'excessive, monstrous, and human-like forms in the novel'[26] –

thus at once as metonymy for the milieu from which they spring and as a replication or *mise-en-abyme* of the text in which they figure. Hugo goes on to contrast the Saint-Antoine barricade with that of the Faubourg du Temple – 'le tumulte des tonnerres' / 'the thunderous tumult' of the former and the silence of the latter – separating the insurrection into 'une colère et une énigme'[27] / 'an anger and an enigma', and likening the Faubourg to a dragon in contrast to the Temple's sphinx.

Among the numerous cinematic adaptations of *Les Misérables*, Raymond Bernard's (1934) is the most impressive I have seen. Four-and-a-half hours long, and recently released on DVD, it features an outstanding performance by Harry Baur – one of French cinema's most neglected stars – as Jean Valjean. Bernard's film features the *quartier* in the sequences depicting the 1832 riots, in which a furniture shop is clearly visible and we are told of fighting around the Bastille and in the Faubourg Saint-Antoine, while demonstrators carry a banner proclaiming 'L'Armée des Bastilles'. As a general rule, however, filmic adaptations make little specific reference – clearly in part at least through constraints of time – to the Faubourg, though the elephant figures in three known to me: Marcel Bluwal's 1972 version, the first made for French television; the 1982 film directed by Robert Hossein; and a curious 1966 animated short from the Soviet Union, *Gavroche*, directed by Irina Gourvitch. This, which describes Gavroche as the 'symbol of the French people', begins and ends with Édith Piaf's *Hymne à l'amour* – one child of the streets invoked to celebrate another, though Piaf's song is markedly less political (to put it mildly) than Hugo's fierily radical novel. His Faubourg Saint-Antoine, the most striking and memorable of the area's numerous cultural representations, is at one and the same time a force of nature, elemental in its disorder, and a historically and sociologically determined phenomenon – the lair of the *classes dangereuses* at their most politically menacing.

The canonical writer of nineteenth-century Paris, of course, is Balzac, but the Faubourg plays scarcely any part in his work. As Hazan points out: 'Aucun personnage important de *La Comédie humaine* n'habite l'est de Paris'[28] / 'No important character in *La Comédie humaine* lives in the East of Paris'; the title character of *Le Cousin Pons* lodges in the Marais (not a well-off area in those days), but the boulevard Beaumarchais is an all-but-impassable barrier. The only exception I have discovered is the 1836 short story *Facino Cane*, whose narrator lives (as Balzac himself had briefly done many years before) in the rue Lesdiguières, on the Marais side of the Place but close to the Faubourg. Thence he sets out to follow the denizens of the area ('j'allais observer les moeurs du faubourg, ses habitants et leurs caractères'[29] / 'I went to observe the ways of the Faubourg, its inhabitants and their characters'), selecting a workman and his wife on their way back from one of the many popular theatres in the boulevard du Temple (maybe they have been to see Garance or Frédéric from Marcel Carné's film *Les Enfants du paradis*, set on the boulevard at about that period). Balzac – or at least his narratorial alter ego – empathizes with their poverty ('je pouvais épouser leur vie, je me sentais leurs guenilles sur le dos, je marchais les pieds dans leurs souliers percés'[30] / 'I could identify with their life, I felt their rags on my back, I walked with my feet in their shoes full of holes'), which triggers a brief but characteristically expansive evocation of the Faubourg as habitat of *classes laborieuses* and *classes dangereuses* alike:

> Je savais déjà de quelle utilité pourrait être ce faubourg; ce séminaire de révolutions qui renferme des héros, des inventeurs, des savants pratiques, des coquins, des scélérats, des vertus et des vices, tous comprimés par la misère, étouffés par la nécessité, noyés dans le vin, usés par les liqueurs fortes. Vous ne sauriez imaginer combien d'aventures perdues, combien de drames oubliés dans cette ville de douleur! Combien d'horribles et belles choses![31]

> I already knew how useful this faubourg could be; this revolutionary seminar which brings together heroes, inventors, practical scholars, rogues, scoundrels, virtues and vices, all straitened by poverty, stifled by need, drowning in wine, worn out by strong liquor. You could not imagine how many lost adventures and forgotten dramas there are in this city of pain! How many horrible and beautiful things!

We may be reminded of the celebrated assertion at the beginning of Balzac's best-known novel, *Le Père Goriot*: '[C]e drame n'est ni une fiction, ni un roman. *All is true*'[32] / 'This drama is neither a piece of fiction nor a novel. *All is true*'; but *Facino Cane* takes its readers in a very different direction from the realistic social anatomy to be found in *Goriot*. The narrator finds himself at a proletarian wedding in a grimy café in the rue de Charenton, where music is provided by a string trio of blind musicians from the nearby Quinze-Vingts hospital. One of these, eighty-two years old, is a Venetian named Facino Cane – a descendant of the notorious (real-life) fourteenth- and fifteenth-century *condottiero* of the same name. He has fled Italy sixty years before, having stumbled upon the hidden treasure of the Republic of Venice behind a wall in the jail in which he is imprisoned and carried off with him as much as he could in his escape. Now he invites the narrator to return there with him as his 'eyes' and share the remainder of the treasure with him; alas, he is to die before they can make the journey.

This fairly preposterous story, whose teller journeys from Venice to Paris by way of Smyrna (now Izmir, in Turkey), London, Amsterdam and Madrid, is related to the narrator as the two men sit beside the Canal Saint-Martin, whose 'eau dormante'[33] is compared to that of Venice's canals. Balzac's Faubourg, unlike Hugo's, has little or nothing revolutionary about it. It is there to serve as sombre contrast to the glamour of Facino's picaresque life before his sorry institutionalization:

> Mais ni les physionomies de cette assemblée, ni la noce, ni rien de ce monde n'a trait à mon histoire. Retenez seulement la bizarrerie du carde. Figurez-vous bien la boutique ignoble et peinte en rouge, sentez l'odeur du vin, écoutez les hurlements de cette joie, restez bien dans ce faubourg, au milieu de ces ouvriers, de ces vieillards, de ces pauvres femmes livreés au plaisir d'une nuit![34]

> But neither the faces at this gathering, nor the wedding, nor indeed anything of that world has to do with my story. Just remember how strange this setting was. Imagine the hideous red-painted café, smell the wine, listen to those shrieks of joy, stay here in the Faubourg, among those workmen, those old men, those poor women handed over for a night's pleasure!

The Faubourg in which we shall stay, active as it was in four major uprisings in the space of less than twenty years, is a somewhat more protean and less miserabilist world than that conjured up – to memorable effect – by Balzac. The hegemony of haut-bourgeois taste characteristic of the July Monarchy meant that the furniture industry prospered during this period. In January 1833 there appeared a periodical bearing the Faubourg's name, and proudly proclaiming that '… ce titre représente à lui seul les grands principes qui ont amené l'accomplissement de nos glorieuses révolutions de 1789 et 1830' / '… this title of itself represents the culmination of our glorious revolutions on 1789 and 1830'.[35] This first among, as we shall see, a number of community magazines to be published in the *quartier* was at once political – it called for equality and dismissed the Chambre des Députés as a mockery – and practical, giving in its three issues tips on how to brew stronger beer, whiten ivory (!) and make everlasting putty. Of particular note is its international dimension, for it carried news from England and Italy which would not always have been easy to come by at the time.

It was in 1836 that one of the most fascinating of the *quartier*'s denizens moved into 104 rue du Faubourg Saint-Antoine – Agricol Perdiguier, a carpenter from Avignon who was to become the leading light of the *compagnonnage* movement. This was an early form of trade unionism with affinities to guild socialism, which sought not only to organize workers in defence of their rights but also to educate them in the skills of their chosen trade by way of the *tour de France* – not a cycle race but an odyssey around France to meet senior craftsmen and learn from their experience. At least two of the characters in Diwo's novel trilogy embark on this, a tradition traceable back as far as the fifteenth century. Perdiguier published the first book on *compagnonnage* in 1839, attracting the attention of Hugo, Lamartine, Eugène Sue and George Sand, and played an important part in uniting what had often been an extremely fractious movement. On his retirement from manual work he opened a bookshop in the rue du Faubourg Saint-Antoine, and was active in the 1830 and 1832 uprisings before being elected a deputy in the 1848 parliamentary elections. His literary output includes songs, manuals for craftsmen, a play, political treatises and seven out of a projected twelve-volume *Histoire démocratique des peuples anciens et modernes*. The aftermath of Louis-Napoleon's coup in 1851 drove him into exile successively in Belgium, Germany and Switzerland; he returned to Paris in 1855 and opened a bookshop near the Gare de Lyon, served as deputy mayor of the 12th *arrondissement* in 1870 and died, alas in dire poverty, in 1875. His funeral was accompanied by an enormous crowd. Jacques Rancière in *La Nuit des prolétaires* pays extensive tribute to the self-taught working-class writers and thinkers of nineteenth-century France, many of whom were nourished by the *compagnonnage* movement. Perdiguier is undoubtedly one of the greatest of their number, and an emblematic figure of the Faubourg's culture and traditions.

It was the revolution of February 1848 – after which Agricol Perdiguier was elected to parliament – that ended the reign of Louis-Philippe, and thus marked the last time France was ruled by a king (though the Second Empire was to last twenty years). The exhaustion of the Orleanist regime and the poor economic situation, with up to two-thirds of building and furniture workers unemployed, fuelled discontent which erupted when a political banquet planned for 14 February was banned by the prefect of police. Demonstrations outside the house of Louis-Philippe's unpopular prime minister Guizot led to the killing of twenty workers from the Faubourg, and on the night of 23–24 February barricades went up all over the area. Faubourg deputations paraded carrying red flags, though the poet Lamartine, a minister in the provisional government set up after the king's abdication, was hostile to this and attempted to impose the tricolour in their place. 'In two days, France had gone from a conservative constitutional monarchy to a republic dedicated to the "right to work".'[36]

That 'right to work' came under attack with the closure of the *ateliers nationaux*. The Convention decreed on 21 June that all male workers aged between eighteen and twenty-five would be conscripted into the army – a provocation which led to the uprising of 23–25 June. A parliamentary commission of inquiry reported that a locksmith's in the Faubourg had been transformed into an ad hoc munitions factory, and the *quartier* was – as might have been expected – the nerve-centre of the uprising. Racary, a mechanic arrested on a Faubourg barricade and condemned to hard labour for life, proclaimed his defiance with the cry: '"Je suis républicain. Eh bien! l'avenir est à nous. Vive la République démocratique et sociale!"'[37] / 'I'm a republican. Well! the future is ours. Long live the democratic and social Republic!"' If the June Days have been neglected by establishment historians and in school textbooks, this, for Hazan, is because 'leur fantôme est toujours aussi encombrant'[38] / 'their ghost is still as much of a nuisance'. A politically committed writer of a very different stripe, Alexis de Tocqueville, who had backed the violent suppression of the uprising, nevertheless regarded it as the most important event in post-Revolutionary French history, since its aim was not to change the mode of government, but to bring about a qualitatively new social order. The June Days have come to be associated primarily with the death of the archbishop of Paris, Monseigneur Affre, killed by a stray bullet at the entrance to the Faubourg while trying to mediate between insurgents and soldiers, but their political as well as human dimension should not be underestimated.

The description of the place de la Bastille in June by Daniel Stern / Marie d'Agoult, quoted in the Introduction, shows how significant in this would-be second French Revolution the *quartier* was. Négrier, the general whose division was charged with quelling the uprising in the Faubourg, was killed nearby along with the deputy Charbonnel; Stern – a friend of Lamartine's and of the 'utopian socialist' Louis Blanc, who bemoaned the June Days in the name of a more tranquil reformism – gives a fulsome account of his seemingly courageous, but suicidal, confrontation with the rioters: 'Rien ne le protège, rien ne le masque; l'ombre de la Colonne de Juillet trace seule une ligne étroite sur le sol inondé de lumière'[39] / 'He is unprotected and unconcealed; only the shadow of the July Column traces a narrow line of the ground drenched in light.' The column here appears in a sinister rather than celebratory perspective, in keeping with its role as sepulchre for many of the dead of 1830 and February 1848. Stern claims to have drunk a toast with some of the workers to 'la République *démocrate et sociale*'[40] / 'the *democratic and social* [NB not 'socialist'] Republic', but such cross-class conviviality was to count for little in the face of the savage repression carried out by General Cavaignac, who, his task finished, was to announce proudly: "'Il n'y a plus de lutte dans Paris'"[41] / "'There is no longer a struggle in Paris.'" Until the next time, three years later ...

The painter Ernest Meissonier's *Souvenir de la guerre civile*, depicting a barricade strewn with corpses (no live human beings are to be seen), is the best-known artistic reproduction of the June Days. Meissonier painted it immediately after the events, modelling it on a water-colour done at the scene. Its small size and low-key realism, a long way removed from the rhetorical sweep of Delacroix, lend it an almost minimalist poignancy, certainly by contrast with the heavily stylized contemporary depiction on the cover of Jean-Michel Fabre's *Mgr Affre: un évêque au pied des barricades!* representing the dying archbishop in a martyr's pose. This comparison is explicitly made by Stern when she says: 'Le martyre de l'archévêque de Paris allait renouveler, à la face du monde, ce grand spectacle, qui fut la force et qui restera la gloire de l'église Chrétienne'[42] / 'The martyrdom of the archbishop of Paris was going to renew, before all the world, that great sight which was the strength and will remain the glory of the Christian Church.' The 'sight' in question is clearly the martyrdom of Christ.

Affre was a genuine intellectual – a former professor of philosophy at the seminary of Nantes – and in many respects a progressive figure, who had inaugurated parishes in working-class areas such as Ménilmontant (in the north of Paris). Who fired the bullet that killed him remains uncertain, with much contradictory evidence. What is not in dispute is that he was attempting to mediate between the two sides, though it is questionable whether his reported words to the rioters – a plea to the 'pauvres ouvriers' / 'poor workers' to 'cesser une lutte impie'[43] / 'stop your impious struggle' – were the best calculated to calm their wrath. His last words, after a two-day agony, were a plea that no more blood should be spilt. As many as 200 000 mourners are reported to have joined his funeral procession.

Apart from a glutinous poem in rhyming couplets by one P. Barret, published in 1862, Affre's death would appear to have had few literary repercussions – at least directly. Yet his seemingly Christ-like demeanour may seem to foreshadow that of Monseigneur Myriel, the bishop of Digne who redeems Jean Valjean through his beneficence at the opening of *Les Misérables*. Myriel takes in the newly released convict for the night and is rewarded by the theft of his silver candlesticks; the police catch Valjean red-handed, but Myriel assures them that he had made him a gift of the silverware. This story is said to be based on the real-life action of Monseigneur de Miollis, bishop of Digne between 1805 and 1838. Miollis's successor was Marie-Dominique-Auguste Sibour, who was to succeed Affre as archbishop of Paris – perhaps no more than a coincidence, but a serendipitous and intertextually resonant one.

The June Days were followed by Louis-Napoleon's election as president in December 1848, defeating Cavaignac in a surprising landslide victory. Three years later he staged a coup, dissolving the Assembly and occupying Paris with 50 000 troops – the prelude to the establishment of the Second Empire. France's last non-republican regime, in December 1852. There was less spirited opposition to Louis-Napoleon in the Faubourg than might have been expected, perhaps because of a lingering respect for the memory of his grandfather. Such at least is Jean Diwo's suggestion in *Le Génie de la Bastille*, where he comments in mildly cynical vein on Victor Hugo's call for support for an insurrection: 'Il n'existait qu'une faille dans ce cri généreux: personne dans les faubourgs n'avait envie de charger son fusil!'[44] / 'There was only one flaw in this glorious appeal: nobody in the faubourgs wanted to load their gun!'

Among the members of the committee of resistance set up by republicans was Jean-Baptiste Baudin, a doctor who represented the department of Ain (between Lyon and the Swiss border) in the 1848 Assembly. Baudin and several of his parliamentary colleagues – including Victor Schoelcher, the prime mover in the 1848 abolition of slavery in France's overseas territories* – joined a barricade erected on 3 December in the rue Saint-Marguerite, now the rue Trousseau. Suspicious workers from the Faubourg taunted the deputies by asking whether they expected them to get themselves killed for the sake of twenty-five francs per day – a reference to the parliamentary salary at the time. Baudin allegedly responded: 'Vous allez voir comment on meurt pour vingt-cinq francs!' / 'You'll see how to die for twenty-five francs!' and was promptly killed in an exchange of gunfire between insurgents and troops. The police refused to hand Baudin's body over for burial until his next-of-kin gave an undertaking that he would be buried immediately and in secret. The location of the grave (in the Montmartre cemetery) quickly became known, however, and in 1868 a subscription was launched to pay for a monument there. Those responsible, including the journalist Charles Delescluze, were prosecuted; Delescluze's defence was led by the young lawyer Léon Gambetta, later to become one of the most prominent figures of

---

* Schoelcher's tomb in the Pantheon, along with those of the assassinated socialist leader Jean Jaurès and the Resistance hero Jean Moulin, was visited by François Mitterrand on the day he assumed the Presidency (21 May 1981).

the early days of the Third Republic. Gambetta's eloquence at the trial made him famous overnight, but Delescluze was less fortunate, being imprisoned and in 1858 deported to Devil's Island for two years. He was to die on the barricades of the Commune in 1871, so that the bullet that killed Baudin can in a sense be said to have claimed two victims.

Baudin has become a celebrated figure largely through Victor Hugo's *Histoire d'un crime*. The crime in question is Louis-Napoleon's coup, in protest against which Hugo went into exile – first to Brussels, then to Jersey and finally, for fifteen years, in Guernsey, returning to Paris only on the fall of the Emperor. The text's sub-title, 'Déposition d'un témoin' / 'A witness's statement', suggests a live eye-witness account, but in fact pressure of other work and the appearance of a number of other works about the coup meant that it was not completed and published until 1877, though Hugo had begun work on it only ten days or so after Baudin's death. It enjoyed instant and immense success, but in more recent times has been difficult to get hold of; the left-wing publishing-house La Fabrique, one of whose directors is Éric Hazan, issued a new edition in December 2009.

Hugo's text has been described by Graham Robb as 'one of the great examples of history as boy's adventure',[45] which captures the vivacity of his 'live-broadcast' account perhaps at the expense of its political seriousness and moral indignation. He waxes highly cynical about the attempts of right-wing politicians such as Falloux (who had taken the lead in proposing the 1848 abolition of the *ateliers nationaux*) to curry favour with the working class ('Se figure-t-on Falloux tribun soufflant sur le faubourg Antoine?'[46] / 'Can we imagine Falloux as a tribune stirring it up in the Faubourg Antoine?' – Hugo is here using the secularized form of the area's name briefly introduced after the Revolution, an ironic reference to Falloux's role in giving the Catholic clergy much greater responsibility for education).

Hugo describes himself upbraiding the armed soldiers who filled the place de la Bastille, in the name of the National Assembly of which he had been elected a member three years before. As his coach makes its way through the Faubourg the tension mounts, and he asks his driver to head in the direction of the shots that ring out. The writing is terse and staccato, with much laconic, almost stichomythiac dialogue; we are a long way from the epic expansiveness of the barricades in *Les Misérables*, as when we learn of Baudin's death from the mouth of an acquaintance of Hugo's:

Cet homme intrépide était pâle.
    – N'allez pas plus loin, me dit-il, c'est fini.
    – Comment, fini?

— Oui, on a dû avancer l'heure; la barricade est prise, j'en arrive.
Elle est à quelques pas d'ici, devant nous.

Et il ajouta:

— Baudin est tué.

La fumée se dissipait à l'extrémité de la rue.

— Voyez, me dit Alexandre Rey.

J'aperçus, à cent pas devant nous, au point de jonction de la rue
Cotte et de la rue Sainte-Marguerite, une barricade très basse que les
soldats défaisaient. On emportait un cadavre.

C'était Baudin.[47]

That fearless man was pale.

— Don't go any further, he said, it's all over.

— What do you mean, over?

— Yes, they must have brought things forward; the barricade has
been captured, I've just been there. It's a few steps from here, ahead
of us.

And he added:

— Baudin has been killed.

The smoke was lifting at the other end of the street.

— Look, said Alexandre Rey.

I saw, a hundred feet ahead of us, where the rue Cotte meets the
rue Sainte-Marguerite, a very low barricade being taken down by the
soldiers. They were carrying off a corpse.

It was Baudin.

Hugo follows with a gripping account of the barricade erected in the
Faubourg and events around it, including the peaceful confiscation under
Schoelcher's leadership of weapons and ammunition from soldiers who protest
that they will gladly change sides and fight alongside the protestors, but are
not trusted because of a similar promise broken in June 1848. Resonances
of 1789 are plain in Schoelcher's suggestion that the insurgents should not
seek to build a barricade in the rue de Montreuil ('Où allons-nous? nous
tournons le dos à la Bastille. Nous tournons le dos au combat'[48] / 'Where
are we going? We're turning our backs on the Bastille. We're turning our
backs on the fight'). Schoelcher appeals for solidarity ('Quand l'armée et
les faubourgs se battent, c'est le sang du peuple qui coule des deux côtés'[49]
/ 'When the army and the faubourgs fight, it's the people's blood that flows
on both sides') and seeks to open discussion with the troops. It is at this point
that some of the workers denounce the twenty-five francs of a deputy's salary,

and that Baudin makes his celebrated retort. He is not killed instantly, for Schoelcher – as much the hero of this account as Baudin – first denounces Louis-Bonaparte's violation of the constitution, the 'crime' of Hugo's title. The captain threatens to shoot unless the insurgents retreat, but the soldiers are initially reluctant until an (unattributed) bullet kills one of their number, whereupon they open fire, more it would appear in despair than in anger. No prisoners are taken – the insurgents scatter into side-streets and nearby 'safe houses' – but the Faubourg's discouragement is all but terminal, as Hugo relates in a paragraph worthy of extended quotation:

> En présence du fait de la barricade Saint-Antoine, si héroïquement construite par les représentants, si tristement délaissée par la population, les dernières illusions, les miennes, durent se dissiper. Baudin tué, le faubourg froid, cela parlait haut. C'était une démonstration suprême, évidente, absolue, de ce fait auquel je ne pouvais me résigner, l'inertie du peuple; inertie déplorable, s'il comprenait, trahison de lui-même, s'il ne comprenait pas, neutralité fatale dans tous les cas, calamité dont la responsabilité, répétons-le, revenait, non au peuple, mais à ceux qui, en juin 1848, après lui avoir promis l'amnistie, la lui avaient refusée, et qui avait déconcertée la grande âme du peuple de Paris en lui manquant de parole. Ce que la Constituante avait semé, le Législative le récoltait.* Nous, innocents de la faute, nous en subissions le contre-coup.[50]

Faced with the Saint-Antoine barricade – so heroically built by the elected representatives, so sadly abandoned by the population – the last illusions, at least mine, were inevitably dispelled. Baudin had been killed and the Faubourg remained cold – that said it all. It was a supreme, self-evident, absolute demonstration of something to which I could not resign myself, the people's inertia; a deplorable inertia if the people understood, a betrayal of themselves if they did not, a neutrality which in any event was fatal, a calamity whose responsibility lay, let us say it again, not with the people, but with those who in

---

* The first term refers to the assembly that drew up the constitution of the ill-fated Second Republic in 1848, the second to the parliament elected in 1849 and dissolved by Louis-Napoleon as part of his coup. The amnesty referred to, which would have applied to all those deported to Algeria for their participation in the June Days, had been proposed by among others Victor Schoelcher, but was voted down by the Assembly.

June 1848 had promised an amnesty that was then refused, and who had disconcerted the great soul of the Parisian people by breaking the word given to them. What the Constituent Assembly had sowed, the Legislative Assembly was to reap. We, innocent of any fault, endured the consequences.

The best-known pictorial representation of Baudin's death, or at least the moment that preceded it, is Ernest Pichio's painting in the Musée Carnavalet, in which the deputy, wearing his sash of office, is shown before a fairly rudimentary barricade, with the July Column in the background. This was not painted until 1869, and was initially refused by in the autumn Salon exhibition organized by the Académie (roughly equivalent to the Royal Academy). Republican newspapers protested to such effect that the Academy was forced to rescind its decision the following year. The sale and distribution of photographic reproductions, however, was prohibited until the fall of Napoleon III – evidence, for all the liberalization that marked its second decade, of how authoritarian a regime the Second Empire was. Karl Marx was famously to observe that Louis-Napoleon's coup, fifty-two years after his uncle's, was an instance of history repeating itself 'the first time as tragedy, the second time as farce'.[51] Perhaps it was that sense of the farcical, and the weariness it may have engendered after five major uprisings (1789, 1830, 1832, 1848 and 1851) that caused this must tumultuous period in the *quartier*'s history to peter out into what seems to have been a sullen acquiescence. Jean Diwo – ever an authorial voice on the side of placid moderation – has it that: 'Comme toujours après s'être trouvé engagé, souvent malgré lui, dans une bataille perdue, le peuple de la scie et du rabot aspirait au calme et à l'ordre, conditions évidentes d'un retour à la prospérité perdue'[52] / 'As always after having been caught up, often in spite of themselves, in a losing battle, the people of the saw and the plane aspired to calm and order, the obvious conditions for a return to the prosperity they had lost.' The considerably more radical Éric Hazan asserts soberly: 'Pour Paris rouge, c'est une parenthèse de vingt ans qui commence'[53] / 'For red Paris, a twenty-year hiatus was beginning.' The Faubourg had one more would-be revolutionary shot in its locker, but other immense, if less sanguinary, changes were to take place before that was to be fired.

Chapter Four

'Where is the noise of the storm that I love?': The Second Empire from Haussmann to the Commune

THE TWO DECADES of the Second Empire were marked by a kind of revolution in Paris, but of a very different kind to the hurly-burly of the previous eighty-two years. The key figure was Baron Georges-Eugène Haussmann, though it might be more appropriate to refer to him as 'Baron', since his title may well have been self-conferred, resting on the fact that his maternal grandfather, Baron Dentzel, had no male heirs. Haussmann, an early example of the classic French *fonctionnaire* or state employee who though unelected can wield immense influence, made his career as prefect – the appointed representative of central government in a French department – first in the Var, on the western Riviera, and then in Yonne (Burgundy) before being nominated prefect of the Seine – the department that in those days encompassed Paris and its suburbs – in 1853. He was to occupy this post for seventeen years, falling from grace only a few months before his master Napoleon III.

Edmone Texier's *Tableau de Paris*, published in the year Haussmann assumed responsibility for the city, is the most comprehensive survey known to me of what pre-Haussmannian Paris was like. To read his assertion that 'la large et longue rue du Faubourg Saint-Antoine commence déjà à donner une idée de la splendeur de la cité dans laquelle le voyageur pénètre'[1] / 'the broad and long rue du Faubourg-Saint-Antoine already begins to give us an idea of the splendour of the city the traveller is entering' might make the unwary reader think that Texier was writing about Paris after Haussmann. The Faubourg's German inhabitants also get a good press, described as 'ouvriers intelligents et laborieux' / 'intelligent and diligent workmen', and as such favourably contrasted to the pseudo-intellectuals – 'la classe des lettrés ou soi-disant tels'[2] / 'the lettered classes, or at least those who claim to be so' – who are identified as the other major category of German immigrants to

Paris. Texier's was not, however, the only or even the dominant view of the *quartier*, as is evidenced by the writer Paul Féval – a Catholic royalist, but also, perhaps incongruously, a friend of Charles Dickens – who describes in his *Les Nuits de Paris* (first published in 1851) a bizarre hallucination in which he 'saw' the spirit of the Faubourg in rags, carrying a torch and with the handle of a dagger protruding from its sleeve. This was the vision of the Faubourg as *dangereuse* rather than *laborieuse*, perceptible as we have seen in *A Tale of Two Cities*, that Haussmann wanted to dispel.

More than any other individual figure, and despite the changes of the past 140 years, Haussmann can be described as responsible for the Paris we know today. He had predecessors, such as Meynadier whose plan for large new boulevards was mentioned in the previous chapter, but none with the financial means and political authority at his command. He was mandated by Louis-Napoleon to transform the city from a picturesque, but unhygienic and often dangerous, warren into a modern metropolis to rival post-Great-Fire London. The wide boulevards and open squares, such as the place de la République and the place de l'Étoile, that characterize the contemporary city were his doing, while he was also responsible for the laying-out of the Buttes-Chaumont park, in the north-east of the city, along with the building of two major railway stations, the Gare du Nord and the Gare de Lyon, and the much smaller Gare de la Bastille, opened in 1855 and serving the Seine-et-Marne department to the south-east of Paris until the old steam trains were replaced by the electrified RER line in 1969.

For most of those who have expressed an opinion of him, Haussmann is either villain or hero. The not-so-hidden political agenda behind the developments he initiated was to control the *classes dangereuses* by eliminating the dense network of narrow streets that afforded them cover and flushing them into the light of day. Two new barracks, near the Hôtel de Ville and in what is now the Place de la République, were built on his watch to add to those in the boulevard Henri IV and the rue de Reuilly, so that the Faubourg was well and truly hemmed in by the military. Michel Foucault, in *Surveiller et punir*, analyses the shift in disciplinary technique at the end of the Ancien Régime from a system which locked prisoners away out of sight in dungeons to one which relied on surveillance and visibility. Haussmann's reinvention of the city, while it was clearly not carceral, undoubtedly aimed at making it harder for potential malefactors and disruptive elements to go about their nefarious business in secret and easier for troops to move swiftly against them. Éric Hazan emphasizes Haussmann's political purpose when he says: 'Le faubourg Saint-Antoine, le quartier Popincourt et le faubourg du Temple formaient au milieu du XIXe siècle un ensemble où les classes laborieuses et dangereuses se trouvaient concentrées de manière inquiétante. C'est pourquoi cettre région de Paris fut l'objet de toute l'attention de Haussmann'[3] / 'The Faubourg Saint-Antoine, Popincourt and the faubourg du Temple were in the mid-nineteenth century an area in which the *classes laborieuses et dangereuses* were concentrated to a disturbing extent. That is why this part of Paris was the major object of Haussmann's attention.' Haussmann's own memoirs, whose tone is egotistical to say the least, recount the Emperor's enthusiastic response to his proposal to cover over the Canal Saint-Martin, which enabled 'l'établissement, "à plein voyant", d'un bout à l'autre, de la ligne magistrale d'où l'on pourrait, au besoin, prendre à revers tout le Faubourg Saint-Antoine'[4] / 'the clearly visible establishment of the direct line of sight from which it would be possible if need be to attack the whole Faubourg Saint-Antoine from the rear'. His measures to tame the *quartier* took administrative as well as architectural form, for when he reorganized the *arrondissement* system in 1860 the Faubourg, hitherto part of the 8th, was split between the 11th and the 12th – clearly a 'divide-and-rule' strategy.

Yet not all commentators, even on the left, were hostile to an urban project which made Paris a far healthier city than heretofore, destroying 20 000 insanitary buildings, laying 600 kilometres of sewers and making further cholera epidemics like that of 1849 impossible. So strong an adversary of Louis-Napoleon as the republican deputy Jules Simon – removed from his lecturing post at the Sorbonne in 1851 for his public denunciation of the coup – praised Haussmann for making the city an airier and less noisome place. The Marxist geographer David Harvey distils the potential contradictions in Haussmann's approach when he says that: 'He wanted to make Paris a capital worthy of France, even of Western civilization. In the end he simply helped to make it a city in which the circulation of capital became the real imperial power.'[5] In this respect he prefigured capitalist development in a host of cities, of which Victorian London and its post-imperial epigone in the Docklands development of the 1980s may well be the most familiar to readers of this book.

What is certain is that Haussmann rendered the Faubourg a safer place in two respects – safer for its inhabitants, whose living conditions were markedly less unsavoury than before, but also safer for the autocratic regime whose servant he was. Not only was activity such as the building of barricades made considerably more difficult, but those who would have been most likely to have engaged in it – the impoverished proletariat – began to find themselves, in a movement that has continued unabated right to the present day, priced out to the suburbs. This has been the major factor in the development of what became known as *la banlieue rouge* – the 'red suburbs' such as Saint-Denis or Ivry, mostly to the east of Paris, with a large industrial working-class population which makes them nowadays among the last bastions of the Communist Party. Bernard Marchand makes a forceful etymological point in stating that 'La banlieue parisienne représente exactement le "lieu du ban", l'endroit où l'on est banni' / 'The Paris *banlieue* represents precisely the "place of the ban", the spot to which one is banished'[6] – one reason perhaps why the term has always had less secure and salubrious resonances in French than its closest English equivalent, '(the) suburb(s)'. Today's Paris bears the imprint of Haussmann not only in its layout and architecture, but in its changed social composition – something to which the erstwhile Faubourg's transformation into Bastille, or even 'Bastoche', bears onomastic witness.

Not that the area which bears that name today was entirely urbanized in the mid-nineteenth century, for Joseph Charlemont – champion and leading light of French boxing, a combat sport in which feet as well as fists are used – wrote of his childhood at 139 rue de Charonne and of his marauding activities in 1850 among 'les vignes de Charonne, les belles pêches de Montreuil et les succulentes reines-claudes de Bagnolet'[7] / 'the vines of Charonne, the fine peaches of Montreuil and the succulent greengages of Bagnolet'. Two of those areas have now been absorbed into the *banlieue* – *rouge* for Bagnolet which is a long-standing Communist stronghold, *vert* for Montreuil which has had a Green mayor since 2008 – while Charonne forms part of the 20th *arrondissement*. All are now entirely built-up, and it requires a real effort of imagination to conceive of such rural riches as Charlemont describes on the doorstep of the Faubourg. The area changed from about 1865 onwards, which saw the construction of larger buildings with industrial workshops grouped around a courtyard and residential accommodation above – a distribution still common in the *quartier*. 1864 had seen the opening of what has remained one of the iconic Parisian brasseries, Bofinger (actually in the Marais, but often associated with Bastille because of its location in the street of that name) – an illustration of how the area was transformed under Haussmann.

Modern Paris had arrived, but that is not to say that the Faubourg's revolutionary traditions had been altogether swept away. The comparative tranquillity of the Second Empire, already under threat from Louis-Napoleon's absurd imperial adventure in Mexico between 1864 and 1867, came to an end in 1870 with the declaration of war on Germany, a war comprehensively lost by France within six months, precipitating the Emperor's abdication. Paris was besieged by the Prussian armies from September 1870 until the signing of the armistice in February 1871 – a period of even more intense hardship than usual for the city's working class, some of whom dug up corpses from whose powdered bones they made a meagre broth that was their only sustenance. The terms of the final treaty were seen as humiliating, the more so as they had been conceded by a conservative majority in the new republican National Assembly which went on to raise taxes. When troops moved to seize cannon in Montmartre that had been bought by public subscription for the defence of Paris, wounded patriotism and class resentment combined in the revolutionary moment known ever after as the Commune. That term, used administratively to refer to a town or village, had strong republican connotations, since it had not come into official use until after 1789. On 28 March 1871, by which time large numbers of better-off Parisians had fled the capital, the Commune de Paris was proclaimed from the steps of the Hôtel de Ville – an effective secession of the city from the now Versailles-based national government, led by Adolphe Thiers. It lasted, however, only two months, a period characterized by popular euphoria but also a lack of serious planning which made it relatively easy for the Versaillais troops to set about retaking Paris on 22 May. As they advanced into the city, the Communards retaliated by setting fire to many of its most celebrated buildings; the Hôtel de Ville and the Tuileries Palace – Napoleon III's residence – were both burnt to the ground. Colin Jones points out an irony – quite possibly a conscious one – here when he says: 'The regime which had lived by and for new buildings found its nemesis in an orgy of incendiary demolition.'[8] It is as if the angry Parisian masses had found a way of showing that despite Haussmann's best efforts they were still capable of the kind of 'urban guerrilla' activity his redevelopment had been designed to prevent.

The Communards' largely symbolic violence attracted a savage riposte in the form of the *semaine sanglante* or 'bloody week', in which something like 30 000 were shot (Versaillais losses were about 900). The Commune itself has remained an important moment in Parisian popular memory – because of its spontaneous nature, because of the appalling ferocity of the government's vengeance and not least because it was probably the last time full-scale political revolution appeared to be on the agenda. Needless to say the Faubourg was in the forefront of the action, but less prominently so than the less easily cut-off areas of Belleville and the Faubourg du Temple; Haussmann had done his work all too well. Jean Diwo's assertion, in *Le Génie de la Bastille*, that the Faubourg was 'complètement mort'[9] / 'completely dead' in March 1871, may appear to lend credence to this view, though as we have seen earlier Diwo's political perspective is generally a somewhat dulcet one. As early as 17 March, on which date Thiers moved the government to Versailles, there was a demonstration of protest in the place de la Bastille, virtually the first sign of popular discontent in the capital. On the following day Victor Hugo's son

Charles, a left-wing journalist who had shared his father's exile in Guernsey, was buried, and an ominous silence fell over the Place as Hugo – back in France only seven months before – accompanied the coffin.

The Commune itself saw a large barricade at the junction of the place de la Bastille and the rue du Faubourg Saint-Antoine and another covering the rue de Charenton and the rue de la Roquette. The latter street as we have seen housed two of the major Parisian prisons, in the larger of which six hostages were detained in April 1871 and, after attempts at exchanging them for the revolutionary socialist Blanqui who was imprisoned in Brittany, shot on 24 May. Their number included the president of the Court of Appeal (Bonjean), three Jesuits, the parish priest of the Madeleine church and, most notoriously, the archbishop of Paris, Georges Darboy, who is said to have died blessing his executioners. However, the socialist historian, and sometime fiancé of Karl Marx's daughter Eleanor, Prosper-Olivier Lissagaray took a somewhat more cynical view: 'Ce n'est plus le prêtre orgeilleux glorifiant le 2 Décembre;* il balbutie: "Je ne suis pas l'ennemi de la Commune, j'ai fait ce que j'ai pu; j'ai écrit deux fois à Versailles"' [10] / 'He was no longer the proud priest glorifying 2 December; he stuttered: "I'm no enemy of the Commune, I did what I could; I wrote to Versailles twice."' The photographer Eugène Appert produced a photo-montage reproduction of the execution, accompanied by one of the shooting in reprisal of three leading Communards, Rossel, Bourgeois and Ferré. Bertrand Tillier points out that these restagings were constructed from an overtly Versaillais point of view, whereas 'les images contemporaines d'édifices en ruine et de communards arrêtés qu'a portraiturés Appert servirent d'épouvantail aux vainqueurs et d'icônes aux vaincus' [11] / 'the contemporary images of ruined buildings and arrested Communards whose portrait Appert gives us acted as spectres to frighten the victors and as icons for the vanquished'. The ideological battle of the Commune was refought in the realm of the image, as it was to be more than 130 years later when the cartoonist Jacques Tardi produced a four-volume illustrated adaptation of Jean Vautrin's 1999 novel *Le Cri du peuple*. Tardi's illustrations feature at one point or another all the major Communard sites, including the Place de la Bastille and the Roquette prison, though the Left Bank – the real centre of the insurrection – figures as prominently if not more so, almost by way of a suggestion that the Faubourg's revolutionary preeminence was no longer uncontested. Two TV films, by Jean Prat (1966) and Serge Moati (1977), have told the story of Louis Rossel, the only senior officer to have gone over to the Communards, who

* The date of Louis-Napoloon's 1851 coup.

was executed in 1871. I have been unable to access copies of either of these so cannot say whether the Faubourg features in them. The British, though since 1994 Lithuanian-based, director Peter Watkins's 2000 *La Commune (Paris, 1871)*, also made for television, runs for six-and-a-quarter hours and is, on the evidence of the parts of it I have seen, a remarkable mise-en-scène not only of the events of 1871 but of the role of the media, for it purports to be the work of a Communard TV station set up in opposition to the official Versaillais line. The film was shot in Montreuil, in the studios of the early silent director Georges Méliès, but uses non-professional actors, many drawn from the Popincourt area contiguous with the Faubourg.

Among literary evocations of the Commune, the work of Jules Vallès ranks alongside Zola's *La Débâcle*, whose Commune scenes are set on the Left Bank, as the most remarkable. Vallès was a prominent Communard activist – founder of *Le Cri du peuple*, which ephemeral though it may have been was in February and March 1871 the capital's most-read daily newspaper, and an elected member of the Commune (for the 15th *arrondissement*). Two men are indeed reported to have been executed by the Versaillais in mistake for him. A street near the Charonne Métro station appropriately bears his name. His *Jacques Vingtras* trilogy, whose eponymous character is largely modelled on the author, has been described as the tale of a sacrificed generation – that which underwent the successive crushing of its revolutionary aspirations in 1848, 1851 and 1871. The third volume, *L'Insurgé*, existed only as a draft at the time of Vallès's death in 1885, and was prepared for publication by his secretary and lover, the feminist journalist Séverine. Louis-Ferdinand Céline, whose political views to put it mildly differed somewhat from those of Vallès, praised the work highly, observing: 'La littérature française ne délire presque jamais' [12] / 'French literature is hardly ever delirious.' His own work of course was to prove the definitive exception to that rule, and Vallès's disjointed, staccato first-person mode of writing foreshadows *Voyage au bout de la nuit* more strikingly than any other text known to me. Vallès's own dual career, as writer / journalist and as political revolutionary, is at once pungently and poignantly evoked in his alter ego's cry:

Mais ces gazettes que voilà sur ma table – comme des feuilles mortes!
– elles ne frémissent pas et ne crient point!
    Où donc le bruit d'orage que j'aime? [13]

But these gazettes here on my table – like dead leaves! – they don't quiver, they don't shout.
    Where then is the noise of the storm that I love?

Vingtras, like his creator, is a revolutionary journalist – a prefiguration of the committed intellectual later to be supremely typified by Sartre – which prompts some pre-Sartrean reflections on his possible relationship with that working class represented inter alia by the (duly desanctified) Faubourg:

Et que lui dirai-je à ce faubourg Antoine? A ces gens de Charonne, à ces blousiers de Puteaux, comment parlerai-je? – moi qui vais jeter, dans la balance, des théories à peine mûres et que je n'ai guère eu le loisir de peser dans mes mains de réfractaire.[14]

And what will I have to say to that Faubourg Antoine? To these people of Charonne, to those manual workers from Puteaux,* how am I going to speak? – I who am going to throw into the balance scarcely mature theories which I have hardly had the time to weigh in my refractory hands.

The novel ends with Vingtras fleeing France and imagining Paris as 'une grande blouse inondée de sang'[15] / 'a great overall drenched in blood'. The would-be revolution is over; a would-be revolution it was destined to remain, in part at least, because of the spontaneity and inclusiveness which made it such an iconic moment.

Alphonse Daudet paints a picture of the *quartier* in 1871 as an exhausted epigone of its old fiery self in 'Au Faubourg Saint-Antoine' – part of his series of short texts evoking the Franco-Prussian war and the Commune, *Les Contes du lundi*. He recounts finding in the area 'les anciens de 48, égarés éternels, viellis mais incorrigibles, l'émeutier en cheveux blancs, et avec lui le vieux jeu de la bataille civile, la barricade classique à deux et à trois étages, le drapeau rouge flottant au sommet, les poses mélodramatiques sur la culasse des canons, les manches retroussées, les mines rébarbatives'[16] / 'the old guard from 1848, forever lost, older but incorrigible, the white-haired rioter and with him the old game of civil battle, the classic two- or three-storey barricade with the red flag flying on top, the melodramatic poses on the breeches of the cannons, the rolled-up sleeves, the rebarbative faces'. 'Du Trône à la Bastille, ce ne sont qu'alertes, prises d'armes, perquisitions, arrestations, clubs en plein vent' / 'From the Trône to the Bastille there are only alarms, weapons being seized, searches, arrests, clubs blown by the

* Puteaux is a western suburb of Paris, in Vallès's day a working-class bastion though now gentrified and for more than forty years indeed run by an authoritarian right-wing municipality.

wind.' The revolutionary action of the Faubourg is now firmly under the heel of the Versaillais; the 'clubs' to which Daudet refers are the political discussion-groups which have often played a significant part in the formulation of radical thought and strategy in Paris, now at the mercy of the wind of their own verbiage. Intriguingly, the major exception Daudet cites is the rue de Lappe, which was to become so important as the heart of the area's nightlife. For Daudet it is 'une espèce de ghetto auvergnat' / 'a kind of Auvergnat ghetto', for which the insurrection could be 'à mille lieues' / 'a thousand leagues away'[17] – an observation which appears to postulate a division between the peaceful provincial craftsmen bent over their labours and the ever-volatile Parisians, now it would seem a spent force. Henceforward the revolutionary volcano that had erupted five times in less than a century was to become dormant, though emphatically not depoliticized as its response to the election of left-wing governments in 1936 and 1981 was to show. The Faubourg's transformation into Bastille had begun.

Chapter Five

'Satan's bagpipes': La Belle Époque's forty-three years of peace

T HE TERM La Belle Époque – broadly cognate with the English 'naughty nineties' – can be narrowly defined as spanning the period between 1896, when France emerged from a prolonged economic depression, and the outbreak of the First War in 1914. It is sometimes, if inaccurately, extended as far back as 1871, doubtless because that date inaugurated forty-three years of peaceful constitutional stability. That may seem a modest achievement to an Anglophone readership, but after the turmoil of the 'short nineteenth century' since the Revolution of 1789 it was something new for France, and the romantic aura with which the phrase is surrounded owes a great deal to the political calm and, in its second half, the economic prosperity characteristic of the period. Entertainment became an increasingly important and diversified part of the *quartier*'s life, notably the *bals-musette* of which I shall say more shortly. The cinema, invented in 1895, rapidly became an important entertainment medium, with numerous movie-theatres opening, sometimes fleetingly, in the area, ranging in size from the 1000-seater Cyrano in the rue de la Roquette to the Kinéma Bijou under the railway arches, which seems to have operated only in 1911, and the Keller in the place Voltaire (now the place Léon Blum), which proudly proclaimed itself the smallest cinema in Paris during its five-year lifespan from 1907.

If revolutionary fervour in the Faubourg waned after the suppression of the Commune, this may have been at least in part because France had once again become, as it has remained to this day, a republic. Léon Gambetta, the most prominent republican political figure of the post-Commune decade, made a speech in 1872 in which he denounced 'la véritable Bastille: le Moyen Age, le despotisme, l'oligarchie, le royaume!'[1] / 'the real Bastille: the Middle Ages, despotism, oligarchy, monarchy!' – the Empire evidently subsumed under these categories, the hated fortress acting as synecdoche for the variously tyrannical systems under which France had suffered for so long. It was on 27 July 1880 that the newspaper *Le Citoyen*, a vehicle for the ideas of the revolutionary socialist Jules Guesde, proclaimed; 'Il nous reste à démolir beaucoup de bastilles {sic}: la magistrature, le code, i'ignorance, le Sénat, la présidence de la République, royauté borgne'[2] / 'We still have a great many Bastilles to demolish: the magistracy, the Code,* ignorance, the Senate, the presidency of the Republic, the kingdom of the one-eyed' – a litany whose institutional components are still in place, and in the case of the presidency substantially strengthened. This was the year in which 14 July was proclaimed a national holiday and which also saw the first public celebration of the fall of the fortress since the proclamation of the Second Empire. Many nevertheless remained staunchly hostile to such manifestations, seen by parts of the right as the 'modèle des saturnales révolutionnaires'[3] / 'model for revolutionary saturnalia'. For early twentieth-century disciples of the Catholic nationalist and authoritarian Charles Maurras, the storming of the Bastille was a Masonic plot ('Masonic' here being closely aligned with 'Jewish'), and this conspiracy theory gave rise to the anti-Masonic paper entitled *La Bastille*, which appeared weekly between 1902 and 1914. This publication viewed the Republic as 'une nouvelle Bastille dont le rempart est sévèrement gardé par les francs-maçons'[4] / 'a new Bastille whose ramparts are severely guarded by the Freemasons' – a further indication of how far in an enduringly republicanized France the fortress had come to serve as an icon, for good or for bad.

The major political bone of contention in France during this period was undoubtedly the Dreyfus affair of 1894, in which a Jewish officer in the French Army was wrongfully accused of passing military intelligence to Germany and imprisoned on Devil's Island in Guyana. His acquittal and release was largely the result of a campaign spearheaded by Émile Zola, whose article 'J'Accuse!' appeared in the newspaper *L'Aurore* in 1898. The affair split France in two, *Dreyfusards* on the left – including a significant number of intellectuals – bitterly opposed to the *anti-Dreyfusards* who were generally motivated by a toxic amalgam of militarism and anti-Semitism. There were brawls in the Popincourt area, leading to the sacking of a church in 1899, and Daniel Halévy – a leftist writer and militant *dreyfusard*, though he became a pessimistic conservative in later life – was to proclaim: 'Aussi longtemps que dura la crise dreyfusienne, le Faubourg Saint-Antoine fut notre forteresse'[5] / 'For as long as the Dreyfus crisis lasted, the Faubourg Saint-Antoine was our fortress.' Yet the most significant impact of the affair on the Faubourg and elsewhere in working-class Paris was an indirect one

---

* This refers to the Code Napoléon or Code Civil – still the foundation of civil law in France after more than two hundred years.

– the setting-up of the 'popular universities' which aimed to bridge the gap between intellectuals and the working class and were to play a significant part in the working-class movement between 1896, when the first one was founded in Montreuil, and 1914. The importance of the committed intellectual in France, exemplified above all by Jean-Paul Sartre and Simone de Beauvoir, has often been traced back to the Dreyfus affair and the manner in which it led a great many teachers and writers, inspired by Zola's example, to identify themselves politically with the left. Daniel Halévy was a leading light in the founding of the Société des Universités Populaires in 1898, at the height of the controversy over Dreyfus. The Société defined itself as 'une association laïque qui se propose de développer l'enseignement populaire supérieur, qui poursuit l'éducation mutuelle des citoyens de toutes conditions, qui organise les lieux de réunion, où le travailleur puisse venir, sa tâche accomplie, se reposer, s'instruire, se distraire'[6] / 'a secular association whose goal is to develop higher education for the people, to promote mutual education by citizens of all conditions, to organize meeting-places where workers can come when their day is finished to rest, learn and entertain themselves'. The first such university was founded in the Faubourg in October 1898, and among its adherents was the Ukraine-born socialist activist and historian, later a staunch anti-Stalinist, Boris Souvarine.

The popular universities were a logical extension of the Faubourg's long tradition of working-class self-education, evoked in earlier chapters. They lost momentum with the First War, but have experienced something of a revival since the 1980s. There are now something like a hundred in France, though only two so far as I can ascertain in *intra-muros* Paris, one located in the 20th *arrondissement* not far from the Faubourg – perhaps reflecting the vacating of the *quartier* by the artisans so influential in the founding of the movement.

For Christophe Charle, Paris after the Commune became a virtual theme-park – an allegation made in the present day, we have seen, by those for whom more cosmopolitan and less ossified cities have taken its place among the metropolitan elite. Charle describes the *fin-de-siècle* city as 'un théâtre dont les acteurs miment les révolutions, les contre-révolutions ou des faux coups d'État'[7] / 'a theatre where actors mimed revolutions. counter-revolutions or false coups d'état', but it is noteworthy that he grants a partial exemption to the still largely working-class suburbs in the east, stating that 'les itinéraires des défilés et les pèlerinages symboliques sont maintenant limités à une partie de la capitale: Bastille, Nation, Père-Lachaise'[8] / 'the routes of marches and symbolic pilgrimages were by now confined to one part of the capital: Bastille, Nation, Père-Lachaise'. The funerals of the revolutionary socialist Louis Blanqui and of Jules Vallès passed down the rue de la Roquette in 1881 and 1885 respectively on their route to Père-Lachaise, where the Mur des Fédérés against which 147 Communards had been summarily shot in 1871 became, as it has remained, a rallying-point for left-wing commemorations.

The Place de la Bastille itself, however, remained at least until its redevelopment around the Opéra from 1989 more amorphous and less clearly laid out than its near neighbours République (thus baptized in 1879, before when it had been known as the place du Château d'Eau) and Nation, previously place du Trône-Renversé, renamed and rebuilt in the 1870s. These two squares were each endowed with an eponymous allegorical statue as their centrepiece – République's by Léopold Morice, Nation's by Jules Dalou – whose political and iconographic significance was far clearer than that of the Bastille column, as though to immobilize and memorialize the forces of revolution in less strife-torn spaces. Pierre Pinon's musings in 1989 suggest the square's curious lack of a clear identity, doubtless a reflection of its uncomfortable revolutionary heritage: 'Une place commémorative, une porte de ville, un carrefour de rues, de boulevards et de faubourgs, le dégagement d'une gare d'eau? On ne saura jamais ce qu'aurait dû être la place de la Bastille. On sait seulement ce qu'elle est: une place introuvable' / 'A commemorative square, a gateway to the city, a meeting-point of streets, boulevards and *faubourgs*, the unloading-point for a waterway station? We shall never what the place de la Bastille should have been. We know only what it is: an unidentifiable square.'[9] Géraldine Rideau observes: 'Chargée d'un lourd passé historique, la place possède un lien plus symbolique que morphologique avec le faubourg'[10] / 'Bearing the burden of a heavy historical past, the square's link with the *faubourg* is symbolic rather than morphological', suggesting perhaps a topographical correlation of the difference between the Faubourg of working-class militancy and the Bastille *quartier* of racy night-life. The latter avatar doubtless came more fully into its own with the opening of the eponymous Métro station – nowadays the ninth busiest in all of Paris – in 1905, making it more natural to say that one was going to 'Bastille' rather than to the Faubourg Saint-Antoine.

The Faubourg's fiery reputation meant that the prefects of Paris continued to treat it with caution. Numerous plans for its redevelopment were mooted, whose goal is well summarized by Jean-Paul Blais:

> Il s'agit toujours de faire le pari d'intégrer le faubourg à la ville, de chercher à masquer cette immense esplanade battue des vents pendant l'hiver et inondée de soleil pendant l'été et de casser la coupure entre

la ville prestigieuse du Marais et son faubourg artisanal, entre deux mondes, caractéristiques de la vie parisienne, la place des Vosges, les cours industrielles du meuble, bordées par le canal Saint-Martin et frôlée par les flots de vapeur venus de la gare de chemin de fer.[11]

The goal was always to integrate the Faubourg with the city. to try to mask this vast esplanade battered by winds in the winter and flooded with sunlight in summer and to do away with the sharp break between the prestigious urban Marais and its artisanal faubourg, between two worlds both characteristic of Parisian life: the Place des Vosges and the industrial courtyards of the furniture industry, bordered by the Canal Saint-Martin and brushed by puffs of steam from the railway station.

Much new building went on during this period, often of a high standard. The maison Le Bihan, at 25 rue du Faubourg-Saint-Antoine, is a splendid glass-and-steel construction built as a furniture workshop and sales outlet, and originally incorporating two apartments. It still sells furniture, nowadays from an extremely up-market designer range – one among many examples of the area's gentrification. In 1904 the Rothschild Foundation erected new blocks of flats in the square Trousseau, towards the east of the Faubourg, which were nicknamed 'the Louvre of working-class housing', and featured a crèche, a dispensary and a kitchen selling nutritionally beneficial hot dishes. This communitarianism of this undertaking, obviously rooted in the Foundation's ethos, also mirrored, and may even have been influenced by, the strong community traditions of the *quartier*, which find their clearest expression in its courtyards. We shall be visiting some of the best-known of these in the final chapter; they became increasingly important in the area during the period currently under discussion. Éric Galmot, at the time deputy mayor of the 11th *arrondissement* with responsibility for urban planning, opined in 1997: 'La cour ancienne est un *melting pot*, une exception dans les mégalopoles tentés par le ghetto'[12] / 'The old-style courtyard is a melting pot, an exception in megalopolises tempted by the ghetto' – a remark whose pertinence to the Faubourg, itself a melting pot of sorts which has by and large not succumbed to ghettoization, is plain. The courtyard can justifiably, if also today a touch romantically, be seen as a microcosm of the Faubourg, and Patrick Bloch's assertion: 'Dans ses quartiers s'est forgée – durant deux siècles – l'identité républicaine et sociale de la France'[13] / 'Within its boundaries was forged, over two centuries, the republican and social identity of France' could apply to the courtyard as microcosm as much as to the area of which it forms part.

The furniture industry offered few apprenticeships in the faubourg during this period. Workers would typically receive their training in the provinces (Grenoble and Metz were favoured cities), and then make their way to Paris with support from their *compagnonnage*. The industry received an important boost – one which must have helped to counteract the decline in apprenticeships – in 1886 with the opening of the École Boulle in the rue Pierre Bourdan – hard by the place de la Nation, slightly to the east of the Faubourg, but integrally linked with its economic life and traditions. The École was named after Louis XIV's master cabinet-maker André-Charles Boulle – a character as we have seen in Diwo's *Les Dames du faubourg* – and originally trained carpenters and upholsterers before extending its scope to encompass engraving, work in bronze and other less functional, more decorative crafts. The high-tech establishment of today, offering courses in woodworking, jewellery and work in precious metals, continues and perpetuates the Faubourg's artisanal traditions in a form more appropriate to the twenty-first century. At the opposite end of the scale was the Saturday *trôle* or furniture market, which took place weekly at the intersection of the rue du Faubourg-Saint-Antoine and the avenue Ledru-Rollin from about 1850 through to the 1930s. This was an early kind of informal flea-market selling inexpensive furniture, ranging from writing-desks to *guéridons* or circular bar-tables, which artisans had made themselves – a species of IKEA *avant la lettre* whose name lingers on in the annual Fête de la Trôle organized in May by La Commune Libre d'Aligre. The market which gives its name to that community organization, built to replace an earlier covered market in 1843, was by the end of the nineteenth century second only to Les Halles for food sales. Trade – not always of a respectable kind, as we shall see – remained fundamental to the area throughout this period.

For an idea of what the Faubourg was like in the period shortly after the Commune, I shall turn to Jules Vallès's *Le Tableau de Paris* – the title a conscious reference to Mercier and Texier. Vallès's text was originally published between 1882 and 1883 in the daily newpaper *Gil Blas*, which in 1884 was to serialize Zola's *Germinal;* it was illustrated, somewhat misleadingly, with images by Daumier, Gustave Doré and others taken from Texier's text of thirty years before. It focuses on the working-class areas of the city, dismissing for instance the Latin Quarter as 'un ghetto de la fausse culture'[14] / 'a ghetto of false culture'. The Faubourg thus figures prominently, and Vallès's view of it is several degrees less bland than Texier's, though by the same token considerably more pessimistic. He devotes a section ('Les

Bastilles') to prisons in and near the *quartier* – not only the original Bastille, here as in the texts cited earlier in this chapter serving as a synecdoche for authoritarian carceral regimes, but Mazas, in the boulevard Diderot, and La (Grande) Roquette. Solitary confinement, in the second half of the nineteenth century the norm in France, is denounced, and Vallès gives a grim account of an execution at La Roquette. He views the Faubourg as archetype and mythical distillation of proletarian dissent ('Toutes les douleurs comme toutes les colères sociales ont tenu dans ce faubourg Antoine' [15] / 'Every kind of pain and social anger resided in the Faubourg Antoine'), regretting the disappearance of skilled working-class traditions such as the Tour de France* and ruefully observing that 'Le Faubourg Antoine n'est plus ce qu'il était, et ce n'est pas du fond de ses entrailles noires que partira désormais le grand cri des agitations populaires' [16] / 'The Faubourg Antoine is no longer what it used to be, and it is not from the depth of its dark entrails that the great cry of popular agitation will now be heard.'

The most striking – indeed shocking – divergence between Vallès's *tableau* of the Faubourg and that of Texier is to be found in their attitude towards the foreign, particularly German, workers in the area. Texier, we have seen, praises their diligence and seriousness, whereas Vallès's attitude, for all his radicalism, reeks of a nationalism – not to say racism – that may remind us why he was so influential on Céline. In this he was probably affected by the caricatural anti-Prussianism characteristic of the French press before 1871. He bemoans the high rents in the *quartier*, which have supposedly driven French workers out ('Nous allons y trouver des Bretons qui vendent de l'ail bénit, des Italiens qui montrent des marmottes, et des bataillons d'Allemands!' [17] / 'We'll find Bretons selling holy garlic, Italians exhibiting marmosets, and battalions of Germans!').† His diatribe against the Germans ('De loin même, l'Allemagne tire sur les travailleurs du quartier Saint-Antoine et les blesse au flanc, et leur envoie de la mitraille de misère au ventre!' [18] / 'Even from afar off, Germany is firing on the workers of the Saint-Antoine *quartier*, wounding them in the side, sending a hail of wretched bullets into their very bellies!') is so to speak balanced by his stigmatization of the Italians, seen as indolent and inanely pious.

One important category of French workers whose presence in the Faubourg become more marked during this period was the Auvergnats.

---

* Not a cycle-race but the journey round France accomplished by young apprentices to learn the tricks of their trade from craftsmen throughout the country.

† Italians from the Alpine region and Savoyards often made a living exhibiting marmosets, sometimes trained to dance, in travelling fairs.

A survey conducted in February 1883 revealed that in the passage Thiéré, parallel to the rue de Lappe, only five out of 1225 inhabitants had not been born in Auvergne. Auvergnats worked not only in the wood- and metalworking industries but also, classically, as *bougnats* – running bars which doubled as outlets for the sale of coal and wood, making them a twofold linchpin of their community. Their presence also made itself felt, as it continues to be, by the foundation of what is one of the longest-lived of Parisian weekly newspapers. *L'Auvergnat de Paris*. This was started by Louis Bonnet on 14 July 1882 and, apart from a three-month break in 2009 when it went into liquidation before finding a new proprietor, has continued to appear ever since. It remained in the hands of the same family for virtually a century, Bonnet's son and grandson successively taking on the editorship. The paper, whose headquarters were in the boulevard Beaumarchais, campaigned vigorously in its early days at least against the stereotyped portrayal of Auvergnats as avaricious hayseeds. 1886 saw the foundation, also by Bonnet, of the Ligue auvergnate de Paris, with branches from every district of the province, which between 1904 and 1939 ran special trains to bring Auvergnats living in Paris back to their *pays* in the spring and summer months.

The president of the Ligue auvergnate de Paris in 1925 was Pierre Laval – then a socialist member of parliament, twenty years later to be executed for his activities as head of the Vichy government. This perhaps indicates the political ambiguity of the Auvergnat community, in some sense external to the Faubourg's revolutionary traditions. Roger Girard states that Auvergnats often began on the left but moved rightwards, yet asserts that 'aucun Auvergnat de Paris [...] n'acceptera la collaboration'[19] / 'no Paris-based Auvergnat would accept collaboration' – Laval presumably constituting an exception. Bonnet himself was successively a supporter of General Boulanger (whose populist nationalism posed a threat to the Third Republic in the late 1880s), a socialist sympathizer and an anti-Dreyfusard, which makes Girard's description of him as a left-wing Bonapartist appear the only adequate one even if it poses as many questions as it answers.

The Auvergnat community contributed to the life of the Faubourg in another important way through its *bal musette* tradition of popular dance music, originally played on a kind of bagpipe from the province but later also influenced by the Italian population of the *quartier* and more generally using the accordion in the twentieth century. In 1879 there were a recorded 130 such establishments in Paris, twenty-six in the 11th. Tensions that had been manifest between Auvergnats and Italians in the Faubourg seem to have been alleviated by the common cultural ground they found in the *bal musette*, described by Marie-Claude Blanc-Chaléard as the 'expression d'un brassage que réalise, presque malgré lui, le peuple de Paris dans son quartier de prédilection, le Faubourg Saint-Antoine' [20] / 'the expression of a mingling brought about by the people of Paris almost in spite of itself in the *quartier* it most favoured, the Faubourg Saint-Antoine'. The *bal musette* was particularly identified with the rue de Lappe, the street more than any other associated with the night-life of the *quartier*. The exclamation of Vallès – himself an Auvergnat – that 'la rue de Lappe est la fosse commune des instruments du Travail et de la Guerre!' [21] / 'the rue de Lappe is the common grave of the instruments of Work and War!' doubtless owes something to that street's reputation for nocturnal jollity, which was to spread to the remainder of the *quartier* and has formed an important part of its identity right through to the present day.

The colourful Parisian night-life of the Belle Époque, epitomized by the can-can – which in fact dates back to the early nineteenth century – the paintings of Toulouse-Lautrec and the songs of Aristide Bruant, is above all associated with Montmartre, an area often visited by inhabitants of the *beaux quartiers* who savoured its boisterous raffishness. Bastille's night-life, by contrast, was less touristic, though during this period it began to attract visitors from further afield. The Bal de la Rosière, founded in 1858 at 66 rue de Charenton, might sound suspiciously sedate, for a 'rosière' was a young woman rewarded in many French villages for her virtuous reputation. However, Emmanuel Patrick, in *Le Courrier de Paris* (16 March 1886), paints a slightly less staid picture:

> Les rosières du numéro 66 se rencontrent, à la nuit tombante, sur la place de la Bastille, où elles turbinent consciencieusement, et à une couronne virginale dont elles ne savent que faire, elles préfèrent un peu de *galette* ou un verre de mêlé-cassis, versé sur le zinc du mastroquet. [22]

> The 'rosières' of number 66 meet as night falls in the place de la Bastille, where they go hard to work, and to a virginal crown of no interest to them they prefer a slice of waffle or a glass of brandy and blackcurrant up at the counter of the local bar.

Other establishments were to become more widely known outside the *faubourg* during the Belle Époque. In 1887 Aristide Bruant founded a music-hall on the boulevard Beaumarchais, later called Le Concert Pacra after its subsequent owner, which until its closure and demolition in 1972 hosted the greatest names in French show-business, from Fréhel to Charles

Aznavour. The best-known of the rue de la Roquette's venues in the early twentieth century was Le Bousca – originally Le Chalet – founded by the Auvergnat Antoine Bouscatel, a bagpipe-player who looked down his nose at the accordion until the Marseillais Charles Péguri, of Italian origin, allegedly walked into the premises one day in 1904 and 1905 and prevailed upon Bouscatel to join him in a duet. Thenceforth the combination of instruments was to prove irresistible, as Bouscatel's reported response to Péguri attests:

> Alors! les gars. Qu'en pensez vous? C'est du merveilleux qui nous tombe du ciel. C'est une révolution qui se prépare. Avez-vous entendu? C'est rond, c'est chaud, c'est vivant. Et c'est tout un orchestre, cet instrument du diable! Il vous a mis les tripes à l'air ce biniou de Satan. Alors écoutez ce que va vous bailler Bouscatel. C'est décidé. Dans mon bal de la rue de Lappe, on y jouera de l'accordéon avec ce phénomène de Péguri. Et je vous dis foi d'Auvergnat, je refuserai du monde à ce bal. Des gens viendront de Pigalle! De Montrouge! de Passy! des Batignolles! Il en viendra aussi de Bordeaux! de Marseille! de Strasbourg! [23]

> Well, lads, what do you think? This is a miracle from heaven. There's a revolution on the way. Did you hear that? It's full-sounding, it's warm, it's lively. This devil's instrument is an orchestra all to itself. Satan's bagpipes have gone straight to your guts. Now listen to what Bouscatel's going to tell you. My mind's made up. In my rue de Lappe dance-hall we'll have this extraordinary Péguri playing the accordion. And, on my word as an Auvergnat, I'll be turning people away. They'll come from Pigalle! From Montrouge! From Passy! From Les Batignolles!* They'll even come from Bordeaux! From Marseille! From Strasbourg!

Bouscatel's hyperbolic enthusiasm had some justification, for a while at least; Le Bousca attracted a large clientele until he sold it in 1910, moving to the rue de la Huchette in the Latin Quarter. It was sold again, to a family called Carcanague, in 1919, and moved rapidly up-market. The Faubourg's internationalism, so reviled by Vallès, had important cultural as well as political consequences. Alas, Bouscatel and Péguri were to be overshadowed by the more sophisticated types of entertainment that came to the fore after the end of the First War. Péguri committed suicide in his workshop in 1930,

---

* Well-off areas or suburbs of Paris.

while Bouscatel died forgotten and in poverty in 1945. They can perhaps be seen as among the first victims of the *quartier*'s transformation from the Faubourg into Bastille – a shift that began during the Belle Époque and has continued steadily ever since.

That shift went hand in hand with a transformation, for better and for worse, of women's place. Between 1870 and 1900 155 000 women in Paris were officially registered as prostitutes, but 725 000 others were arrested during the same period for clandestine activity. The courtesans for whom the Belle Époque is celebrated were to be found in more up-market areas than the Faubourg, where unlicensed prostitution was rife. The triangle of the place de la Bastille, the boulevard Richard-Lenoir and the boulevard Voltaire was one of the city's most notorious areas in this respect, one particularly notorious spot being outside a large clothing shop on the Marais side of the Place. Gay male prostitution was also reported near the boulevard Bourdon and around the Gare de Vincennes, whose toilets were a popular cottaging venue.[24] The 11th *arrondissement* was reported to have the highest number of unregistered female prostitutes – in large part, according to Alain Corbin, the result of 'la terrible misère sexuelle dont souffre une large fraction de la société urbaine'[25] / 'the terrible sexual misery from which a large proportion of urban society suffered'. That misery, of course, was likely to affect the prostitutes even more than their clients; Victor Hugo, it is interesting to note, expressed his support for the English abolitionist Josephine Butler, but the sale of women's sexual services was too important a part of the urban economy, in Paris as elsewhere, for such campaigns to stand any chance of success. Jules de Neuville had written in 1860 of how 'la petite ouvrière du quartier Saint-Antoine, après avoir été la grisette favorie du bal des Délices, après avoir été lorette, après avoir trôné aux courses, va se cacher perdue de dettes dans une maison publique'[26] / 'the working-class girl from the Saint-Antoine *quartier*, after being the favourite *grisette* of the bal des Délices,* after being a kept woman and a star attraction at the races, will hide herself away, hopelessly in debt, in a brothel'. The career traced here – from honest working girl by way of *grisette*, a liminal category which included such figures as Murger and Puccini's Mimi from *La Bohème*, to 'lorette', so called because many such women were set up by their lovers in flats near the church of Notre-Dame-de-Lorette, between Saint-Lazare and Pigalle – ends in financial and probably also emotional ruin, something which undoubtedly befell many young women from the Faubourg in the Belle Époque and indeed before.

---

* This was one of the major popular Parisian balls of the time.

The iconic figure of working-class prostitution during the Belle Époque is undoubtedly Amélie Hélie, the 'Queen of the *Apaches*', known for her striking blonde hair as Casque d'Or and immortalized in Jacques Becker's wonderful 1951 film of that name, in which she is played by Simone Signoret. *Apaches* was the name given to the street gangs of Bastille and other nearby areas in the early twentieth century (the term appears to date from 1902), living on the proceeds of robbery, swindling and prostitution and renowned for their flashy mode of dress. The term – 'Orientalist' in Edward Said's use of the term albeit in a different hemisphere – has its roots in French colonizing dreams of the nineteenth century, to which obstreperous native Americans – or 'Peaux-Rouges'/ 'Red Indians' as they would have been known at the time – constituted an unwelcome obstacle.[27] The concomitant fascination with the 'Wild West' sparked off a host of popular magazines devoted to colourful 'cowboys-and-Indians' serials, an echo of which appears in Renoir's Prévert-scripted, and Marais-set, 1936 film *Le Crime de Monsieur Lange* when the publishing cooperative enjoys huge success with their contribution to the genre, *Arizona Jim*.

A lurid cover-drawing in *Le Petit Journal* of 20 October 1907, clearly designed to arouse a sense of moral panic, depicts an *apache* – described as 'la plaie de Paris'[28] / 'the plague of Paris' – towering over a policeman less than half his size. Dominique Kalifa's *Les Crimes de Paris* features a number of other similarly highly seasoned lithographs, posters and drawings dishing up the *classes dangereuses* as matter for titillation.[29] Kalifa also quotes a newspaper story about a driver attacked in the rue du Faubourg Saint-Antoine by 'rôdeurs'/ 'prowlers' who strung a noose round his neck before being thwarted by the intervention of the police.[30] Aristide Bruant, as mentioned in Chapter One, devoted one of his best-known songs, 'A la Bastoche', to the life and death of a (fictional) *apache*, 'La Filoche', guillotined for robbing and killing a bus-driver; another, 'Nini Peau d'Chien', written for the centenary of the fall of the fortress, tells of a young woman who walks in the evening with her group of friends along the boulevard Richard-Lenoir. Popular in the area for her kind heart, she is almost certainly a colleague – or even rival – of Casque d'Or. Hélie's main centre of activity was initially Belleville, then Popincourt, but her first 'protector', Marius Pleigneur, universally known as Manda, ran a criminal empire which is said to have extended from Montmartre to Bastille, while when she deserted him for his amorous and economic rival Leca the couple set up home in the rue Godefroy Cavaignac, at the northern limit of the Bastille area. Manda, played by Serge Reggiani, is guillotined at the end of the film for the killing of Leca; his real-life counterpart, whose victim recovered from his wounds, served eight years in a Guyana penitentiary where he was to die. Hélie eventually married a varnisher – a trade of course, like Manda's original work as a polisher, practised in the Faubourg – before dying of tuberculosis in 1933.

Hélie became a media figure *avant la lettre* with her appearance in a play based on her story in 1902, in which year her life-story, allegedly in her own words, was serialized in the weekly *Fin de siècle*.[31] The voyeuristic appeal of the Parisian underworld – distilled in romanticized form in Marcel Carné and Jacques Prévert's 1830s-set film masterpiece *Les Enfants du paradis* (1945) – contributed greatly, as Casque d'Or's story and Bruant's songs show, to the *quartier*'s image as at once enticing and perilous, a place where real human misery and want were transmuted into the stuff of exoticism and myth.

Yet the role of women in this period, in the Faubourg and elsewhere, was not so consistently wretched as we might be tempted to suppose. The first self-styled French feminist, Hubertine Auclert, organizer of the first campaign for female suffrage and a lifelong campaigner for gender equality, lived in the rue de la Roquette until her death in 1914. Even Casque d'Or has not always unproblematically been perceived as a victim, for Sarah Leahy avers that despite Hélie's exploitation by men and 'lack of solidarity with her fellow prostitutes […] she does nonetheless offer a rare public glimpse of an unashamed sexuality'[32] – a striking instance of the transformation of women's status in this period. The rapid development of public transport – the Métro opened in 1900 – made it easier for them to roam the city in safety, while economic expansion opened new possibilities of employment for them. The last of the great universal exhibitions organized in Paris opened with a literal embodiment of the new status of woman, as subject and object alike. To quote Diana Holmes and Carrie Tarr:

> The deployment of women's bodies as spectacle reached its apotheosis with the twenty foot high stucco figure of *la Parisienne*, a statuesque creature gorgeously dressed by a leading couturier, above the entrance gate of the 1900 Exposition. But the pose of *la Parisienne* suggested movement, not passivity: she was clearly on her way to explore what the city had to offer, the consumer as well as the object of consumption, hence subject as well as object of new ways of looking.[33]

The *flâneuse*, it might be said, came into her own at this time alongside her well-established (if that is not an oxymoron) male counterpart. Yet the world of exploitation and misery is never far from such an emancipatory view of the *quartier* and the city. Adrian Rifkin writes: 'Commonly, Paris is imagined as *the* City of the People. At the same time, it "procures pleasures" for the rich'[34] – a symbiosis which as the wanderings of Mercier and Restif show had long since existed, which is indeed almost certainly a constitutive part of any modern metropolis, but which reached its apogee in the real and mythical city, the two no longer entirely distinguishable if indeed they ever were, of the Belle Époque.

The most sombre episode in the *quartier*'s life during this period was the Soleilland affair. Albert Soleilland was a cabinet-maker from the rue de Charonne, who in 1907 lost his job and on the very same day violated and murdered Marthe, the twelve-year-old daughter of friends whom he was taking to a concert at the Bataclan music-hall in the boulevard Voltaire (where Maurice Chevalier was later to enjoy his first major success). The girl's body was found in a suitcase deposited at the Gare de l'Est, and Soleilland was the obvious suspect. The trial, held in public, attracted large numbers of well-off spectators and figures from the world of entertainment ('pleasures for the rich ...'), the newspaper *Le Petit Parisien* advocated Soleilland's lynching and a veritable moral panic ensued in which the popular press stridently claimed that Paris had become 'un véritable "coupe-gorge"'[35] / 'a real thieves' alley'. The trial revealed a miserable life; Soleilland's first two children had died in infancy, he drank absinthe and had allegedly attempted to rape his sister-in-law and his wife, Juliette, occasionally prostituted herself to raise the family income. The President of the Republic, Armand Fallières, was a convinced opponent of capital punishment and commuted numerous death sentences during his period of office, including Soleilland's. He was deported to Cayenne, in French Guyana, where he became paralysed after being stabbed by a fellow prisoner and died half-mad in 1920.

The case dealt a severe blow to attempts to abolish capital punishment in France; a parliamentary vote on the question the following year opted to retain the death penalty by 330 votes to 201. Juliette wallowed in the attention the case brought her, selling her intimate confidences to *Le Matin* in an early example of cheque-book journalism and receiving a proposal of marriage from a shipyard worker in Toulon. The case and its effects have a gruesomely contemporary ring to them, as modern though not so sensational as that of Henri Landru or 'Bluebeard', guillotined in 1922 after murdering eleven women for their money. One of his early victims was killed in the rue Crozatier, near the Aligre market, a fortnight after answering a personal advertisement from a gentleman seeking a wife; the day after the murder Landru was seen moving out of the building, to continue his career for a further six years.

The Grande Roquette prison was pulled down in 1900, and the guillotine moved to the Left Bank in 1909, so that this period saw the last executions of men in the *quartier*. Among the most noteworthy victims were the anarchist Auguste Vaillant, who threw a nail-bomb into the Chambre des Députés in 1893, wounding fifty people but killing nobody, and the swindler and quack doctor Henri Pranzini, executed for the murder of three women in 1887, out of whose skin wallets were reputedly made for the two senior officers in La Sûreté, the national police force.

Between the squalid and the glittering, the everyday working life of the Faubourg went on. The Commission du Vieux Paris, set up by the municipality in 1897, commissioned the photographer Charles Lansiaux to take numerous pictures of the *quartier* in 1920 and 1921, but these will disappoint seekers after risqué or proletarian images, for – perhaps in emulation of the great Parisian photographer Eugène Atget who frequently worked in the very early hours when streets were deserted – they depict the Faubourg almost as a ghost-town, its passages and courtyards drained of life. More evocative by far is the description given by the biographer and literary journalist André Billy of the area as it was in 1905 – a mixture of the old and the new, the cour Damoye from 1780 and the 1830s column cheek-by-jowl with the more recent suburban trains and – by the standards of those days – high-rise buildings:

> La foule des travailleurs, débarquée des trains de banlieue, se disperse déjà dans la direction du boulevard Beaumarchais, du boulevard Richard-Lenoir, de la rue de la Roquette, du faubourg Saint-Antoine dont les premières maisons, petites et bariolées de teintes neutres, restent, sur la place de la Bastille, le seul vestige du passé. Entre le rue de la Roquette et le boulevard Richard-Lenoir, la voûte de la cour Damoye s'ouvre au flanc d'une haute construction à sept étages. Dans ce repaire obscur se tapit le commerce des brancards, des roues, des ressorts d'occasion, avec celui des comptoirs d'étain à l'usage des limonadiers. On est en train d'enlever les volets des magasins, et des hommes, aux casquettes enfoncées sur les oreilles, un cache-nez autour du cou, les mains rouges de froid, sortent un à un de leurs réduits les comptoirs dont le métal a des reflets morts. Ils les alignent sur deux files, le long des ruisseaux de la cour. Et soudain un individu jailli d'une porte me prend le bras, l'air à la fois insolent et obséquieux; il me fait des offres; il a des occasions superbes; quel prix désiré-je mettre? Il est persuadé que je suis venu lui acheter un comptoir d'estaminet. Ma retraite le déçoit.

Contemplée du boulevard Richard-Lenoir, la colonne de Juillet trace, sur l'immensité blafarde que déploie derrière elle le canal Saint-Martin, un trait épais, noir. Un vague rayon dore les membres du Génie.[36]

The crowd of workers, getting off their suburban trains, is already scattering towards the boulevard Beaumarchais, the boulevard Richard-Lenoir, the rue de la Roquette, the Faubourg Saint-Antoine whose first houses, small and daubed with neutral hues, are the only trace of the past remaining on the place de la Bastillle. Between the rue de la Roquette and the boulevard Richard-Lenoir, the vault of the cour Damoye opens in the side of a tall seven-storey building. In this dark den lurks a trade in cart-shafts, wheels, second-hand springs, zinc counters for bar-owners. The shutters of the shops are just being taken down, and men with caps pulled down over their ears and scarves round their necks, their hands red from the cold, are removing one by one from their cubbyholes the counters whose metal offers a dead reflection. All of a sudden a man leaping out from a doorway takes me by the arm, his bearing at once insolent and obsequious; he makes me offers; he has superb bargains; how much do I want to spend? He is convinced that I am there to buy a bar counter from him. When I move away he is disappointed.

Looking from the boulevard Richard-Lenoir, the July column forms a thick black line against the vast pallid space of the Canal Saint-Martin behind it. A vague ray of sunlight gilds the statue's limbs.

Today's workers get off the Métro, or sometimes the bus, rather than off suburban trains; traces of the past around the Place are fewer still than in Billy's day; the assorted dealings in wood and metal are a thing of the distant past, like the mufflered workmen; and the zinc bar-counters survive only as period trappings in a few cafés. The July column looks down on a very different setting from that evoked by Billy, at a time when the metamorphosis of the *quartier* from Faubourg to Bastille was far less marked than it was to become.

Chapter Six

'Villains, stars and everybody in between': The First War and the *entre-deux-guerres*

FRANCE lost more lives in the First War than any other Allied country bar Russia – almost 1 700 000 – and more than 4 000 000 French soldiers were wounded. I have not been able to find an area-by-area breakdown of these statistics, but it seems reasonable to suppose that the Faubourg suffered as much as other *quartiers* if not more, given that its largely working-class population would have fought in the trenches rather than enjoying the greater security of an officer's life. The end of the war was marked by victory celebrations on 14 July 1919, in which the far Left alone refused to participate.

The flavour of working life in the Faubourg during this period is evoked in Laurent Azzano's *Mes joyeuses années au Faubourg*. Azzano came from an Italian family of cabinet-makers installed in the rue de Lappe, and his account – alas short on precise dates – is rich in industrial and social detail, making clear how poor many of the *quartier*'s dwellers were. He evokes the 'immonde et puante'[1] / 'foul and stinking' Cité Lesage-Bullourde, largely inhabited by poor Jews, where overcrowding and tuberculosis were rife, yet also reminds us of the insurrectionary traditions of the Faubourg whose Auvergnat blacksmiths forged the lances of the Revolution. The worker who told his boss after a row: '[J]e t'emmerde, ton boulot, je chie dessus et toi avec, fais-moi mon compte, je ne veux plus voir ta gueule'[2] / 'Fuck your work, I shit on it and you too, work out what you owe me, I don't want to see your ugly face again' was evidently a worthy descendant of theirs, while many of the Italian incomers to the 11th and 12th *arrondissements* in the 1930s were fleeing the Fascist régime.

The area's night-life has its predictable cortège of prostitutes (seen as upwardly socially mobile), bars (twenty-seven in 500 metres of the rue de la Roquette) and dances (Azzano favoured those in the rue de Lappe, their

rivals in and around la Roquette being supposedly the preserve of *apaches*).
There was violence, often taking the form of knife-fights, but these
appear to have followed a certain code, stopping the minute somebody
was wounded. Non-venal sexual activity also figures in the form of a
220-pound woman accused of attempting to rape an apprentice who was
delivering her a mattress, a widow who made love in street doorways to
show how much she missed the services of her husband, and cottaging in
the tunnels under the boulevard de la Bastille, to say nothing of a woman
who used the clearly shocked Azzano as a 'dress-rehearsal' for her wedding-
night. This amalgam of seaside-postcard bawdy and honour among thieves
may arouse suspicions of sentimentalization, but a political edge is often
there to offset this. Thus, a Jewish worker cheated out of money by his
employer led his workmates to go on strike and join a trade union; this
latter, however, could do little for them when they were arrested since
they were foreigners. *Plus ça change* ...

Azzano's view of the area at the time he was writing (1985) is to a large
extent a spectatorial and touristic one, recommending places to visit and
concluding with a craftsman's pride: 'Car malgré vents et marées, ou plutôt:
émeutes, révolutions, inondations et guerres, le Faubourg est devenu la plus
grande et la plus prestigieuse exposition des plus beaux meubles du monde,
du gothique au contemporain'[3] / 'For through hell and high water, or rather
riots, revolutions, floods and wars, the Faubourg has become the largest and
most prestigious exhibition of the world's finest furniture, from the gothic
to the contemporary.' The abatement of the *quartier*'s radical traditions is
subsumed, just at the time when the Mitterrand government was about to
take a rightward turn under the pressure of adverse economic circumstances,
into an extolling of its craftsmanship. The choice of the word 'exposition /
exhibition', rather than say 'atelier' (= workshop), seems revelatory in this
regard. Nobody has ever accused the Faubourg of becoming a theme-park,
but Azzano, doubtless in spite of himself, suggests how that view night find
some measure of justification.

So too in a different way does Jean Diwo's autofictional memoir *249,
faubourg Saint-Antoine*, named for his childhood home. The term 'autofiction',
coined by the novelist and literary critic Serge Doubrovsky, refers to texts
which invite us to read them at once as fiction and as autobiography – an
amalgam of genres (though of course any autobiography is necessarily in some
degree fictional) signalled here by the character of Jean-Baptiste Benoist,
modelled on Diwo's father but 'un personnage largement imaginaire, comme
les autres acteurs de cette comédie parisienne'[4] / 'a largely imaginary
character, like the other actors in this Parisian comedy'. Diwo views the

Faubourg's working class as at once autodidactic (his father had been to see Fellini's *La Strada* at a local cinema on the very day he died at the age of eighty-three, and an elderly neighbour, Monsieur Laurent, had amassed a vast amount of material which he was planning to turn into a history of the area) and perhaps surprisingly restricted in their topographical horizons. None of his acquaintances had a car, and his own knowledge of Paris as an eight-year-old went no further than the 11th and 12th *arrondissements*; the furthest he had strayed from home was to the department-store La Samaritaine, close by the Louvre. Yet alongside this parochialism (by no means uncommon in large cities at the time) sat a kind of internationalism typified by an absence of racism and a mild degree of gastronomic cosmopolitanism. The influx of workers through the centuries from Germany, Flanders, Poland and Italy left its mark on the *quartier*'s eating habits, with eastern European spices, *flamiche* (a species of quiche from northern France) and pasta common alongside more traditional Parisian dishes.

For the rest, Diwo's tone is imbued with the slightly sentimental bonhomie that characterizes his *Dames du faubourg* trilogy, with periodically more sombre notes. Thus, he evokes one Marcel Bloch who had bought a plot of land in the avenue Ledru-Rollin to set up a furniture factory. This he did for two years 'avant d'inventer des avions, d'être déporté avec sa femme Madeleine et de devenir le grand Marcel Dassault, son nom de résistant'[5] / 'before inventing aeroplanes, being deported with his wife Madeleine and becoming the great Marcel Dassault, his Resistance name'.

A sometime classmate of Diwo's, Marc Dumas, dedicated his 2001 memoir *Voie royale: le faubourg Saint-Antoine* to him, along with one Raoul Dubois who lived through the Popular Front period there. This rehearses well-worn clichés about the area's traditions, both artisanal and radical ('Territoire d'exception ce faubourg de gloire, ce faubourg des barricades, ce faubourg laborieux resté le creuset des idées nouvelles. De là ont jailli les principes de Liberté, d'Égalité, de Fraternité qui ont ébranlé le monde'[6] / 'It's an exceptional territory, this glorious Faubourg with its barricades, this hard-working Faubourg which has remained the breeding-ground for new ideas. It's from here that the principles of Liberty, Equality and Fraternity set out to shake the world'), along with a potted history which reveals that the Faubourg covers approximately a ninth of the total area of Paris. Perhaps the young Diwo really did not need to stray far outside its limits. The title's 'voie royale' harks back to the rue du Faubourg Saint-Antoine's origins as the major eastern entry to Paris. A photograph of a crowd greeting troops at the Liberation knits together the hieratic and the political, giving the 'lieu privilégié des entrées solennelles'[7] / 'privileged place for solemn entries' a more contemporary resonance of a piece with its long-standing radical traditions.

The only work of fiction I have come across dealing specifically with the *quartier* during the First War years is a comparatively recent one – *Les Mutins du faubourg* (1999), by Alain Bellet, written for a younger readership. Bellet's novel, as its title suggests, takes a disabused view of the conflict, focusing on inhabitants of the area who refused to serve in the army or were resistant to orders once conscripted, sometimes at the cost of their lives. The *trôle* has been declared illegal, resources being concentrated on the war effort, but local furniture-makers decide to defy the ban, leading to a set-to with mounted police in the rue de Charonne. Meanwhile the conscripted woodworker Jacques Rioux is imprisoned for mutiny, but released to join his beloved, Marthe, herself incarcerated in La Petite Roquette for aiding his desertion, thanks to his rescue of a young girl foully kidnapped by the 'roi du meuble'[8] / 'king of furniture' Prosper Chaussat. Chaussat's premises are then burnt down by a furious crowd, and the tale ends with the main characters setting off for a celebration in a passage just off the rue du Faubourg Saint-Antoine.

Anger at the slaughter of war is thus echoed by rage at capitalist exploitation, in all probability sexual as well as economic though given the age of the target readership this is not spelt out. Chaussat may suggest a faint echo of Renoir and Prévert's licentious magazine-owner Batala in *Le Crime de Monsieur Lange* of 1936 – a cinematic foreshadowing of the Popular Front government that was to come briefly to power later in that year. Bellet's Faubourg is not, however, entirely a bastion of proletarian righteousness, as one character hints when gleefully announcing the final celebration ('Même les apprentis apaches de la rue de Lappe et ce sacré Victor qui se prend pour leur chef seront là, ce soir!'[9] / 'Even the trainee *apaches* from the rue de Lappe with that so-and-so Victor who thinks he's their boss will be there tonight!'). The less salubrious – though perhaps more fascinating – side of the *quartier* makes an appearance right at the end of the novel, foreshadowing how it would come to the fore in later decades. Jean Galtier-Boissière's autobiographical novel *La Fleur au fusil* (1928), based on his experiences as a foot-soldier in the First War, had alluded to a sentry-box in the rue de la Roquette to which it was common practice to bring prostitutes; even the war years, it would seem, could not tame the area entirely.

The *quartier* was seen by and large as offering comparatively little for visitors apart from its night-life. According to Évelyne Cohen's survey of tourist guides to Paris, the 1930 *Guide Larousse* recommended only Père-Lachaise and the place de la Bastille as worth seeing in the eastern part of the city, the latter for historical rather than aesthetic reasons. Working-class areas were clearly too lowly and the night-life of the area too insalubrious to be brought to the attention of the respectable visitor, for whom *classes laborieuses* and *classes dangereuses* alike were deemed to hold little attraction.

The *classes laborieuses* were, however, to become more prominent in literature after the First War with the appearance of specifically proletarian fiction, largely under the energetic aegis of the anarchist novelist, polemicist and literary editor Henry Poulaille, who was born at 195 rue du Faubourg Saint-Antoine. One of his characters, Louis Magneux in *Seul dans la vie à quatorze ans* (not published until 1980), attends an anarchist meeting in the Faubourg, while in *Pain de soldat: 1914–1917* (1937) the population of the Faubourg respond less militaristically and chauvinistically than other Parisians to the soldiers, on twenty-four-hour home leave, who join the 1917 Bastille Day parade. The term 'proletarian literature' is normally used to refer to writing produced by self-educated writers from a working-class background, such as Poulaille himself, but the working population of the Faubourg figures in a number of texts which may go beyond this fairly narrow focus written during or set in the period under discussion. The poet Jean Follain waxes nostalgic about 'les révolutions déferlant du faubourg Saint-Antoine là où les varlopes courent sur le coeur de chêne'[10] / 'the revolutions streaming out of the Faubourg Saint-Antoine where planes are wielded on hearts of oak' – this in the year preceding the election of the left-wing Popular Front government. Jules Romains – a graduate of the prestigious École Normale Supérieure and thus anything but an autodidact – published a collection of working-class short stories, *Le Vin blanc de la Villette* (1923), set for the most part as the title suggests in an area well to the north of the Faubourg but studded with references to the *quartier* as both proletarian area and budding centre for *apaches* and night-life. One of the final volumes of Romains's immense novel-cycle *Les Hommes de bonne volonté, Françoise* – published in 1946 but set in 1933 – presents a considerably more benign view of the *quartier*. Pierre Jallez, one of the cycle's two central characters and like Romains a Normale Supérieure graduate, meets his fiancée-to-be Françoise in a café entitled Le Canon de la Bastille. Georges Simenon's celebrated detective Maigret, who lived on the boulevard Richard-Lenoir, also pays a visit to the now-vanished café of that name, evoked also by Follain in *Paris*. Jallez's view of the Faubourg is suffused with the romanticism of a 'class tourist', as when he compares the place d'Aligre to the central square of an old provincial village or claims that only the Croix-Rousse district of Lyon, for long the centre of the silk industry, gives a similar sense of artisanal tradition. The Croix-Rousse was, like the Faubourg, an area characterized by working-class militancy, and the 1831 and 1834 uprisings of the *canuts* or silk-workers count among the most prominent instances of industrial revolt in nineteenth-century Europe. Jallez's vision, less roseate than it may appear on an uninformed reading, is in any event tempered by the furniture Jallez and Françoise see in the shops, which 'ont longtemps résisté aux modes nouvelles, car le faubourg aime la tradition et le style. Mais vous voyez, le virus des "arts décoratifs" a fini par les gagner. Les bourses modestes ont droit aux cubes et aux surfaces nues'[11] / 'for a long time resisted new fashions, for the Faubourg likes tradition and style. But as you can see, the "decorative arts" virus has finally got to them. Modest purses are entitled to cubes and bare surfaces' – the sentiments of a Prince Charles *avant la lettre*, perhaps finally little less nostalgic than the neo-provincial terms in which the *quartier* is described.

A writer of a very different political stripe, Léon Daudet (son of Alphonse), who was an extreme right-wing monarchist, knew the area well since he was born in the adjacent Marais and many of his family lived in the 11th; his autobiographically based *Paris vécu* describes the rue de la Roquette, along which he had accompanied his father's body to Père-Lachaise, as 'la principale voie douloureuse de Paris, le chemin des enterrements' / 'the major *via dolorosa* of Paris, the route for funerals', and glumly opines: 'Aucun voleur à la tire ne s'aventure rue de la Roquette. Qu'y volerait-il? Des épluchures, ou des pipis d'enfant?'[12] / 'No pickpocket ventures into the rue de la Roquette. What would he steal there? Potato peelings, or children's wee-wee?' Of the route from the cemetery to the Faubourg he says: 'Il est préférable de ne pas s'y risquer après onze heures du soir, sauf si l'on aime le poivre dans les yeux, les coups de feu et les coups de couteau'[13] / 'It's preferable not to take your chance there after 11 p.m., unless you like pepper in your eyes, gunshots and knife-attacks' – an aristocratic fear of the *classes dangereuses* clearly informing his response.

Sociological observation from a similar ideological perspective is to be found in the Maurrassian Jacques Valdour's *Le Faubourg* of 1925. Valdour, the widely travelled son of a well-off family, initiated what he dubbed 'the concrete method' in social sciences, grounded in close personal familiarity with the milieu to be studied. Thus, in a manner that foreshadows Simone Weil or indeed many Maoist militants of the years after 1968, he took a variety of manual jobs – as coal-miner in Saint-Étienne, metalworker in

Saint-Denis and among others cabinet-maker in the Faubourg. This led him to adopt the Catholic-corporatist ideology with which *Le Faubourg* is impregnated. Despite its title much of the work actually deals with the 20th *arrondissement* near Charonne, where Valdour disapprovingly notes than a newsagent sold 150 far-left papers – a category that includes the Communist *L'Humanité* – out of a daily total of 650. He reports a conversation between two workers one of whom complains of having risked his life in a capitalist war while the other bemoans the 'invasion' of the *quartier* by foreigners – Italians predictably, but also Germans, as we have seen a long-standing presence, who now pass themselves off as Polish or Swiss, presumably because of lingering post-war nationalist prejudice. There are also dialogues between Communist sympathizers and opponents, indicating that while there was no significant unrest in the Faubourg of the time political discussion and debate continued unabated. Valdour expresses sympathy for the workers, isolated and subject to exploitation (meals and laundry are both described as expensive), but his discourse reeks of xenophobia. The fall of the Bastille is imputed to 'bandes recrutées parmi les gens suspects et les étrangers, surtout les Allemands, qui pullulaient au Faubourg'[14] / 'gangs recruited from among suspicious individuals and the foreigners, especially Germans, with whom the Faubourg teemed', while we are regaled with a sinister evocation of the number of Italian newspapers sold in the kiosks on the Place de la Bastille and a predictable dose of anti-Semitism. A great many Jews from Central Europe took up residence in and around the rue de Lappe after the First War, though the most visibly Jewish *quartier* of Paris was, as to a degree it has remained, the Marais, but I have been unable to find any other reference to the supposed 'ghetto' Valdour mentions near the square Trousseau, in the east of the *quartier*.

Valdour's solution to these assorted woes is a corporatist localism by definition vehemently hostile to Bolshevism. His close sociological observation leads to a Manichean view of the Faubourg as a 'pays de mission'[15] / 'an area ripe for conversion', currently in the hands of the forces of darkness:

> Idées fausses et propagande révolutionnaire, images menteuses et sensibilité affolée, journaux, discours, manifestations dans la rue, bals et spectacles, toutes les forces d'erreur et de mal sont déchaînées et liguées contre ce peuple du Faubourg, si riches de qualités naturelles, si obstiné à retenir au moins un peu de l'abondant trésor de ses traditions que ce n'est pas trop de l'alliance de tous ces ennemis pour les lui arracher par morceaux.[16]

False ideas and revolutionary propaganda, mendacious images and a panic-stricken frame of mind, newspapers, speeches, street demonstrations, dances and variety-shows – all the forces of error and evil are unleashed in concert against the people of the Faubourg, so rich in natural qualities, so determined to hang on to at least a little of the great treasure of their traditions that all these enemies need to band together to wrench it from them piece by piece.

Bar the diabolical frivolities of dances and variety-shows all these evils were of course to be found in abundance in the political movements with which Valdour aligned himself. The Faubourg, as he suggests, had never been exactly propitious terrain for the kind of organic harmony he preaches, and its hostility to the demonstrations of February 1934 which brought France to the verge of a right-wing coup was to be manifested in a vigorous counter-demonstration by former soldiers.

For genuine proletarian literature about the Faubourg we have to turn to *Faubourg Saint-Antoine: roman,* by Tristan Rémy, a friend and close collaborator of Poulaille's. Rémy had worked as a pork-butcher and railway ticket-clerk before joining *L'Humanité* as a clerical assistant, and it was in that newspaper that he published his first works of fiction. *Faubourg Saint-Antoine* won the Prix du roman populiste – designed to reward a novel which 'préfère les gens du assé comme asséages et les milieux populaires comme décors' [17] / 'prefers ordinary people for its characters and popular milieux for its setting' – in 1936 (the year of the Popular Front). These criteria would appear to have been somewhat flexible, for in 1940 the prize was to be awarded to Jean-Paul Sartre's *La Nausée*.

Rémy's novel, however, is clearly and robustly proletarian, set as much of its first book ('L'Apprenti') is in a cabinet-maker's workshop with excursions to the entertainments of the Richard-Lenoir funfair and a night-club, Le Cadran Bleu. The workers are exploited and a young apprentice, Charles – almost a latter-day Gavroche – moons a supervisor behind his back, leading to a fight. The tale ends happily, however, with a reconciliation and an elderly female worker being placed in charge of the workshop. There is a strong sense of community life but curiously little or no feeling of assertive class consciousness, exemplified by the fact that Charles finds his fellow-workers excessively deferential towards those in charge of them. The second book, 'La Fille', with completely different characters, features a female protagonist, Armande, and strikes a more contemporary note with mention of the Arab population of the area – the first in fiction I have been able to discover – and Armande's search for work including applying for a job as a cinema usherette.

A much later novel set in the area, François Raynal's *Faubourg* of 1950, is included here because its action takes place during the 1920s and 1930s. The *quartier*'s louche aspects come to the fore here through its three main characters: Roger de Beaumoutiers, a former naval doctor and holder of the Légion d'honneur now reduced to a tramp by alcoholism, his former lover Berthe ('Froufrou'), a can-can dancer likewise living on the streets, and their daughter – though this is not revealed until later in the novel – Louise, who works as a hatcheck girl in a night-club. This is the world of the *chansons réalistes* of such as Fréhel and later Édith Piaf, drawing a seedy poetry from down-at-heel urban, often night-time settings. Yet the Faubourg of craftsmanship is also a strong presence, as when Raynal writes: 'Entre la Bastille et la Nation, sur une demi-lieue, la rue du Faubourg Saint-Antoine étend son fleuve d'asphalte qui reçoit le tribut de nombreux passages, rues et cours profondes où l'on entend le chant de la varlope. Là, c'est, bien assis sur quatre quartiers: Roquette, Quinze-Vingts, Sainte-Marguerite et Picpus, l'immense royaume du meuble'[18] / 'Between Bastille and Nation, covering half a league, the rue du Faubourg Saint-Antoine is like an asphalt river receiving the tribute of countless passages, streets and deep-lying courtyards from which you can hear the song of the carpenter's plane. Here, firmly based in the four *quartiers* of Roquette, Quinze-Vingts, Sainte-Marguerite and Picpus, lies the vast kingdom of furniture.'

At the same time, weightlifters demonstrate their prowess in the square, the Italian – largely Piedmontese – community has a restaurant in the place d'Aligre as its focal point and the rue de Lappe, as ever, abounds in cinemas and dance-halls. More sinisterly, Louise is seriously wounded by a frustrated suitor, described as a 'sale petit souteneur de la Bastille'[19] / 'a dirty little pimp from the Bastille', but pulls through, while Roger and Berthe come into money and give the slightly unconvincing family romance a happy ending. 'Alors, tout à coup, le Faubourg semblait sourire de bonheur'[20] / 'Then, all at once, the Faubourg seemed to smile with happiness'; the conflict between the 'good' Faubourg of hard work and happy families and the 'bad' Bastille (though Raynal does not explicitly use this antithesis) of unsavoury night-life and crime is resolved in favour of the former. As some of the diners at the Piedmontese restaurant might have opined in cynical mood: *se non è vero, è ben trovato* ...

The cinema became an increasingly popular form of entertainment in this period, notably with the advent of sound in 1929, but I have not been able to locate any films of the period specifically set in the Faubourg. René Clair's *Quatorze juillet* of 1933 takes place in an obviously working-class *quartier* which given the title it is tempting to assimilate to the Faubourg

Saint-Antoine, but the waltz-song for which the film is widely known is entitled 'A Paris dans chaque faubourg' / 'In every faubourg of Paris', and Clair carefully avoids any overt topographical indication. The slender plot involves a male taxi-driver, Jean, and a female flower-seller, Anna – archetypal figures of the latter-day *classes laborieuses* – whose happiness is jeopardized by the seductress Pola and her *apache* connections. Anna goes to work in a bar, bringing herself perilously closer to the *classes dangereuses* from which Pola comes, but all ends happily for the couple in a resolution similar in tone to that of Raynal's novel (to which I would hasten to add Clair's film, with affecting performances by Annabella, Georges Rigaud and Pola Illery and sets by the two great Parisian designers Lazare Meerson and Alexandre Trauner, is far superior).

The Faubourg of the *classes dangereuses* figures prominently in Claude Dubois's enticingly titled *Apaches, voyous et gonzes poilus: le milieu parisien du début du siècle aux années 60 / Apaches, louts and hairy guys: the Paris underworld from the beginning of the century to the 1960s*. Dubois regretfully observes that 'les bals-musette hantés par les gars du milieu guinchant en casquette ou en chapeau ont disparu'[21] / 'the *bals-musette* frequented by lads from the underworld dancing in their caps or hats have vanished' – a nostalgia symmetrical with that displayed, in very different ways, by Bellet or Romains in their evocations of the *quartier* as bastion of honest working-class craftsmanship. Many such rue de Lappe *bals* visited by credulous visitors on 'Paris by night' coach tours in the hope of finding themselves side by side with gangsters were in fact tourist traps, serving up 'une représentation falsifiée de l'ambience de ces bals: musique ponctuée de bruits de pétards dans une semi-obscurité ou démonstration de danse dite "apache" (laquelle n'a jamais été pratiqué nulle part) exécutée par un couple embauché pour cela'[22] / 'a spurious representation of the atmosphere of such *bals*: music punctuated with what sounded like guns going off in the half-darkness, or a so-called "*apache*" dance show of a kind that never really existed, given by a specially hired couple'.

Dubois provides an at once serious and colourful overview of a world in which an English tourist in 1925 could ask: 'Et cet instrument désagréable qui fait un bruit affreux? What is it? Accordéon?'[23] / 'And that unpleasant instrument which is making such a dreadful noise? What is it? Accordion?', to be told by a (supposed) *apache*: 'Probably.' He identifies two founding myths of the rue de Lappe and its neighbours: the original tale of Casque d'or, seen as the first time the *apache* world had found itself on the front page, and André Picard and Francis Carco's play *Mon homme*, premiered in 1920. Carco – the son of a senior public employee – was the great writer of louche Parisian night-life in the period between the wars, and an habitué of the rue de Lappe and its dance-halls. Carco woud seem to have been largely responsible for the popularity of the slang term 'Paname', sometimes spelt 'Panam',* to refer to the popular – hence primarily eastern – areas of Paris in the years after 1914. Dubois traces this term back to on the one hand the popularity of the eponymous hat among *boulevardiers*, on the other the Panama Canal scandal of 1891 – a plausible enough combination of the elegant and the scabrous. In Carco's book 'La Bastille est une composante essentielle de Paname'[24] / 'Bastille is an essential part of Paname', and his *œuvre* makes a number of references to the *quartier*, though like Zola before him and Léo Malet after his work 'rotates' different areas of Paris; while he is associated primarily with Les Halles or Montmartre his topographical scope is considerably wider. In his collection of reminiscences *De Montmartre au Quartier Latin*, he recalls days not long before the First War when: 'A Grenelle, à la Bastille, dans des meublés ignobles, je logeais plusieurs jours, buvant, fumant et ne m'expliquant pas le goût pénible qui me poussait à fréquenter des filles publiques, leurs amis, des voleurs'[25] / 'In Grenelle on the Left Bank or Bastille, in vile rented rooms, I would stay for several days, drinking, smoking and not explaining to myself the tedious taste that drove me to hang out with prostitutes, pimps and thieves.' He evokes the memory of a young dancing girl – assuredly a euphemism – known as Pépé-la-Panthère who frequented the *bals* of the area and was found murdered in the boulevard Beaumarchais. In 1913 the English writers Katharine Mansfield and John Middleton Murry visited Carco in Paris and spent time with him in rue de Lappe dance-halls, foreshadowing other less intellectual but quite as celebrated foreign habitués of the area, from George Raft to the Duke of Windsor, in decades to come.

The play *Mon homme* is said to have revived the fashion for *apache* stories, which had come to be seen as passé. For Jean-Jacques Bedu it also made the fortune of the rue de Lappe, for all that its action could equally well have been set elsewhere.[26] One of the central characters, Claire, the apparently respectable wife of a Russian prince and diplomat, has in a previous avatar worked as a dancer in the rue de la Roquette and compares herself to Casque d'or. On a nostalgic return visit in her husband's absence she spies Fernand and it is love at first sight, of a self-abasing kind that may

* Carco published a collection of short pieces entitled *Panam* and a novel entitled *Paname*, doubtless to distinguish it from its predecessor. I consider neither here since they are not set in the Faubourg / Bastille though *Panam* includes a vignette describing a *bal-musette*.

recall Mistinguett's celebrated song also called 'Mon homme'. This – later translated into English as 'My Man' and recorded by Billie Holiday – tells of the singer's abiding passion for the man who beats, robs and deceives her, and was an immense success in France in 1920, so much so that the play was rewritten to include a performance of it. Like Mistinguett's alter ego Claire feels helpless before the first man to cause her heart to race for eight years ('Et je n'ai plus qu'un désir: me soumettre à lui, au plus tôt ... à tout risque'[27] / 'And I have only one desire: to submit to him, as soon as I can ... whatever the risk').

Claire returns once more to the *bal-musette*, where she is enraptured by the intoxicating atmosphere, and speaks to Fernand for the first time. A passionate embrace follows, with something like an exchange of vows (FERNAND: Ma femme! CLAIRE: Mon homme![28] / FERNAND: 'My woman!' CLAIRE: My man!). Inevitably, no good will come of this; Fernand, visiting Claire at home, is shot dead by the (male) secretary of her husband, who has attempted to blackmail her sexually, and with his dying breath counsels her to say that she caught him burgling the apartment. The twofold romanticism at work here – female self-abnegation fuelling and fuelled by the *frisson* of upper-class fascination with popular nocturnal Paris – will in all probability appear doubly dated to a contemporary public, especially in the absence of the haunting melody and vocal delivery that make Mistinguett's song still so powerful. Yet the play's considerable success indicates how potent that emotional cocktail was in the Paris of its time, and 'La Bastoche' – which is to 'Bastille' what 'Paname' is to 'Paris' – was an integral part of it.

The best-known address of 'La Bastoche' was unquestionably the dance-hall Le Balajo, at 9 rue de Lappe, which began life under the name Au vrai de vrai but changed its name in 1936. The *quartier* already abounded in dance-halls, of which there were seventeen in the rue de Lappe alone in the 1930s. Most notable in the area were the Bousca-Bal (mentioned in Chapter Five) and Le Petit Balcon, but the Balajo – still there, though now purveying a mixed diet of rock-and-roll, salsa and reggae (www.balajo.fr) – was to become far more renowned and emblematic than either. Robert Lageat's autobiographical memoir *Des Halles au Balajo* purveys anecdotes of the author's tenure of the dance-hall between 1982 and 1994, along with a succinct and racy account of its history before. For Lageat 'en 1925, c'est ça la Bastille: Paname et le milieu!'[29] / 'in 1925, that was the Bastille: Paname and the underworld!' – doubtless an exaggeration of the kind such works are likely to foster, but one whose mythical resonance played a major part in the area's image at the time. Georges 'Jojo' France, previously manager of an *hôtel de passe* (where prostitutes would take their clients) had set up a cabaret entitled La Bastoche at 32 rue de Lappe in 1931, at which time the Balajo was known as the bal Vernet. The murder of a young woman – a prostitute from the rue Jean-Beausire, on the Marais side of the square – led the elderly Vernets to put the cabaret up for sale, and it was bought by Jojo in 1936 and renamed the Balajo in consequence. Diwo evokes this in *249, faubourg Saint-Antoine*, quoting his mother's disapproving comment on the street's unsavoury nocturnal reputation and a friend's response that its dance-halls 'ne sont pas des lieux de perdition et les quelques voyous qui les fréquentent font pour la plupart de la figuration'[30] / 'are not dens of iniquity, and the few rascals to be found there are mostly playing a part' – the *classes dangereuses* once again presented as titillation for visitors. Le Musette, at no 23, catered to a primarily gay clientele, which doubtless made a visit to the street even spicier.

Establishments such as the Balajo bridged, albeit in temporary and often voyeuristic fashion, the gap between the world of 'Paname' and respectable Parisian society. 'Au *Balajo*, truands, vedettes, tout-venant, s'écrasent les haricots pour pénétrer' / 'At the Balajo, villains, stars and everybody in between trampled one another almost to death to get in.' The apaches' sartorial style changed to blend in better with the more up-market tenor of the street, according to Philippe Krümm:

> Peu à peu, leur tenue négligée fut remplacée par le faux col, la régate, la cravate en rayonne, le panama d'été et le feutre d'hiver, la pochette en soie et les chaussures à deux tons en … peau de serpent. Quant aux dames, elles mirent leurs fourrures en écharpe, brandirent des sacs à main en crocodile. Elles montrèrent leurs jambes gainées de soie perchées sur des talons hauts, tout en portent de croquignolets petits bibis en guise de chapeau. Tout ce beau monde se mit à danser la valse à l'envers. Ce qui amena un soir un danseur du Balajo à demander à Jo Privat de lui jouer une valse à l'endroit car il ne savait pas la danser à l'envers![31]

Gradually, their careless mode of dress was replaced by the detachable collar, the sailor knot, rayon ties, the panama in summer and the felt hat in winter, the silk pocket-handkerchief and two-tone snakeskin shoes. As for the ladies, they wore fur stoles and brandished crocodile handbags, showing their silk-stockinged legs perched on high heels and wearing deliciously tiny miniature hats. All these fine folk began dancing the waltz back-to-front, so that one evening a dancer at the Balajo asked Jo Privat to play him a waltz the right way round, since he didn't know how to dance it back-to-front!

This well-heeled enthusiasm no doubt owed something to the presence across the street, at no 12, of Madame Floriane's brothel, listed in the Paris Office du commerce's official *Guide rose*:

Pour ceux qui attrapent des suées au *Bal* sans balancer leur semoule. simple comme bonjour de traverser se faire éponger les amygdales ... encore que pour des amygdales, elles soyent [sic] bas placées les couillettes en question! De belles frangines, cinq francs la passetiquette ... Une affaire en or ce bocard: elles sont cinquante femmes à accomplir chacune ses quatre-vingt passes. ... Vous multipliez: quatre mille ... multipliez encore: vingt mille balles par jour la recette, pas sale![32]

For those who get in a sweat at the Bal without getting their rocks off, it's as easy as anything to cross the street and get your tonsils rubbed down ... even if your bollocks are a little lower-hanging than 'tonsils'! Lovely girls at five francs a shot ... The joint was a goldmine, with fifty women each turning eighty tricks a day. ... Do the sums: four thousand ... and again ... twenty thousand francs' worth of takings a day – not bad!

Brothel visits seem to have been more or less *de rigueur* among literary and artistic milieux in the famously free-living Paris of the time. Thus, Salvador Dali on an early trip to Paris asked the taxi-driver to recommend him a good brothel, fetching up at the celebrated Le Chabanais near the Louvre – a favourite haunt of Edward VII when Prince of Wales – while the great writer and Surrealist fellow-traveller Georges Bataille referred to brothels as his church. Claude Dubois speaks of a brothel frequented by his father in the 1930s at 138 boulevard Richard-Lenoir, Chez Blanche, whose speciality 'était de *casser une lune* – sodomiser'[33] / 'was to *break a moon* – sodomy', and which therefore charged four times as much as more conventional establishments. Jean Follain vaunts the streetwalkers of that boulevard Richard-Lenoir for their vivid slang, notably their habit of addressing a reluctant client as 'miniature des prairies'[34] / 'meadow miniature' – a delicate way of describing him as a 'vache' / 'cow'. This term is used in French slang as an unfocused insult for members of either gender, and when applied to males would also have had overtones of its derisive argotic use to designate a policeman – two (dulcet) insults for the price of one.

Lageat's evocation of the bordello is at once earthier and more materialistic than Bataille's, reminiscent of a production-line – complete with exploited workforce – rather than anything more ecclesiastical. The verve of his writing throws into relief the desolating financial underbelly of the *quartier*'s enticing seediness.

Lageat lists a number of underworld figures often to be seen at Le Balajo, giving a spicily *argotique* account of a fight between two of them that ended with 'le lingue planté dans le joufflu, que le manche qui dépassait!'[35] / 'a knife planted in the fat guy – only the handle left sticking out!' Among the celebrities who flocked there were the expressionist Montmartre painter Gen Paul, the novelists Céline and Marcel Aymé, the film-maker Abel Gance, the actors Arletty and Jules Berry, and unsurprisingly considering the association between the rue de Lappe and *Mon homme* Carco and Mistinguett. The mutual fascination of the worlds of crime and entertainment was to become almost a commonplace after the Second War, as witness Frank Sinatra's alleged involvement with the Mafia or indeed that of George Raft, a Balajo regular. The Balajo would seem to have been one of the first scenes in which this relationship was played out, illustrating how the *classes dangereuses* had lost much of their erstwhile radical edge but none of their menace.

Clément Lepidis's *Les Bals à Jo* gives a colourful account of the life of the accordionist Jo Privat, whose music animated the Balajo (though as we have seen it was not named after him) from the time of its opening in 1936, when he was only seventeen. Privat in an on-line interview evokes the variegated clientele of the twelve dance-halls in the street,[36] yet while Lepidis lists the Bastille as one of Paris's more sordid *quartiers* and the rue de Lappe in particular as a hive of prostitution he does not altogether endorse the romantic aura with which Privat surrounds it: 'Rue de Lappe des années trente [...] chez toi la joie n'était pourtant pas de mise malgré que l'on y dispensait le plaisir'[37] / 'Rue de Lappe of the thirties [...] joy was not really at home with you despite the pleasure that was on offer there.' Privat was a lifelong Communist Party supporter, who regularly offered his services to the annual fête of the Party's newspaper *L'Humanité* but conducted himself in rather less puritanical fashion than the Party leadership would have approved. Bedu tells – who knows if the story is true or not? – of his being picked up by a limousine which carried him off to the up-market, and highly conservative, suburb of Neuilly, where he played the *java*, most popular of the *bal-musette* dances, for a woman who demanded: "'Jo, traite-moi de putain, de salope, je t'en prie!'" [38] / "'Jo, call me / treat me like a whore, a bitch, I beg you!'" Privat was apparently happy to oblige; what else may have followed is not explicitly stated, but the sexual component of the upper-class fascination with the *classes dangereuses*, even in edulcorated musical form, could not be plainer.

The rue de Lappe was celebrated enough to figure on the 'shopping-list' of the three Séeberger brothers – among the first cinematic location scouts. Between 1923 and 1931 they compiled an extensive archive of Paris street photographs which were then shipped to Hollywood, yielding what has been described as 'a visual index of Paris as it appeared in the cinema'.[39] Most of their chosen locations, predictably, were the usual tourist suspects, such as Notre-Dame and the Latin Quarter, but there is a set of photographs of the rue de Lappe, showing:

> Little passages, with wet cobblestones glistening below peeling posters glued to the stone walls; a sinister courtyard entry, partly blocked by a heap of coal; an aging woman whose face reports a hard biography. In one photo a concierge stands rather proudly by the seedy building she tends.[40]

Two dance-halls – the Bal Monteil and the Bal Bousca – also figure,[41] along with a supposed *apache* house and a striking Art Nouveau shop dispensing the German doughnuts known as *krapfen*. These, like the heap of coal in all probability belonging to a *bougnat* from Auvergne and the poster in Hebrew outside an apartment-block, evoke the immigrant population of the area, as we have seen always an important factor in its life. The dance-halls were evidently photographed before they opened for the night's business, as suggested by the four rather bored-looking waiters (reflected in mirrors) who are the Bal Bousca's only inhabitants, while the '*apache* house' appears slightly run-down. Any glamour to these locales is strictly in the eye of the beholder. It is the workaday Faubourg rather than 'La Bastoche' that is set before us here, in such details as the cobbler's-cum-hardware shop glimpsed at the back of a courtyard ot the two men flyposting – doubtless advertisements for theatres or night-clubs, but we can make them out with difficulty if at all – in the passage Thiéré. Andrew and Ungar tell us that the Hungarian-born Istvan Kertész also photographed the street in 1931, convincing Pierre Mac Orlan that he could feel the blood in the gutters. The Séebergers' approach is slightly more low-key, suggesting a *quartier* that has known hard times rather than one where trouble may be just around the corner (taking the form for that inveterate phallocrat Henry Miller of homosexual approaches).[42] Their shots, drawing on 'the melodramas of Hugo, Zola, Eugène Sue, and their less celebrated descendants',[43] set the mould for Hollywood's representation of popular Paris in the years before the Second War, all at once picturesque, sordid and nostalgic.

The seamier side of life in the *quartier* is illustrated by Jacques Borel's autofictional novel *L'Adoration* (1965), recounting his childhood experiences. These for the most part took place on the Marais side of the boulevard Richard-Lenoir, where after the death of his father in the 1930s his mother took him to live with an aunt and uncle who ran a so-called hotel there. Borel's poetic reflections on childhood and adolescence centre on the 'avowal' of the novel's title – his traumatic realization that the establishment where his beloved mother helped out his aunt and uncle was in fact a bordello or at least an *hôtel de passe*. 'Il y avait dans presque toutes les petites rues du quartier où nous habitions des putains en grand nombre qui faisaient le trottoir'[44] / 'There were large numbers of prostitutes walking almost all the little streets of the *quartier* where we lived' – proof that the boulevard did not act as a hermetic seal between a respectable area and a more raffish one. Borel's narration makes it clear that this activity went on not only in the eastern part of the Marais but in Bastille and further north in Popincourt. The young Borel along with his doctor *amour* Geneviève goes to the rue de la Roquette to visit a dying child, in a dirty, run-down apartment block that would not have seemed out of place in the Séebergers' gallery of photographs. A family friend from his former home town of Mazerme – in reality Saint-Gaudens, near Toulouse – plants the germ of suspicion in his mind when she says: '"Vous habitez une drôle de maison. Et un drôle de quartier aussi. J'en ai montré à Madeleine* les errantes prêtresses"' / '"You live in a funny old house. And a funny old area too. I've shown Madeleine its errant priestesses"' – a bizarrely Bataillesque turn of phrase on the lips of an unmarried provincial lady.

His early amorous promenades with Madeleine take them to the east of the boulevard, through streets and passages still dedicated to manual work; the *classes laborieuses* may not figure prominently in his story, but they have not gone away. Even the rue de Lappe is quieter than its reputation would suggest ('si déserte et comme si provinciale certains soirs de semaine'[45] / 'so deserted and almost provincial on some weekday evenings'). The world of prostitution evoked here is a joyless one chiefly significant for the vicarious humiliation it inflicted on the young Borel through what he perceived as his

* An art-student friend of the narrator, later to bceome his wife.

mother's degradation, almost as painful for him as if she had been a prostitute herself. This also affected his response to the Popular Front demonstrations of 1936. The election of a left-wing coalition government led by Léon Blum in May of that year sparked off a wave of strikes and demonstrations which led to immense improvements in workers' conditions – the right to strike, the forty-hour week and paid holidays pre-eminent among them. This euphoria was short-lived, for the government fell in the following year as a result of the Great Depression, but the demonstration of 14 July 1936, culminating at a rally in the place de la Nation, was the largest France had seen. François Lassagne wrote in the left-wing weekly *Vendredi* on 24 July: 'La Bastille fut vraiment prise, ce soir de 1936'[46] / 'The Bastille was really stormed, that evening in 1936', but for Borel this was not cause for rejoicing. His repugnance for the noisy crowd that on that day 'noircissait le boulevard Beaumarchais, les abords du boulevard Richard-Lenoir, la place de la Bastille tout entière'[47] / 'darkened the boulevard Beaumarchais, the environs of the boulevard Richard-Lenoir, the whole of the place de la Bastille' stems from his identification of them with the Lohénec couple who employed his mother in their *hôtel de passe*. '[J]e voyais aujourd'hui autant d'oncles Lohénec dans la foule des manifestants qui tournaient en rangs compacts autour de la colonne de Juillet'[48] / 'I saw on that day a host of Lohénec uncles in the crowd of demonstrators who walked in serried ranks around the July column.' French slang has long used the term 'bordel' to designate a messy or chaotic situation; it is as if the youthful Borel – a near-homonym – were experiencing that all-but-dead metaphor in live form, seeing in the menacing crowd demanding social change the embodiment of the world of disorderly bodies that had brought his beloved mother so low.

His sequel, *L'Aveu différé*, published thirty-two years later, focuses on the life of the *quartier* rather than his sense of abjection, mentioning the Kursaal cinema close to his former home and giving sympathetic portrayals of many of the streetwalkers he had known. Here too the life of the street is painted as tranquil to the point of dreariness, a far cry from the red-light district of myth: 'De temps à autre, pas si fréquents, en fin de compte, les entôlages, c'était bien la seule vie nocturne qui, faiblement, et encore! l'animât, la rue aux putes, pas de bals, comme rue de Lappe, pas un bistrot, et parler à son propos de rue chaude serait décidément abusif'[49] / 'From time to time, not so often really, rip-offs were the only kind of nightlife to be found in the whores' street, and then of a fairly feeble kind – no dances as in the rue de Lappe, not a single bar, and to call it a hot-spot would be quite misleading.' Borel's rueful avowal that 'c'est le moment où putes et bordels disparaissent d'une littérature où ils ont, si longtemps, régné en maîtres, que tu choisis

[...] pour en parler' [50] / 'it's just when whores and bordellos are disappearing from a literature over which for such a long time they reigned supreme that you have chosen to speak about them' further evokes the dispiriting entropy of red-light life that pervades the novel. The Faubourg – which experienced its last political hurrah in 1936 – may have been giving way to the more hedonistic 'Bastoche', but that more recent avatar was by no means an uncomplicatedly joyful one.

Chapter Seven

'Slicked hair and splendid sideburns': Occupation and Liberation

T HE 150TH ANNIVERSARY of the Revolution was commemorated, on 14 July 1939, by a march from Bastille to Nation, organized by the Communist Party, in which 50 000 took part – the last major political demonstration in the Faubourg for several years. I say 'major' in reference to size only, for at 3 p.m. on 27 June 1942, with the Occupation at its height, a remarkable event took place at the corner of the avenue Ledru-Rollin and the rue du Faubourg Saint-Antoine. Some 200 women, mostly Communists, gathered to the strains of the Marseillaise and distributed tracts to passers-by, to be joined later by a rag-doll effigy of Pierre Laval 'hanged' from a gallows improvised from a rod and two bricks. This remained in place all afternoon, for the police mistook the bricks for sticks of explosive and summoned the bomb squad rather than intervening directly.

The 1941 round-ups of Jews and others seen as undesirable saw 8000 arrests in the 11th *arrondissement*, the centre of the August round-up organized by the Paris police in close cooperation with the Gestapo. During this the area was completely cordoned off and all Métro stations between République and Nation were closed. 4000 Jews, 1500 of them French, were seized and sent to an internment camp which had been prepared for them in the north-eastern suburb of Drancy; most were transported from there to Auschwitz. The *arrondissement* was to provide its share of Resistance heroes. Jean-Pierre Timbaud, secretary of the steelworkers' section of the CGT trade union, and the municipal councillor Maurice Gardette were both shot along with other hostages in Châteaubriant, near Nantes, in 1941, to avenge the killing of a German officer. Another councillor and trade-union official, Léon Frot, was similarly killed in 1942, while the Polish-Jewish resistant Marcel Rajman (sometimes spelt Rayman), a member of the now celebrated Manouchian Group which was made up largely of non-French, was shot along with twenty-one others in 1944.* Each of these has a street or garden-square named after him in or near the *quartier*. Arthur Dallidet, a leading Communist party organizer, was arrested at the corner of the rue de Reuilly and the boulevard Diderot – in the 12th *arrondissement* – in February 1942, and died under torture without giving anything away. Others were luckier; on 16 July 1942 a young Communist, Jean Jérôme, was on his way to a clandestine meeting at 39 rue de la Roquette when he noticed large numbers of policemen, conducting the most notorious round-up of all – now known as the 'rafle du Vél'd'Hiv' after the indoor cycle-track where the detainees were held. His contacts, the Zerman family, refused to answer the door to the police, and the *concierge* said that they were away from Paris for a few days. They immediately took refuge in the south, and their son, Julien, joined the Jewish Resistance, to be killed on a mission in 1944 at the age of eighteen. Further to the north, at 54 rue Saint-Sabin, Robert Bernadac, responsible for radio communications for one of the most important northern French Resistance networks, was arrested on 13 March 1943. He was able to flush his contacts notebook down the toilet before being taken to the Gestapo headquarters and deported, surviving to return to France at the Liberation. It was at 2 rue Bréguet, just off the boulevard Richard-Lenoir, that the Resistance network known as the Groupe du Musée de l'Homme (after the museum where many of its principal members worked) had its headquarters between 1940 and 1942. Its principal organizer, the ethnologist Germaine Tillion, was arrested and deported to Ravensbrück in August 1942, but survived and even wrote a satirical operetta in detention. This, entitled *Le Verfügbar aux enfers / At Your Disposal and in Hell*, was given its first professional performance at the Théâtre du Châtelet in 2007, when its author was still alive (I have not been able to discover whether she attended the première). Germaine Tillion died the following year, a month short of her 101st birthday.

The rue Amelot, which runs parallel to the boulevard Beaumarchais up towards République, housed two important Resistance organizations, one of which, the Comité de la rue Amelot, based at no 36, began life as a Jewish charity, distributing 2000 meals per day in 1941, and went on to host undercover political meetings under the umbrella of the Union générale des Israélites de France – a Jewish representative body set up by the Germans along the lines of the *Judenräte* in Poland and other occupied territories. To the north-east, at 16 avenue Parmentier, was the headquarters of a clandestine

---

* The story of this group is told in two feature films – Franck Cassenti's *L'Affiche rouge* (1976) and Robert Guédiguian's *L'Armée du crime* (2009).

printing press which kept going throughout the Occupation, producing publications for the Communist Party and other Resistance organizations, and in a final blaze of glory the posters calling Parisians to arms at the Liberation.

Women too played their part in the Resistance. Up to 4000 woman resistants are estimated to have been held in the Petite Roquette during the Occupation, while many common-law prisoners, some on remand, were evacuated to jails in the south-west, in appalling circumstances.[1] Harrowing testimonies to the dreadful conditions in the Petite Roquette, where up to five women were held in cells designed for one or two and pregnant women were not entitled to extra food until their fifth month, are to be found in France Hamelin's *Femmes dans la nuit*.[2] Among the fifty or so common-law prisoners executed during those years, the best-known was Marie-Louise Giraud, a laundress from the Normandy port of Cherbourg guillotined in the Petite Roquette in 1943 for performing illegal abortions. Her story was made into a film by Claude Chabrol, *Une affaire de femmes* (1988), in which she is movingly played by Isabelle Huppert.

The Petite Roquette was to house political prisoners again at the time of the Algerian War, when a number of members of the network set up by the philosopher Henri Jeanson to provide funds and forged papers for activists in the independence movement were imprisoned there. Best-known of these was the dissident Communist Hélène Cuénat, who along with five fellow militants made a spectacular escape in February 1961, less then a year after beginning a ten-year sentence. Her account of this is reminiscent of Robert Bresson's great film (based on a real-life prison escape by Resistants in Lyon) *Un condamné à mort s'est échappé*.[3]

The Balajo closed its doors on the outbreak of war in September, and the *quartier*'s burgeoning night-life was to disappear all but completely until the Liberation – probably one reason why the area was reputedly disliked by the occupying Germans. If there is a conspicuous dearth of literary and cinematic texts set in or specifically mentioning the area during *les années noires*, this is doubtless because the two spheres in which it was most renowned were during that period in enforced abeyance.

Everyday life in the *quartier*, for the most part, would as in the rest of Paris and other French cities have been characterized by hardship, shortages and the prevalence of the underground economy. *Le Temps* published a story on 1 December 1940 in which the mayor of the 11th *arrondissement*, M. Viet, spoke of the growing number of unemployed in his area – 22 000 at the time. Meat was hard to get, largely because farmers preferred to sell their animals in the provinces where they fetched higher prices, and the only vegetables readily available were potatoes and carrots, while oil and unadulterated coffee could be found only on the black market. Coal was in painfully short supply, and heating in public buildings was not turned on until 15 November, leaving schoolchildren blue with cold. The singer Renée Lebas, the child of Romanian-Jewish parents – a tailor and a dressmaker who worked in the rue du Faubourg Saint-Antoine – recorded in Swiss exile in 1942 Michel Emer's song 'De l'autre côté de la rue', subsequently to become part of Édith Piaf's repertoire. The song tells of the contrast between the singer's 'vieille mansarde' / 'old attic' on the seventh floor and the opulent dwelling of the woman opposite – a contrast alleviated by the true love the singer knows and her neighbour's 'monsieur qu'elle déteste'[4] / 'gentleman she hates'. Given Lebas's origins it does not seem too fanciful to see in the singer's dismal material circumstances an evocation of those that all too many inhabitants of the Faubourg had to endure under the Occupation. Claude Autant-Lara's 1956 film *La Traversée de Paris*, based on a short story by Marcel Aymé, gives a darkly sardonic view of the times through its tale of two men (played by Bourvil and Jean Gabin) transporting four suitcases full of black-market pork from the southern end of the Latin Quarter to Montmartre. Their itinerary, passing as it does through the Marais, takes them close to the Faubourg, and the activities described in the film would undoubtedly have been commonplace there, if less colourful than those depicted by Autant-Lara.

Le Parisien de Paris, by the investigative journalist Claude Blanchard, gives a graphic, and not always edifying, portrayal of what the *quartier* was like after the Liberation. A furniture salesman 'tend au passage, comme une toile d'araignée, le piège de ses paroles'[5] / 'proffers the trap of his words like a spider's web to the passer-by', while furtive traces of the black market – which thrived until 1948, by which time production was back to pre-war levels – surely persist in Blanchard's assertion: 'Plus la maison est sale, plus les carreaux sont cassés, plus ça empoisonne et plus l'homme est riche'[6] / 'The dirtier a house is, the more windows are broken, the more toxic it is, the richer the man [presumably the owner] is.' This seediness sits cheek-by-jowl with the Faubourg we have learnt to know and love, as in his evocation of 'le vieux faubourg des coups durs, dont l'accent traînant, plus encore que celui de Belleville, est la quintessence du langage parigot et qui "perle comme çin"'[7] / 'the old hard-hitting Faubourg whose long-drawn-out accent, even more than that of Belleville, is the quintessence of popular Parisian language and which "talks like this"'.* He interviews one of the last

---

* I have not attempted to transliterate the original onamatopoeic French.

traditional cabinet-makers, who speaks fondly of the custom of knocking off
work an hour early to go to the café — a refinement presumably superfluous
to the bronze-caster in the rue des Taillandiers who by 10 a.m. was already
on his sixth vermouth. Blanchard also takes a leaf out of Jules Romains's
book in comparing the nearby rue Keller to the Croix-Rousse silk-weavers'
quartier in Lyon.

The Faubourg's working-class traditions thus seem to have survived *les
années noires* in battered but recognizable form. As 'Bastoche', the *quartier*
came to life after the Liberation, the Balajo reopening in November 1944
with a gala ball presided over by Mistinguett. Its visitors were to include
Hollywood celebrities such as Rita Hayworth and Robert Mitchum, along
with Édith Piaf who celebrated her 1952 marriage with Jacques Pills there.
The rue de Lappe acquired even greater notoriety in 1950 thanks to a
hit song written by Francis Lemarque and recorded by the cabaret singer
Marcel Mouloudji, which bore its name. Mouloudji was of Algerian Kabyle
extraction, though born in Paris, and had been closely associated before the
war with the Popular Front, remaining committed to the left throughout
his life. Lemarque likewise had progressive political connections, working
closely first with Jacques Prévert, then with the singer and sometime
communist sympathizer Yves Montand.

Lemarque, whose real name was Nathan Korb, was born to a Polish tailor
and a Lithuanian mother at 51 rue de Lappe, literally over the Bal des Trois
Colonnes dance-hall, and spoke only Yiddish until the age of three. His view
of the Faubourg is a benignly cosmopolitan one:

> Dans ce quartier se côtoyaient des individus venus des quatre coins
> du monde. Il flottait dans l'air léger de cette époque un parfum de
> liberté qui m'a appris à comprendre ceux qui venaient d'ailleurs, et à
> fraterniser avec eux.[8]

> In this area people lived side by side who had come from the four
> corners of the earth. There was a whiff of freedom in the light-hearted
> air of this period which taught me to understand those who came from
> elsewhere, and to fraternize with them.

Lemarque claimed that there were comparatively few Jews in the area
(among their number was Renée Lebas, a friend of his from the late 1930s
and later to become a well-known singer) and that he and his family always
got on well with the local Auvergnats, whose accordion music inspired him
and his brother to begin singing and playing themselves.[9] He was to go on

to become one of the best-known Parisian singers and songwriters of the post-war period. 'Rue de Lappe' thus evokes his very earliest memories – of 'frappes' / 'hoodlums', the *bals-musette* and the *java* dance beloved of the *apaches* with their 'cheveux gominés / Avec de belles rouflaquettes' / 'slicked hair and splendid sideburns', like a Parisian equivalent of the British Teddy Boys a few years later, Despite the political affiliations of its author and singer, 'Rue de Lappe' is politically ambivalent, for it paints a primevally sexist picture of gender relationships, saying of the male clientele at the local dance-halls that: 'Avec les gonzesses c'était à / Coups d'trique / Qu'ils discutaient politique' / 'With their lasses they used rods of iron to talk about politics' – the 'trique' referring ambiguously, and in equally unappetizing fashion, to a 'real' cudgel or to its phallic equivalent. At the same time, its final verse derides the 'poulets' or 'cops' who arrested – the French refers to 'un soir de rafle', which has clear Occupation overtones – a convict escaped from French Guiana, in all probability the same Devil's Island where Alfred Dreyfus had been wrongfully imprisoned. The luckless 'frappe' had returned to the rue de Lappe (a rhyme which pervades the song) '[p]our cueillir le cœur d'ces dames / Comme une poire au poirier' / 'to pick fair ladies' hearts / Like a pear from a tree'. His arrest proves only a temporary setback, for while 'ça lui coûtait / Quelques années / Mais il n'les faisait / Mais il n'les faisait / Presque jamais / Rue de Lappe / Rue de Lappe / Quand il rev'nait / Rue de Lappe / Rue de Lappe / Il r'commençait' [10] / 'it cost him a few years, he hardly ever served them, and when he came back to the rue de Lappe he started all over again'. This barely credible escapological cycle is clearly not inviting us to take it literally; rather, it conjures up an unchanging cyclical world of popular festivity whose hoodlums are benign latter-day Artful Dodgers and whose 'ladies' are ever ripe for plucking despite the 'rods of iron' wielded by their escorts.

Jules Romains edited a 1951 volume entitled *Portrait de Paris* in which the Faubourg's radical reputation is mentioned by Robert Garric (at one time Simone de Beauvoir's philosophy teacher), who speaks of Gavroche as the symbol of Paris, 'gouailleur et attendri, grand dans sa fragilité, dépisteur de la sottise et fouineur, inventeur de mots, hirsute et cocasse, parfois héroïque' [11] / 'mouthy yet tender-hearted, great in his fragility, good at detecting bullshit and sniffing things out, verbally inventive, hairy and comical, sometimes heroic'. The whiff of retro sentimentality about this description may be in some degree dispelled when we learn that as late as 1958 a quarter of dwellings in the area had no running water and more than half no inside sanitation; the Balajo and its denizens notwithstanding times were still hard for many *faubouriens*. The photographer Lionel Mouraux's memoir *Je me souviens du 11e arrondissement* gives an only slightly sentimental account of tough-yet-tender life in Popincourt, just to the north of the Faubourg, in his young days (he was born in 1953), which makes plain the lack of material comfort but also the pleasure afforded by the cinema and the open-air fairs held on the boulevard Richard-Lenoir.[12]

No better example of the spirit of solidarity in the *quartier* could be found than the Commune libre d'Aligre, established in 1955 by M. Jeanson, a former chief cook for the French railway sleeping-car company and later a fishmonger at the eponymous market (also known as the Marché Beauvau). That market, at the eastern limit of the Faubourg, was as we have seen a rival to the more central Les Halles in the nineteenth century, and continues to thrive today. *Communes libres*, of which there are at the time of writing more than eighty in France (six of them in Paris), are charitable neighbourhood associations set up under a law passed in 1901, before which date special authorization had been required. The Aligre one organized material help for children and the elderly – down to the inclusion of cigarettes in the hampers distributed to the needy aged in the summer of 1959 – along with 14 July celebrations sometimes involving media stars of the time. One amusing detail was the Assemblée Nationale's vetoing of the offer to lend buses for a weekend outing for local children, made by Les Vins du Postillon – a company that imported cheap, often rot-gut wine from Languedoc to Paris, where it sold widely to the less well-off.

The Commune libre published a monthly journal, *Le Gavroche d'Aligre*, between 1956 and 1962, whose accounts of popular dances, solidarity collections for the families of Belgian miners and the setting-up of the Fédération Nationale des Communes Libres in 1956 resonate with the political traditions of the Faubourg. Less radical perhaps was the call by the journal's film critic, Suzanne Gautier-Derozier, in the summer of 1959 to ban 'subversive' films in order to protect the young. She was particularly severe on Claude Chabrol's *Les Cousins*, stigmatized as 'un encouragement à la veulerie et au vice'[13] / 'an encouragement to spinelessness and vice'. A later number that year called on parents to be vigilant lest their children should become 'blousons noirs' – leather-jacketed rockers who were to become an important youth movement in France, much feared in part because of their enthusiastic embrace of American culture. The then Paris prefect of Police, Maurice Papon – later to be disgraced and imprisoned for his wartime role in the deportation of Jews from Bordeaux – even went so far as to wonder whether rock-and-roll should be banned in France.

Concern for the welfare of the *quartier*'s youth extended to iconography of the past as well as the present, for early in 1957 there was talk of designing a new type of hat for the local *gavroches* to wear on special occasions in place of the Phrygian bonnet, deemed to be too revolutionary. Gavroche would surely have turned in his grave, though he might have been mollified by the fact that some youngsters were photographed in the summer of 1958 defiantly sporting Phrygian bonnets. The Commune also crowned annually its 'Esméralda' – an equivalent to the chaste 'rosière' referred to in Chapter Five, named after the at once seductive and virtuous heroine of Hugo's *Notre-Dame de Paris*. The journal's reach into the past was historical as well as mythopoeic, as in a 1960 issue in which one Théodore Mesure reminiscences about the 1900 14 July celebrations in the place d'Aligre and quotes from a song his grandfather had sung:

> Le génie de la Bastille
> Il n'a pas de parapluie
> Il n'a pas de parapluie
> Ça va bien quand il fait beau
> Mais quand il tombe de la pluie
> Il est trempé jusqu'aux os.[14]

> The genius of the Bastille
> Hasn't got an umbrella,
> hasn't got an umbrella;
> That's all right when it's fine,
> But when the rain falls
> He gets soaked to the skin.

This song was recorded by the humorous singer-songwriter Ricet Barrier in 1969, and the recording credits him and Bernard Lalou with its authorship; perhaps they drew on and elaborated an earlier popular or improvised version. The later avatar also mocks the hapless statue for not being able to shelter himself from the sun ('Il n'a pas de chapeau d'paille / Pour se préserver un peu / Il rôtit comme une volaille / Sous l'éclat du ciel en feu'[15] – 'He doesn't have a straw hat / To protect himself a little / He's roasting like a chicken / Beneath the fiery sky'), displaying a commendably Gavrochian lack of respect for what is after all a significant national icon.

The market also housed a restaurant, La Boule d'Or, which after being well reviewed in the US edition of *Vogue* magazine attracted such celebrities as Clark Gable, Gina Lollobrigida and even Dwight Eisenhower, but closed in the late 1960s, to be replaced by a semi-circular block of flats, Les Jardins d'Aligre. Jeanson died in 1962, widely mourned in the *quartier*, not least because of his political past, for he had joined the Paris socialist delegation in giving an ambulance to the Republicans during the Spanish Civil War and been an active Resistant. The Commune libre became significantly less active after Jeanson's death, though it was revived in 1978 and is still active today.

The period known as *les trente glorieuses* – broadly speaking between the end of the Second War and the oil crisis of 1974–75 – was characterized, in France perhaps even more than in previously more heavily industrialized countries such as the US and the UK, by steady, sometimes spectacular, but often unevenly distributed economic prosperity. France experienced no social unrest on the grand scale between the Liberation and the events of 1968, and the Faubourg was no exception. The Plan d'urbanisme Directeur (PUD) of 1967 has been described as a species of 'Haussmann mark two', though without the authoritarian political agenda of its predecessor; its modernizing zeal – which worshipped the automobile and the high-rise development with quasi-transatlantic fervour – began to make itself felt as early as 1959. In the Faubourg it made its major impact through the 1965 redevelopment of the Hôpital Saint-Antoine by Le Corbusier's former right-hand man, André Wogenscky. The walking-tour proposed in the final chapter will point out other examples of the modernization of the *quartier* in this period.

That modernization also significantly affected the cinema, always a popular form of entertainment in the Faubourg. In the half-century following the end of the war, seventy per cent of Parisian cinemas closed – a cull partially offset by on the one hand the opening of multiplexes, on the other the greater number of cinemas in the *banlieue*. The major closure in the *quartier* was that of the Cyrano in the rue de la Roquette, which shut in 1969 after fifty-seven years to revert to the building's original function as a theatre. In the post-war period there appear to have been three cinemas in the area; the Radio-Cité-Bastille, opened in 1939 and from the 1960s through till 1990 specializing in 'adult' films; the Bastille Palace, which began life as a neighbourhood cinema in 1937 and in the 1970s showed a mixture of 'adult' and Hollywood B-movies; and the Lux-Bastille, later the Paramount-Bastille, a vast edifice in pseudo-Egyptian style with three screens, pulled down to make room for the Opéra in 1984. I have also found references to a cinema in the 12th *arrondissement* called Saint-Antoine, which showed action films dubbed into French, but have been unable to locate it precisely, though the name suggests that it must have been in or very near the Faubourg.

The Radio-Cité-Bastille and the Bastille Palace are still there, but transmogrified by the upmarket evolution of the *quartier* since the advent of the Opéra. They have been renamed now as La Bastille (1990) and Le Majestic Bastille (1995) respectively, and show 'art et essai' works – what would be described in English as 'art' or in a US context 'indie' films. The earlier, more popular cinematic culture of the area is evoked in the first of Cyrille Fleischman's collection of short stories *Riverains rêveurs du métro Bastille*, about 1950s Ashkenazi Jewish life in the vicinity of the Place – in fact on the Marais side (where Fleischman himself was born) at least as much as in the Faubourg. The book 's cover photograph is of the Cyrano, suggesting the importance of cinemas as focal points for the *quartier* – something confirmed by many of Fleischman's stories. The protagonist of the first story, 'Entre le cinéma Saint-Sabin et le cinéma Saint-Paul', Jacques Statisch – owner of a clothes-shop which appears to be located in the 11th – is profoundly loyal to his local cinema, the Saint-Sabin, which he avers has more human warmth to it than any other in Paris. He is reluctant even to walk to the Lux-Bastille or the picture-house at the beginning of the boulevard Richard-Lenoir (unnamed, but clearly the Bastille Palace in its pre-porn guise), and justifies his local patriotism to a neighbour by proclaiming that 'un autre quartier ne pouvait rien avoir de mieux qu'un cinéma comme le Saint-Sabin où l'on ne jouait que des bons films' [16] / 'another neighbourhood could not have anything better than the Saint-Sabin, which showed only good films'. The Lux-Bastille figures in the two following stories, 'Aventure dans le IVe arrondissement', where the husband of the Nachdem couple – unlike his wife who prefers the Saint-Paul, on the Marais side of the Place – avers his affection for 'un Lux-Bastille des années cinquante pourtant déjà promis à une future disparition' [17] / 'the 1950s Lux-Bastille already doomed to disappear', and 'Et aussi la dame du Lux-Bastille', in which a doctor, Karl Shifweg, strikes up a relationship with a war widow he meets at the cinema one Sunday afternoon. His new amour turns out to get on very well with Shifweg's ex-wife, and the three of them make an appearance together at the annual ball of a charitable society in the rue de Rivoli, leading the president of the society to say, in words not unworthy of a schmaltzier Woody Allen:

> Et puis, est-ce que ça compte vraiment, de nos jours, qu'il y ait *une*, *deux*, ou même *trois* madame Shifweg? Pas du tout: le docteur rend tellement de services à tout le monde, que c'est toujours un plaisir de le revoir en famille.[18]

> And then, does it really matter, these days, whether there is *one*, *two*, or even *three* Madame Shifweg? Not at all: the doctor does everybody so many favours that it's always a pleasure to see him with his family.

Fleischman's stories are undeniably sentimental, but conjure up the Jewish attachment to neighbourhood that was an important factor in the identity of the Marais and to a lesser extent Bastille after the Liberation. Another story, 'Un conseil de Balzac', has an inhabitant of the rue de Lesdiguières, in the Marais, visited by the ghost of the novelist, who as we saw in Chapter Three once lived in the same street. Balzac tells his interlocutor that 'tout a changé autour de la Bastille'[19] / 'everything has changed around Bastille' – a Janus-faced utterance, referring in the first instance to the difference between Balzac's day and the 1950s but also looking forward to the barely less immense changes between the 1950s and the time at which Fleischman is writing.

No survey of writing about Paris would be complete if it did not make reference to the work of Léo Malet, who virtually invented the *roman noir* – the French equivalent of hard-boiled detective novels by such as Dashiell Hammett and Raymond Chandler. Malet's private eye Nestor Burma is the focus of his novel-series named, in homage to Eugène Sue, *Les Nouveaux Mystères de Paris* – fifteen novels each set in a different *arrondissement*. Alas, Bastille figures only tangentially, for suffering from health problems and short of inspiration Malet abandoned the series in 1959, leaving his projected tale set in the 11th – *La Méprise de la Bastille* – unwritten, while *Casse-pipe à la Nation* (1957) takes place as its title suggests in the part of the 12th to the east of the Faubourg. *La Méprise ...* was to have been set in a July heatwave and to have included dance-scenes in the rue de Lappe, an episode set in the underground part of the Canal Saint-Martin and a drama involving an unfaithful woman, but Malet found himself unable to draw these various strands together, and the book was never written. *Casse-pipe à la Nation* begins with Burma walking past the July Column 'à la Bastoche',[20] but his steps take him towards the Gare de Lyon and thence to the Foire du Trône, which is to be the centre of the novel's intrigue. What might have befallen Burma in 'la Bastoche' itself – which rather than the Faubourg would surely have been his preferred name for the *quartier* – can only be matter for conjecture.

Georges Simenon's Inspector Maigret, probably the best-known fictional policeman of all time, lived at 132 boulevard Richard-Lenoir, and as we have already seen visited the brasserie Le Canon de la Bastille. The area figures episodically in the seventy-five novels Simenon devoted to him, often as haunt of pimps and toughs, once (in *Maigret et les vieillards* of 1960) described as lower-class and once (*Maigret et son mort* – 1947) as a base for the production of false identity-cards. There would appear to be only one reference to the Faubourg as home of the *classes laborieuses*, when Paul Martin in *Un Noël de Maigret* (1950) is described as having a good job in a furniture store in the rue du Faubourg Saint-Honoré, but even he takes to drink after his wife is killed in an accident.[21] Such a portrayal is only to be expected given the requirements of the detective genre, but it is overwhelmingly the louche and cosmopolitan Bastille rather than the diligent yet seditious Faubourg that is to dominate representations of the *quartier* from the end of the war.

The novelist and playwright Pierre Bourgeade, author of *romans noirs* and of libertine texts influenced by Sade and Bataille, began his publishing career with a collection of short stories, *Les Immortelles* (1966). One of these, 'L'Autrichienne', spans the two dominant identities of the area – political through its interpellation of the statue atop the column ('Salut à toi, obscur symbole, mais qui danses! Je baise le pavé, entre deux flics. C'est là que le peuple français a fait explosion'[22] / Hail to thee, obscure yet dancing symbol! I kiss the cobblestones, between two cops. This is where the French people exploded'), hedonistic through the narrator's boastful cry: 'A moi, rue de Lappe! J'ai treize cents balles. Je vous aurai toutes, bonnes femmes! Suivez le parcours'[23] / 'The rue de Lappe's mine! I've got a pocketful of money. I'll have the lot of you, girls! Follow me!' The two strands come together in the euphoric assertion that 'Balajo, c'est Quatorze-Juillet toute l'année'[24] / Balajo is 14 July all year round'.

Two years after Bourgeade's text was published, 'the French people' – or a substantial number of them – 'exploded' in May 1968. All demonstrations had been prohibited within Paris since 1954, when seven people were killed during a protest against the Algerian war, but one month was to be more than enough to make up for fourteen lost years. The once traditional 1 May march organized by the Communist-dominated CGT trade union between République and Bastille was authorized in 1968 for the first time since 1954, but was to be overshadowed in retrospect by what came to be universally knows as 'the events'. These began with a wave of student protests and occupations, whose brutal repression by police triggered what became the biggest general strike in French history, bringing the country to a halt and provoking fevered speculation about the end of the Fifth Republic and even the capitalist system. On 30 May de Gaulle addressed the French nation, announcing elections within forty days which returned a landslide Gaullist majority. The 'movement' – in reality a heterogeneous variety of movements, whose student and worker wings failed to come together in the revolutionary moment that briefly seemed possible – collapsed as abruptly as it had begun, but had greater long-time political effects than might have appeared in its immediate aftermath, notably de Gaulle's stepping down from power less than a year later and the emergence of new political movements to rival the Communist Party on the left.[25]

Given the Faubourg's radical traditions and penchant for often violent street action, it may at first appear surprising that May all but passed it by, but that is among other things a reflection of social and economic change in the Paris area. Large-scale industry was not a significant presence in the Faubourg by this time, and the major strikes and occupations took place further out, in working-class suburbs such as Boulogne-Billancourt, Saint-Ouen or Flins. The idedological hurly-burly, for its part, was concentrated in the student heartland of the Latin Quarter, notably in and around the occupied Sorbonne and École Normale Supérieure. The night of the most violent demonstrations, 24 May, saw the so-called 'burning of the Bourse' (the Paris Stock Exchange) – in fact a minor local conflagration – which was triggered by the blocking of a march headed for the place de la Bastille. On 30 May the CGT trade union organized a march from Bastille to République, calling on de Gaulle to resign, but this was almost completely overshadowed by the huge demonstration of support for him which filled the Champs-Élysées. The traditional working-class Bastille–République axis was upstaged by new centres of would-be revolutionary ferment, in the universities and other occupied cultural centres such as the Comédie Française theatre and the Paris Cinémathèque. No longer the tempestuous Faubourg of before, not yet the cultural magnet it was to become with the Opéra de la Bastille, the *quartier* was politically marginalized in 1968 as it had been for many years and was to remain – with one glorious exception (as it seemed at the time), to be dealt with in the next chapter.

Chapter Eight

'Let's have some sun!': post-Gaullism and the Mitterrand years

THE MODERNIZATION of Paris went on apace during the presidency of de Gaulle's successor, Georges Pompidou (1969–74). This period saw grandiose modernization projects, many though not all reviled by defenders of traditional Paris: the destruction of the main Paris market at Les Halles, replaced by an underground shopping-mall, the building of the skyscraper Tour Montparnasse, next to and overshadowing the new rail station of the same name, and, less infelicitously, the construction of the Centre Beaubourg (renamed Centre Georges Pompidou after his death and opened in 1977). 'Beaubourg' is a major cultural centre housing an immense public library – now rather upstaged by the Bibliothèque Nationale de France on the Left Bank – Europe's largest museum of modern art, two cinemas and, in an annexe, the centre for musical technology IRCAM. Its planning and execution marked the first step in the growing cultural prominence of the Right Bank over the past thirty-five or so years, of which the Bastille Opéra and consequent changes in the area are the most recent example.

Pompidolian modernization had little direct effect on the Faubourg/ Bastille – I use a compound form the better to emphasize the hybrid nature of the area at this time – though things might have been very different had the plan to honeycomb the city with high-speed urban expressways been fully realized. One of these – the radiale de Bagnolet – was to have cut a swathe through the 20th and 11th *arrondissements*, complete with a flyover in the boulevard de Charonne, near Nation. This, like most of the other routes planned, never came to fruition, and the expressway along the banks of the Seine, which runs for part of its length through the 12th, is the only trace in or near the *quartier* of a project which at one time threatened the destruction of all the façades in the rue du Faubourg Saint-Antoine and its widening to forty metres.

Politically the *quartier* appears to have been fairly quiet during the Pompidou years, with one possible exception. On 19 December 1969 the Farmachi pharmacy – now the Pharmacie de l'Opéra Bastille – at 6 boulevard Richard-Lenoir was held up by an armed robber, who killed the pharmacist and her assistant as well as seriously wounding a customer and an off-duty policeman. Suspicion fell on Pierre Goldman, a leftist militant who had just spent a year as a guerrilla fighter in Venezuela. In the politically paranoid climate of the time this weighed heavily against him, the more so as he admitted to two other burglaries. According to Hervé Hamon and Patrick Rotman, Goldman had returned from Venezuela 'paumé, à la dérive, hanté par une sorte d'esthétique du suicide'[1] / 'a lost soul, adrift, haunted by a kind of suicidal aesthetics'. He had also allegedly planned to rob the (extremely wealthy) psychoanalyst Jacques Lacan, but lost his nerve at the last minute.

Goldman was initially found guilty and condemned to life imprisonment in 1974, to become a cause célèbre on the French intellectual left. His prison autobiography, *Souvenirs olonais d'un juif polonais né en France*, sold 60 000 copies, and its favourable reception along with François Mitterrand's belief in his innocence swung much public opinion behind him. He was acquitted of the murders at a retrial in 1976 and released from prison shortly afterwards, to be shot dead in the street in September 1979. Nobody has ever stood trial for his murder.

Valéry Giscard d'Estaing, President for the seven years between Pompidou's death and the election of Mitterrand, has, largely because he served only one term, been something of a neglected figure, yet his presidential style – fundamentally patrician, but sporting a cultivated veneer of populism with a dash of American-influenced would-be classlessness – marked a significant departure from the loftier Gaullian and post-Gaullian years, and this was mirrored in his inaugural 14 July celebration, less than two months after taking office. This took the form not of the traditional procession along the Champs-Élysées, but of the placing of a wreath at the foot of the July Column – a gesture that as Rosemonde Sanson puts it 'dote le régime d'un certificat de baptême révolutionnaire'[2] / 'bestowed upon the regime a revolutionary certificate of baptism'.

Few can have expected anything remotely 'revolutionary' from Giscard's determinedly centrist approach, the more so as his tenure of office was beset by serious economic difficulties. The metamorphosis from Faubourg to Bastille continued during these years, though the *classes dangereuses* were still in evidence, notably a lone bank-robber identified only as 'Serge' whose car number-plate was noted when in January 1981 he robbed a bank at 148 rue du Faubourg Saint-Antoine. 'Serge', it turned out, was a policeman with four previous raids to his credit. The joys of the rue de Lappe continued to pull in punters, the Balajo celebrating its fortieth birthday in 1976, though a sombre note was struck by a political killing involving Basque émigrés in 1979. The major architectural development in the *quartier* during Giscard's presidency was the demolition of the Petite Roquette women's jail, replaced in 1975 by a garden square to which the former prison gates offer entry. Marguerite Duras had conducted an interview for French television in 1967 with the (unnamed) woman governor, at the time the only female prison governor in France.[3]

Robert Lageat, writing in 1980, is to put it mildly unstinting in his eulogy of the *quartier*'s 'unspoilt' qualities:

> Contre vents et marées la rue de Lappe résiste. Un îlot [...] Perdez dix minutes rue de Lappe, rue de Charonne, vous remontez par le passage Thiéré, reprenez la rue de la Roquette, tournez rue des Taillandiers ... ce sont les mêmes maisons qu'autrefois, basses, un peu crispées, lézardées ... Humez l'odeur XIXe, cette transpiration du passé ... *Les Mystères de Paris* qui collent à ces ruelles pavées, ces cours délabrées, ces bâtisses biscornues [...] Maintenant que le IVe, que mes Halles sont détruites sans espoir de renaissance [...] le XIe arrondissement, je pense, a pris la relève du vieux Paris.[4]

> Through hell and high water the rue de Lappe stays the same – like an island [...] Waste ten minutes in the rue de Lappe or the rue de Charonne, go back up the passage Thiéré, go back down the rue de la Roquette, turn into the rue des Taillandiers [...] Here are the same houses as in days gone by, low, a little huddled-up, their walls cracked ... Breathe in the nineteenth-century aroma, that perspiration from the past ... *Les Mystères de Paris* clinging to these cobbled alleyways, these dilapidated courtyards, these quirky buildings [...] Now that the 4th and my Halles have been destroyed with no hope of resurrection [...] the 11th *arrondissement*, I think, has taken on the mantle of old Paris.

The Eugène Sue reference suggests a self-conscious reading of an imagined, and long-vanished, Parisian past (Sue's *classes dangereuses* inhabit the Ile de la Cité, where the police headquarters is now to be found ...) forward into a present in which it is increasingly menaced and can survive only through an act of intertextual will. Yet the Faubourg's spirit of radical solidarity lived on in changed, often more multi-cultural form, as evidenced by the revival of the Commune libre d'Aligre in 1979 to celebrate the market's bicentenary. This has long been the most multi-cultural part of the Faubourg, largely because of its proximity to the Gare de Lyon, which meant that as early as the 1960s it was home to Auvergnats, Italians, Corsicans, Yugoslavians, Portuguese and Tunisians. The opening of an immigrant hostel in the rue Beccaria in the late 1970s led to some disquiet and even the circulation of a petition, but more recently '[l[es habitants s'accordent pour dire qu'ici la cohabitation est sereine'⁵ / 'the inhabitants are at one in saying that here peaople live calmly side by side'. The area was described by Véronique de Rudder in 1987 as a melting-pot, 'un peu un "condensé" de l'immigration dans la capitale'⁶ / 'something of a "condensed version" of immigration in the capital'. The very lay-out of the market reproduced this, for until it was reduced in size in 1980 it was divided into three sections – one Maghrebi, selling the cheapest produce, one with both French and foreign stallholders whose goods were of intermediate quality and one entirely French-run whose fruit and vegetables were supposedly the best.⁷ It was almost certainly the poverty of some of the inhabitants rather than any retro cultivation of the picturesque that kept the last public wash-house in Paris – probably very similar to that described by Émile Zola in *L'Assommoir*, and itself frequented by the real-life Casque d'or and mentioned in Hugo's *Histoire d'un crime* – open in the rue de Cotte as late as the year in which de Rudder was writing.

Ethnic and class diversification have gone hand in hand – but emphatically not overlapped – in Bastille as elsewhere in Paris since the beginning of the *trente glorieuses*. A gentrificatory straw in the wind was the move of the leading film journal *Cahiers du cinéma* to the passage de la Boule-Blanche, just off the rue du Faubourg Saint-Antoine, in 1974, which has been its base ever since. *Cahiers* had in the wake of 1968 taken a sharp, often recondite and sectarian turn to the revolutionary left, whose direct political impact was on the wane by about 1972. The electoral left, in the form of an alliance between the Socialist Party, the Communist Party and the Left Radicals, was widely expected to win the parliamentary elections of 1978, but was narrowly defeated by a combination of right-wing parties. The fortunes of the French left were thus at a dispiritingly low ebb by the end of the 1970s, but with hindsight it is significant that the Socialists obtained more votes than the Communists for the first time since 1936.

Three years later, the Place de la Bastille was filled with a deliriously celebratory crowd for what remains – possibly for ever – its last great political moment. François Mitterrand unexpectedly defeated Giscard in the second round of the presidential election on 10 May,* and in torrential

* Curiously, while the 11th *arrondissement* voted in its majority for Mitterrand, the 12th was very narrowly in favour of Giscard.

rain the assembled revellers chanted: 'On a gagné!' / 'We've won!' and 'Mitterrand, du soleil!' / 'Mitterrand, let's have some sun!' For many it was as if the promissory note of May 1968, despite the fiercely anti-electoralist tendencies that had often characterized the movement, had finally been redeemed.

Mitterrand himself was in his Burgundy constituency of Château-Chinon, but the future prime ministers Michel Rocard and Lionel Jospin were in the square, along with Gaston Defferre, soon to become Interior Minister. Rocard – a long-standing political and personal adversary of the new President – declared that a new page was in French history was opening, something that seemed to be embodied by the singing of the Internationale along with the Marseillaise (to say nothing of occasional dancing of the Charleston) and by the presence of gay and feminist militants. Many more armchair leftists, however, took refuge from the downpour in the up-market Bofinger brasserie, on the Marais side of the square, among their number the veteran Communist and surrealist poet Louis Aragon, the feminist writer Marie Cardinal and the actor Jean-Claude Brialy. Less well-heeled seekers after shelter were, according to *Le Monde*, turned away by muscular employees. Cries of 'Giscard au chômage' / 'Giscard on the dole' and even 'Giscard plus haut que Bokassa' / 'Hang Giscard higher than Bokassa'* were heard, and those old enough to remember made comparisons with 1936. More cynically, the right-wing commentator Jean Dutourd expressed pleasure that Poulidor had finally triumphed – a reference to the well-loved racing cyclist who was eight times second or third in the Tour de France but never won.

Le Figaro described the rally as resembling a stage-show rather than a political meeting – unsurprising given its informality and the wide range of participants, from militants to delighted sympathizers, but suggesting that the evening's euphoria might be short-lived. The new government soon encountered major difficulties in its attempts to put into practice a fairly ambitious left-wing programme, spearheaded by nationalization and reflation, in the teeth of economic difficulties and the predominance of right-wing administrations in Europe and the US. By 1983 Mitterrand's early ambition to 'finish with capitalism' seemed a distant pipe-dream and a policy of financial rigour was in place, though the reforms of the first few years – the abolition of the death penalty, the lowering of the gay age of consent,

---

* Bokassa was the bloodstained head of the Central African Republic until 1979, whose gift of diamonds to Giscard rapidly became notorious and contributed to the then president's discrediting.

the creation of regional assemblies – remain an abiding legacy. Serge Moati's 1991 documentary film *Dix ans après* ends on footage of a young man dancing beneath the rain in the Place; Mitterrand's close ally and adviser Jacques Attali ruefully observes: 'J'ai peur qu'il soit au chômage' / 'I'm afraid he may be out of work', and by way of atonement the film is dedicated to him.

Louis Chevalier, in the 1985 edition of *Les Parisiens*, vividly articulates how 10 May was in so many respects to be a false dawn. His diatribe, while coat-trailing and contentious as it was surely meant to be, is for that very reason worth quoting:

> Ce qui se déroula lors de cette reprise de la Bastille programmée depuis les coulisses de la rue de Solférino, un Breugel eût pu la peindre, un Rabelais le dépeindre. Pestiférés des sectes groupusculaires au coude à coude avec les batteurs d'estrade de la social-démocratie remise à neuf. Acrobates de la dialectique rompus à toutes les pirouettes idéologiques fraternisant avec des autogestionnaires en proie à l'autosuggestion. Convalescents de la déstalinisation en quête de potions de synthèse, cul et chemise avec les rebouteux de l'antipsychiatrie. Écologistes daltoniens qui croyaient avoir vu le feu passer au vert, alors que le rose était de mise.[8]

What happened when the Bastille was recaptured, according to a programme devised in the back-rooms of the rue de Solférino, could have been painted by Breughel or described by Rabelais. Plague victims from tiny groups and sects stood side by side with reconditioned social democrats strutting their stuff on the platform. Dialectical acrobats accustomed to all manner of ideological pirouetting fraternized with advocates of workers' control who were the dupes of their own illusions. Recovering Stalinists looking for artificial magic potions went hand-in-glove with the bonesetters of anti-psychiatry. Colour-blind ecologists thought that the lights had turned green when pink was more appropriate.

Some degree of gloss may be in order here. The rue de Solférino houses the headquarters of the Socialist Party, who had organized the rally. The sects referred to are the various Marxist groupings that had come to the fore in and after 1968, and felt that their hour might have come round at last. The social democrats – Rocard and Jospin their most prominent representatives on the night – were of course the antithesis of revolutionary, and were to be the major beneficiaries of Mitterrand's election, to the disappointment of those who had set their hopes higher. Workers' control was a theme associated with the non-Communist left, to be rendered largely obsolete by the rise of the global capitalist economy, while the 'recovering Stalinists' refers of course to the Communist Party and the 'bonesetters of anti-psychiatry' to the disciples of Gilles Deleuze and Félix Guattari to whom conventional forms of therapy were anathema in their supposed reconciliation of the individual with capitalist society.

France's revolutionary political culture, so important as we have seen through the Faubourg's history, for long nourished the dream of 'le grand soir' – the 'great evening' which would see the triumph of a new and fairer society. The expression would seem to date from no earlier than 1890, though its roots stretch back to Christian eschatology and the Apocalypse, and 14 July and the Commune stand as respectively successful and unsuccessful manifestations of it. The distinctiveness of 10 May 1981 perhaps lies in its carnivalesque fusion of 'le grand soir''s last hurrah with an unexpected but emphatically reformist electoral triumph, to be followed within a few years by the collapse of many of the political hopes raised. For Chevalier, the rainstorm was certainly an omen, but not in the sense so ardently desired by the ecstatic crowd, 'car c'est le socialisme que l'on s'apprêtait à enterrer'[9] / 'for it was the burial of socialism that was being prepared'. In November 1984 workers from the *banlieue rouge* succeeded in occupying the top of the column – long closed for safety reasons – to protest against their sacking by a multi-national corporation, but this attracted considerably less attention than the previous summer's vast demonstration in protest against the proposed partial absorption of private – including Church – schools into the state sector. This, largely backed by the political right, filled the Place de la Bastille on 24 June, and is generally held responsible for the resignation of Prime Minister Pierre Mauroy shortly afterwards and his replacement by the less radical Laurent Fabius. The contrast with three years before could scarcely have been more telling. Twenty-three years later, when carrying out research for this book, I was living in the rue des Tournelles – parallel to the boulevard Beaumarchais, on the Marais side – and hosted a soirée, of a distinctly non-celebratory kind, on the evening of 6 May, when the right-wing Nicolas Sarkozy was elected President of the Republic. My friends on their homeward journey fell foul of tear-gas deployed against protestors in the Place de la Bastille, and the air was still rancid with its fumes as I dolefully took out the empty bottles the following morning. *Sic transit gloria mundi* ...

Jacques Fansten's 1986 film *États d'âme*, featuring Jean-Pierre Bacri and François Cluzet, is an at once nostalgic and cynical evocation of 10 May

1981, on which date five left-wing friends from high-school days form part of the crowd in the Place. The narrative owes much to Julien Duvivier's *La Belle Équipe* of 1936, a key film of the Popular Front years, about five unemployed workers who win the lottery and open a riverside café together. Fansten's quintet, as befits the Mitterrand *Zeitgeist*, are firmly ensconced in the superstructure and the post-1968 middle class. Their entrancement on 'le grand soir' and subsequent disabusal are recounted along with their overlapping romantic involvements with Marie (Sandrine Dumas). The film's shaky gender politics are as much of its time as its sedulous evocation, less sardonic than Chevalier's, of post-1981 disillusionment. The twentieth anniversary of Mitterrand's election was marked by a celebration in the Place, with street performers, world music and short films, beneath a giant portrait of the six-years-dead President. France had had a socialist Prime Minister (Lionel Jospin) for four years, but the 2001 festivities were markedly more subdued than those of twenty years before.

Jean-Paul Blais dates the gentrification of the *quartier* back to 1983, in which year, following on from the revival of the office of Mayor of Paris in 1977, each *arrondissement* first elected its own local council and mayor. The fading of the Faubourg's political traditions is illustrated by the fact that the 11th was held by the right until 1995, when it fell to the left, as did the 12th in 2001 – an unexpected result which clinched Socialist control of the Paris council. Both have been controlled by the left ever since. The Paris municipal council, chaired by the then mayor and future French President Jacques Chirac, launched a plan in 1983 to develop, economically and culturally, the eastern areas of the capital – something which chimed with Bastille's changing identity, vividly if a touch sweepingly evoked by Blais:

> Sculpteurs, artistes peintres, musiciens, *designers*, publicistes, 'communicants' ou gens de mode remplacent les menuisiers, ébénistes, ferblantiers, chaudronniers, bronziers, vernisseurs, gainiers, passementiers, peintres en bâtiment, miroitiers ou doreurs.[10]

> Sculptors, painters, musicians, interior decorators, advertising agents, 'communicators' or fashion designers replaced furniture- and cabinet-makers, tinsmiths, boiler-makers, varnishers, corset-makers, soft-furnishers, house-painters, mirror-dealers and gilders.

The Parisian art world is notoriously peripatetic; Saint-Germain-des-Prés and the Marais have long been among its epicentres, along with Montmartre, Montparnasse, Les Halles and Beaubourg, and the 1980s saw as Blais suggests a number of galleries and dealers – of the artistic kind – open in Bastille. An association called, in a slightly threadbare reference to the statue atop the column, La Bastille a du Génie began organizing open days in workshops in the *quartier* as early as 1982 – the year in which the decision was taken to build the Opéra.

Chapter Nine

'A building, not a monument':
the construction of
the Bastille Opéra

THE BASTILLE OPÉRA was one of François Mitterrand's *grands projets*, also known as *grands travaux* – a dozen or so highly ambitious architectural realizations which left the President's mark on Paris in a manner sometimes described, not flatteringly, as reminiscent of the monumental schemes of the Egyptian Pharaohs. Three of these – the Institut du Monde Arabe, the Musée d'Orsay (both on the Left Bank) and the Cité des Sciences at La Villette, in the north-east of the city – had in fact been embarked upon under Giscard, though they were completed during Mitterrand's first term. Among the others, the best-known are the Grand Louvre, centred on a glass pyramid, which gave the museum sorely needed new space; the Grande Arche out at La Défense, in the western suburbs, inaugurated during the 1989 bicentennial celebrations; and the Bibliothèque de France, where much of the research for this book was carried out. This was not opened until December 1996, when Jacques Chirac named it the Bibliothèque François Mitterrand in homage to the instigator of the project.

The Opéra's history is a chequered and frequently internecine one, in which political manoeuvring seems to loom larger than musical or aesthetic considerations. Before its opening Paris's main opera house had been for 114 years the opulent Palais Garnier, in the 9th *arrondissement*, which was utterly unsuited to contemporary music and concentrated on extremely costly sets and productions, only one of which could be housed at any one time. This along with the restricted supply of seats – fewer than 2000 – in turn led to mind-bogglingly high ticket prices. Nor was it by all accounts a happy place to work, described by Maurice Fleuret (director of music at the Culture Ministry from 1981 to 1986) as 'un antre de haine et de violence'[1] / 'a cavern of hatred and violence'. It was simply not in the same league as Milan's La Scala or London's Covent Garden; while in itself this may not have mattered overmuch to the President, whose indifference to music is a matter of record, cultural politics were an important trademark of his administrations, epitomized by his flamboyant Culture Minister Jack Lang.

The decision to locate the new opera house in the Place de la Bastille was far from politically innocent, evoking as it did the Revolution of 1789 and the triumphant evening of 10 May 1981. Frédérique Jourda, in one of the more enthusiastic studies of the Opéra, refers to the square as a 'carrefour indécis'[2] / 'uncertain crossroads' between the old Paris of the Marais, the Hausmannian boulevard Richard-Lenoir and the Faubourg, seen as still part of the working-class east. This topographical liminality corresponded also to the ideological agenda behind the project, which smacked both of Lang's bold populism and of the mission of André Malraux, Culture Minister under de Gaulle, to bring high culture to the people. For François Chaslin the choice of the Place was emblematic of a 'mélange d'esprit festif (soixante-huit et la fête de l'*Huma*, à chaque rentrée) et de goût pour les célébrations empreintes de gravité (héritées de l'imagerie républicaine, radicale et socialiste)'[3] / 'a blend of festive spirit (1968 and the fête of *L'Humanité* each September) and of a taste for celebrations imbued with more gravity, inherited from republican, radical and socialist imagery' – as might be said an amalgam of Langian pizazz and Mitterandesque gravitas.

The writer and diplomat Pierre-Jean Remy was asked to chair the first working party on the new Opéra, which he wanted to see move away from the international star system towards 'l'idée d'un Opéra populaire poussée jusqu'à ses réelles onsequences'[4] / 'the idea of a popular opera house carried to its logical conclusion'. Remy also, however, wanted the new house to open with Mozart's *The Magic Flute*, Berlioz's lengthy *Les Troyens* or even a new work by the (comparatively) avant-garde Olivier Messiaen, but 'surtout pas *Carmen*!'[5] / 'anything but *Carmen*!' – seemingly in flat contradiction to 'the idea of a popular opera house'. Remy was not to stay long enough to attempt to resolve this incompatibility, for dissatisfied with his salary and the working conditions in his office he decided to leave the job in December 1982 – the first of a string of resignations that were to plague the Opéra in its early years.

The new house was to have two auditoria, one of 2700 seats and a smaller one with a flexible layout (the 'salle modulable') of between 300 and 1200, for more experimental work, along with purpose-built facilities for making costumes and scenery. A competition to choose the architect was launched in 1983, attracting 756 entrants but 'pas un seul projet enthousiasmant'[6] / 'not a single exciting project'. The new building was to occupy the site of the old Bastille railway station (which had become an exhibition venue), and space on the square was at a premium, which in turn cramped the architects' style considerably and largely accounted for the uninspiring array of designs submitted. These included one by the Hong Kong architect Rocco Sen Kee Yim, believed to have the approval of Pierre Boulez, whose view as France's leading composer-conductor and director of the important modern music centre IRCAM would have carried a great deal of weight. The proposal, allegedly 'plein de métaphores à la gloire de la révolution, un peu naïves'[7] / 'full of slightly naïve metaphors to the glory of the Revolution', including a glass courtyard calling to mind the guillotine, was not, however, accepted, though Yim was one of three architects invited to submit more detailed proposals. The other two were Dan Munteanu, whose projected design was more swashbuckling still, and one which the selection committee, for whom the proposals were anonymized, wrongly suspected was the work of the celebrated US architect Richard Meier. In fact it was by the hitherto little-known Carlos Ott, born in Uruguay but resident in Canada, whose proposal was accepted in November 1983.

This design supposedly did not please Mitterrand, who is reported to have compared it to a factory or a garage, but in the deteriorating economic climate Ott's declared wish to 'faire un bâtiment, pas un monument'[8] / 'make a building, not a monument' won the day. The railway station was demolished in 1984, along shortly afterwards with the Paris-Bastille cinema and the only pre-Revolutionary building on the square, a restaurant called La Tour d'argent. The restaurant of this name on the Left Bank is among the most famous in Paris, dating back to 1582, and granted its Bastille namesake permission to use the name in 1932. The Bastille Tour d'argent was markedly less prestigious, and taxi drivers were reputedly encouraged by its management to take unwary tourists there rather than to the original – and substantially costlier – establishment. The building was reconstructed along its old lines after the Opéra was completed, and now trades as Les Grandes Marches.

Ott's building has been much criticized, Marie Delarue calling it a 'fort belle illustration d'"architecture de pissottière" [sic]'[9] / 'a fine illustration of "pisspot architecture"', and even Jack Lang allegedly took exception to it. It nevertheless seems to me – especially after having seen models of many of the other submitted designs – to have been the least worst solution to the problem of how to reconcile the need for a world-class opera house with restrictions imposed by space and finance. The strength of Ott's design lies in its comparative discretion – not a characteristic of many of the other *grands travaux*. Sébastien Maréchal gives a succinct account of the building which situates it in its particularly sensitive architectural and iconographic context:

L'architecte, Carlos Ott, a conçu son édifice à l'écart de la place de la Bastille pour ne pas faire ombre à la colonne de Juillet, monument emblématique. Il ne cherche donc pas à 'recomposer la place'. Bien au contraire, l'opéra se situe dans un espace différent. Pour la façade, le monument est légèrement en retrait par rapport aux immeubles voisins: une arche de granit reprend la forme de l'édifice voisin, pour ne pas faire un contraste d'échelle trop brutal. La forme extérieure de l'opéra exprime sa fonction interne. En façade, le volume cylindrique renferme la grande salle d'opéra tandis que les formes cubiques renferment les salles techniques.[10]

The architect, Carlos Ott, designed his building to be slightly removed from the Place de la Bastille in order not to overshadow the July Column, which is an emblematic monument. So he did not seek to 'recompose the square'. On the contrary, the Opéra is situated in a different space. The monument's façade is set slightly back from the neighbouring blocks, and a granite archway reproduces the shape of the building immediately next door, so that the contrast of scale is not too abrupt. The Opéra's outward shape expresses its internal workings, the cylindrical part of the façade housing the main auditorium while the cubic shapes house the backstage activities.

Beaubourg had of course gone much further a decade and more earlier in deconstructing the outside-inside opposition, putting its air conditioning, electricity and water supplies on the outside of the building along with the escalators. The Opéra might well have appeared timorous by comparison, but as we have seen material constraints made anything more grandiloquent problematic, and to have built Europe's largest opera house in such circumstances was a feat in itself.

Controversy and contention nevertheless marked the project from its earliest days, in terms of both cultural politics and more workaday issues of governmental and financial manoeuvring. There was always a degree of conflict between Lang's penchant for an 'image-conscious, media-wise fun culture'[11] and the perceived status of opera as the most elitist of the performing arts. Italy remains the only Western country in which opera has ever been a popular art-form, and one project, however ambitious, was scarcely likely to alter that situation. Saint-Pulgent's 1991 assertion that 'il ne reste plus trace de l'opéra populiste et révolutionnaire annoncé en 1982'[12] / 'not a trace remains of the populist, revolutionary opera announced in 1982' thus suggests a fundamental incompatibility between a Langian and a Malrauxian view of cultural politics, neither of them realized or indeed realizable in the completed project.

Baser political factors were also to bedevil the Opéra, starting with the election of a right-wing government in 1986. This led to 'a trial of strength between Léotard* on the one hand and Chirac and his Finance ministers on the other, from which Léotard emerged the somewhat dog-eared winner, having saved the opera house itself but sacrificed the *salle modulable* and the scenery workshops'.[13] Further horse-trading led to the reinstatement of the two latter in more modest guise, fortunately without the briefly mooted plan to include a hotel on the premises in order to balance the books. Daniel Barenboim, since 1975 chief conductor of the Orchestre de Paris, was appointed musical and artistic director on a five-year contract, but the reelection of the left in May 1988 led to the appointment of Pierre Bergé, head of the Yves Saint-Laurent fashion house and a strong ally of Mitterrand's, as president of the Opéra. Bergé wanted a greater voice in artistic decision-making than Barenboim, whose planned programme was strongly modernist, was prepared to concede, and the conductor stepped down in 1989, to be replaced by the Korean Myung-Whun Chung.

Such combined political and artistic turmoil meant that there was a race against time to get the building ready for its gala opening in July 1989, a jewel in the bicentennial crown. Chirac objected to the idea that the first performance should be a celebratory concert for the heads of state who were in Paris for the festivities, on the grounds that 14 July was the people's day. The gala opening on 13 July was a spectacle devised by the American Bob Wilson, while on 'Bastille Day' itself there were concerts conducted by Leonard Bernstein and Georges Prêtre, the latter of which featured the Te Deum by Berlioz, perhaps an echo of the July column's inauguration to his *Symphonie funèbre et triomphale*. (Dumont's statue atop the column was regilded for the occasion). The 'people' had their moment at 10:30 p.m., with a concert featuring the accordionist Yvette Horner – one of whose successes was a waltz entitled *Balajo* – and the recently formed world-music-cum-rock group Les Négresses vertes.

The first operatic performance – *Les Troyens*, as we have seen a suggestion of Remy's – had to wait until 17 March the following year, while the first full season did not begin until that September. Major technical and industrial-relations problems continued to beset the Opéra to such a point that Hugues Gall, hitherto in charge of the main opera house in Geneva, felt moved to tell a press conference in November 1993, before taking over as

* François Léotard succeeded Jack Lang as culture minister in the new government.

director: 'Le discrédit de l'Opéra Bastille à l'étranger va au-delà de tout ce qu'on peut imaginer en France; l'évocation de son seul nom suscite sourires et dérision'[14] / 'The discredit of the Opéra Bastille abroad goes beyond anything we can imagine in France; the mere mention of its name provokes smiles of derision.' Myung-Whun Chung's removal as musical director in 1995 and continuing industrial strife pitting Gall against what he described as 'Stalinist' trade unions meant that the Opéra's blighted reputation continued for some years to come. The covering of the façade, the fire doors and the soundproofing all required costly work – the result of the building's over-hasty completion in 1989. Yet by 2000 it was attracting far bigger houses than Garnier, with ninety-five per cent of seats sold during the year. The 'salle modulable' had effectively paid for itself through the greater number of performances it made possible. Moreover, while '[d]e là à être devenu le grand Opéra populaire annoncé, il y a de la marge'[15] / 'from this to the great popular opera house we were promised there is some way to go', the clientele was considerably younger than its predecessor's. Joachim Pflieger, assistant to the then director Gérard Mortier (the current incumbent is Nicolas Joel) said in an interview with me in 2007 that Bastille was far more 'democratic' in its presentation than Garnier, emphasizing in particular its still popular free Thursday lunchtime concerts.

A working-class presence redolent of the Faubourg's traditions made itself felt in on 27 May 2010, when a thousand undocumented migrant workers staged a sit-in on the steps at the front of the building. This 'occupation d'un lieu symbolique, la Bastille!'[16] / 'occupation of a symbolic spot, Bastille!' was interrupted when they were evacuated by police after a week, with forty-three arrests, though no charges were brought and many of the occupiers returned the following day.

The vicissitudes just described, important as they are for the history and development of the area, say more about cultural, political and financial conflicts within late twentieth- and early twenty-first-century France than they do about the *quartier* into which the vast design was inserted architec-turally but not socially. When I interviewed Olivier Dortu, a local community councillor, in 2007 he told me that no invitations to attend the Opéra had been issued to local inhabitants, nor had they ever been offered preferential tariffs for seats. The building is emphatically, though perhaps unavoidably for an institution of international import, in the Place de la Bastille rather than 'Bastille' or a fortiori the Faubourg. Yet its impact on the make-up of the area, both economic and cultural, has been immense, as we shall see in the next chapter.

Chapter Ten

'A real earthquake': the impact of the Opéra on the *quartier*

I N July 1998 Philippe Denis, president of the association SOS-Paris which was founded in the late 1970s to defend the capital's architectural heritage, stated: 'La construction de l'Opéra-Bastille a provoqué dans le quartier un véritable séisme'[1] / 'The building of the Opéra-Bastille caused a real earthquake in the *quartier*.' It unquestionably brought about the most dramatic changes in the area since the days of Haussmann, hastening and intensifying the process of yuppification that has characterized eastern Paris over the past thirty or so years.

The changes in the area over the past twenty or so years are a microcosm of those that Paris, in common with virtually every large Western city, has experienced, but because of the Faubourg's radical traditions and the catalytic effect of the Opéra they have probably been more dramatic than in any other part of Paris. The great film critic Serge Daney, interviewed on video in a Bastille café in July 1991, spoke of the area as his 'vraie patrie' / 'real homeland', for he was born there into a modest milieu, received his early film education in the local cinemas and between 1974 and 1981 worked there for *Cahiers du cinéma*, thus embodying the end of the old *quartier* and the onset of the new. The population of the administrative area known as Sainte-Marguerite, bounded by the rue du Faubourg-Saint-Antoine and the rue de Charonne, was 23 per cent working-class in 1954; by 1990 this figure was down to 9 per cent, and the quality of the housing stock had risen significantly. Pinçon and Pinçon-Charlot adduce three locally specific reasons for this change, already touched upon in previous chapters: the replacement of light industry such as wood- and metalworking by artists' workshops, the area's long-standing festive traditions which made it a popular destination for an evening's entertainment and 'la volonté politique affichée de rééquilibrer Paris à l'est'[2] / 'the declared political wish to shift the balance of Paris eastwards', the latter of course exemplified by the Opéra.

Nature – even if of a highly cultivated kind – has played its part along with culture in the *quartier*'s redevelopment. The railway line that until 1969 went from the old Bastille station to La Varenne-Saint-Maur, some ten miles to the south-east, ran for almost three miles of its length along a viaduct beside the avenue Daumesnil, on which work began in 1988 to convert it into what is now known as the 'promenade plantée' / 'tree-lined walk', for many years the world's only elevated park. There is a pedestrian route on top of the old viaduct for much of the promenade's length and a cycle-track at ground level, with craft shops in the arcades. The claim, made in 1996, that the promenade might make the avenue Daumesnil the Champs-Élysées of eastern Paris [3] seems extravagant to put it mildly, but while comparatively little known to tourists it has great appeal in particular to those interested in cultural topography, since 'les promeneurs situés à huit mètres au-dessus du sol, aperçoivent la trame urbaine qui s'est construite au fil des siècles' [4] / 'walkers twenty-five feet above ground level can see the urban network as it has developed through the centuries'. The promenade would appear to be an ideal cinematic location, but the only film I have seen in which it figures is Richard Linklater's *Before Sunset* (2004), where it is the setting for a 'love-and-life' conversation not dissimilar to those often found in Éric Rohmer's work between Jesse (Ethan Hawke) and Céline (Julie Delpy). There is a reported sighting in Sophie Fillières's *Un chat un chat* (2009), but I have not been able to view this film at the time of writing.

For the rest, the *quartier* changed not only architecturally, with at least twenty-five per cent of its buildings demolished betweem 1970 and 1994, but also economically and socially. There is what it would scarcely be an exaggeration to describe as a whole discourse of nostalgia for a vanished Paris – the province of the hagiographers to whom reference is made in the Introduction – which has been lavishly deployed to bemoan the supposed decline of Bastille. Thus, the novelist Denis Tillinac – a close friend of Jacques Chirac, under whose mayoralty many of the changes he deplores took place – waxes elegiac:

> On a défiguré la Bastille avec cet infâme opéra en forme de camembert. Il faut s'aventurer dans la rue de la Roquette pour retrouver l'ambiance canaille de la grande époque du Balajo; ou dans le faubourg Saint-Antoine qui a gardé son naturel au-delà de Ledru-Rollin, du côté du square Trousseau. Il y a des bars à titis où des dactylos aux lèvres abusivement peintes tolèrent un abordage à l'ancienne.[5]

Bastille has been disfigured with this revolting Camembert-shaped opera house. You have to take a trip down the rue de la Roquette to rediscover the saucy atmosphere of the Balajo in its prime, or along the rue du Faubourg Saint-Antoine which has remained its old self beyond Ledru-Rollin, near the square Trousseau. There you can find rapscallion bars where secretaries with over-painted lips tolerate an old-fashioned pick-up.

Nostalgia for the 'old-fashioned pick-up' might be felt to be a slightly dubious emotion, and even the 'saucy atmosphere' of the rue de la Roquette is nowadays redolent of the theme-park. The novelist and essayist Charles Dantzig also finds himself in young fogey mode when deploring the 'rues banales, où croupissent des artisans, des bistrots à skaï orange. Ici aussi les cafés du Commerce sont remplacés par des cafés pensifs, les galeries succèdent aux boutiquiers'[6] / 'banal streets in which craftsmen and bistros with orange leatherette seats stagnate side by side. Here too old-style bars have been replaced by philosophers' cafés, and art-galleries have succeeded shopkeepers.' The photographer Jean-Claude Gautrand, finally, bemoans the fact that:

> La Bastille, à son tour, est aujourd'hui saccagée. Sites détruits, habitants chassés au-delà du périphérique, ce vieux quartier à l'urbanisme labyrinthique, à la population vouée à l'artisanat et à la petite industrie, tend à devenir le périmètre artistico-intellectuel à la mode.[7]

> Bastille, in its turn, is nowadays devastated. With its old sites destroyed and its inhabitants driven out beyond the ring-road, this old area with its labyrinthine lay-out and its population devoted to craftsmanship and light industry is on its way to becoming the fashionable artistic and intellectual area.

The use of the term 'devastated' to describe an area in which living conditions are unquestionably better than they were half a century, or even twenty-five years, ago may appear tendentious, and the whole discourse on which Tillinac, Dantzig and Gautrand draw to be mired in a backward-looking sentimentalism. Seen in a different ideological light, however, it can in fact provide material for a powerful political critique of the role of unfettered capitalism in the evolution of the *quartier*. Pinçon and Pinçon-Charlot draw a comparison between three areas of Right Bank Paris which is worth quoting at some length to emphasize how this role differed from one part of the city to another:

> A la Goutte d'Or, l'intervention publique a remplacé un habitat dégradé, réhabilité ou remplacé par des logements sociaux, et a conduit à une diminution des densités résidentielles. Autour de la Bastille, la conquête d'une partie du Paris prolétarien, celui des journées révolutionnaires et des barricades, par une population jeune et diplômée, s'est effectuée selon les lois du marché immobilier. La reconquête du vieux Marais aristocratique par de nouvelles couches sociales aisées est un cas intermédiaire. L'intervention publique, par la médiation du plan de sauvegarde et de mise en valeur établi en deux étapes, en 1969 et 1976, a été à l'origine d'une réhabilitation de bâtiments d'une grande valeur historique.[8]

> In the Goutte d'Or,* the public sector replaced decayed housing-stock, which was renovated or replaced by social housing, leading to a decrease in population density. Around Bastille, part of working-class Paris – the Paris of revolutions and barricades – was taken over by a young graduate population using the private housing market. The takeover of the old aristocratic Marais by the new well-off middle class is somewhere between these two extremes. Public-sector intervention, by way of the protection and renewal plan introduced in two stages – 1969 and 1976 – catalysed the renovation of buildings of great historical value.

The gentrificatory process inaugurated by the alliance of the new middle class and the private sector has not, however, gone uncriticized. Complaints about spiralling rents began to be heard as early as 1986, and nearly a quarter-century later the popular touristic web-site Paris-Balades points out:

> Le tissu urbain est un mélange de vieux immeubles décrépis, d'anciens bâtiments en train d'être restaurés, notamment depuis la mise en place de l'OPAH† du Faubourg Saint-Antoine, et de constructions neuves

---

* A working-class area, part of the Barbès *quartier* to the east of Montmartre, latterly with a large Maghrebi and Black African population, whose housing stock was substantially renewed from 1983 onwards.

† 'Opération programmée d'amélioration de l'habitat' – a publicly funded scheme to encourage investment in the improvement of a *quartier*.

des années 1980 et 1990 (qu'on peut qualifier de 'post-modernes', car les bâtiments, sobres, blancs, se veulent respectueux de la rue et de l'habitat existant). Cependant ces nouvelles constructions sont critiquées car elles provoquent un renouvellement de la population: les logements neufs (ou même seulement réhabilités) sont bien plus chers que les immeubles dégradés, qui constituaient un 'parc social de fait'. Même quand il s'agit de logements sociaux, rien ne garantit le maintien des anciens habitants. D'où le malaise, qui se traduit par l'éclosion de nombreuses associations de défense.[9]

The area is made up of old and decrepit blocks, elderly buildings in the process of restoration, especially since the setting-up of the Faubourg Saint-Antoine OPAH, and new buildings from the 1980s and 1990s, which can be described as 'post-modern' since their sober whiteness respects the street and the existing environment. Yet these new buildings have been criticized because they lead to a change in the population. New or even simply renovated dwelling-units are much more costly than the run-down buildings which were effectively social housing. There is no guarantee that the former inhabitants will remain in place even in social housing. The discontent this leads to is manifested in the many tenants' associations that have been set up.

The tendency to yuppification has affected the *quartier* in its non-residential respects too. The former furniture factory at 46 rue du Faubourg-Saint-Antoine was originally earmarked to become the Maison de l'Artisanat, designed to foster craftsmanship in the area (and now at no. 30), but in 1999, despite a petition with 3750 signatures, it opened its doors as the Barrio Latino (incongruously, 'Latin Quarter' in Spanish), then and thereafter a fashionable restaurant and night-spot. Small wonder that in July 1998 the monthly bulletin of SOS-Paris bemoaned the 'dégradation extrêmement rapide du faubourg Saint-Antoine',[10] whose transformation into Bastille was by now a fait accompli. The OPAH succeeded in preserving the *quartier*'s most distinctive features, such as the exceptionally high number of courtyards (Jean-Luc Nothias in a *Le Figaro* dossier of April 1996 estimated that it was home to half of those in Paris), but its social and cultural composition had irreversibly changed.

The literary representations of the area during this period that I have been able to trace are all in the *polar* genre – a term, deriving from 'police', that refers to the detective novel, particularly in its hard-boiled guise. Three of the four – which include one graphic novel – also grant an important place to foreign exiles, variously Argentinian, Iranian and Russian. Reflecting the increasing cosmopolitanism of Paris, especially after the fall of the Soviet bloc, this may also be a strategy to restore to the *quartier* some of the edge it was felt to have lost after its yuppificatory homogenization – what is known in French as *boboisation*, a portmanteau coinage from 'bourgeois' and 'bohémien'. Jean-François Vilar's *Bastille Tango* (1986) sets its contorted political intrigue among Argentinian exiles in the *quartier*, drawn there by a tango club in the rue de Lappe. For Vilar, a left-wing militant of long standing, this is perhaps by way of compensation for the dispirited state of French leftist politics at the time, manifested when the narrator muses: 'Le quartier Saint-Antoine était devenu bien sage'[11] / 'The Saint-Antoine area had become very well-behaved', or in his account of the dismal 1 May gathering in the square, which 'méritait mieux que la manifestation clairsemée qui finit par s'ébranler vers la République'[12] / 'deserved better than the scattered demonstration which finally pulled away towards République'. One character describes the proposed construction of the Opéra as 'une foutue connerie'[13] / 'a fucking stupid idea', while an old hand-written poster is spotted in the rue de Charenton calling on local inhabitants to band together against the project. The pulling-down and reconstruction of the Tour d'Argent is also denounced ('On détruit du vrai et on reconstruit du toc'[14] / 'They're pulling down what's real and rebuilding a fake'), while the narrator relates that until the Revolution the original building featured a tower with two exits, to facilitate the clandestine rendez-vous it often accommodated. I have not been able to verify the accuracy of this story, but as often in urban history *se non è vero, è ben trovato*. The changes in the *quartier* are distilled when a gallery-owner, Baxter, recounts to the narrator his plans for an artistic centre in the premises of a defunct clothes-shop:

> Ici, on pourrait compulser des catalogues, des livres d'art, manger, boire, se retrouver entre amis, discuter, rencontrer des artistes. Je connaissais au moins dix personnes, nouvelles venues dans le quartier, qui avaient des plans similaires.
> — Vous ne m'aimez pas tellement, n'est-ce pas?
> — Pas tellement, non.
> Je ne le détestais pas non plus.[15]

> Here, you could thumb through catalogues and art-books, eat, drink, talk, meet your friends or artists. I knew at least ten people, recently arrived in the area, who had similar plans.
> — You don't like me much, do you?

– Not a lot, no.
I didn't hate him either.

The juxtaposition of Jack Lang-speak – about which Vilar, as an erstwhile Trotskyist, might have been expected to have not a few reservations – with the laconic bourbon-soured cynicism of the *roman noir* lends this passage a disabused piquancy characteristic of the novel as a whole. Such Chandleresque 'mean streets' as there may have been in the *quartier* were, we have seen, being busily swept away as Vilar wrote, but the overall sense of the area that emerges from his novel is one of tangled urban turmoil. In this respect he is an heir to Léo Malet, clearly the inspiration for a minor character, Maleo, who like his 'original' has toyed with the idea of writing a book entitled *La Méprise de la Bastille* – a play on 'prise' / 'capture' and 'méprise' / 'misunderstanding'. 'Paris foutu, c'était sa rengaine'[16] / 'Fucked-up Paris was his theme-tune' – as indeed it is of *Bastille Tango* as a whole.

José-Louis Bocquet's *Sur la ligne blanche* of 1993 – the first novel by one better known as a *bande dessinée* story-writer – likewise gives us a Bastille made exotic by the presence of foreign exiles, notably the Iranian Ali whose family were murdered in the Islamic revolution and who is a professional hitman in Paris, as well as dealing the heroin to which the title makes none too subtle allusion. Any political dimension here takes a back seat to the bloodthirsty drug-trafficking intrigue, set in a *quartier* which by now is exerting a gentrificatory influence on its neighbours ('L'effet Bastille gagnait la République. Dans l'immeuble ce n'était plus que lofts occupés par des antiquaires, des photographes, des galeristes, des artistes'[17] / 'The Bastille effect was getting to République too. In the block there were nothing but lofts occupied by antique dealers, photographers, gallery-owners and artists').

Alain Bellet, whose *Les Mutins du faubourg* was dealt with in Chapter Six, published in 2003 a *polar*, *Fausse commune*, much of which takes place in the Faubourg. The plot hinges on a series of murders whose victims turn out to be descendants of those who had crushed the 1871 uprising to which the title – also a laboured pun on 'fosse commune' / 'common grave' – makes reference. The elderly writer on Paris Michel Ravelle bemoans that 'Bastille n'est plus Bastille'[18] / 'Bastille isn't Bastille any more', comparing the area to an old prostitute and bemoaning the destruction of the railway station. His predictably dyspeptic remarks on the Opéra are to find an ironic counterpart in the praise it receives from a couple of English tourists in the Café des Phares, on the square. The vision of the area may by now seem depressingly commonplace, with the rue de Lappe ('pleine de jeunes gens branchés'[19]

/ 'full of trendy young people'), the rue de la Roquette which 'ne cessait de se transformer au gré des faiseurs de mode' / 'changed all the time with the whims of fashion' and the quite simply 'sinistre'[20] avenue Ledru-Rollin all present and correct. The murders can in this context be read as an attempt to restore to the *quartier* its lost radical edge – an at once nostalgic and seditious revenge of the revolutionary past on the suavely homogenized present.

The area is also the setting for a graphic novel, *Rififi à la Bastille* (2001), the first of a series of two entitled *Beluga* written by Thierry Robberecht and drawn by Alain Maury. As the series title suggests a non-French presence is once again crucial to the plot – not political exiles this time but the Russian mafia, a common plot device in French films of this period, which in *Rififi à la Bastille* controls all the criminal activity of the *quartier*. Among the foci for this are a night-club called La Lune Noire and a bar, Le Petit Bastille, with an old-style hole-in-the-floor toilet. Crack-dealing is masterminded from a Russian Orthodox church and the drugs are imported by barge along the Canal Saint-Martin. This is of course an entirely imaginary topography, creating a fantasy Bastille whose closest approach to contemporary reality comes at the end, when the 'native' criminals of the area assert: 'Il faut toujours défendre le commerce local contre les multinationales!'[21] / 'We must always defend local traders against multinationals!'

For a more realistic, less highly spiced view of the *quartier* in this period of transformation, we must turn to the cinema, and Cédric Klapisch's *Chacun cherche son chat* of 1996. The film's central character, Chloé (Garance Clavel), is a make-up assistant at a modelling agency, and hence occupies a very lowly position in the hierarchy of the so-called artistic professions that have moved into the area. When she takes a holiday – her first for three years – she entrusts her pet cat, Gris-gris, to an elderly neighbour, Madame Renée, but he goes missing, and the film's narrative is organized around her search for him, which involves an increasing number of the local inhabitants before Gris-gris is finally found alive and well, trapped behind Madame Renée's cooker.

Feelgood alarms are likely to be going off loudly by now, but Klapisch's plot is little more than a pretext for the sensitive and often melancholy study of a *quartier* in the throes of transformation. Cranes feature prominently in the opening shot, from the flat Chloé shares with her gay friend Michel, and sometimes the area appears little more than a building-site. Several scenes focus on the demolition of the reinforced concrete church of Notre-Dame-d'Espérance in the rue de la Roquette – an impressive late 1920s building which by the mid-1990s was in dangerously poor condition and was pulled down to be replaced by the contemporary glass-fronted building. Chloé's friends and neighbours are of modest means, and three of them at different times – an elderly widow, Michel's new lover Claude and the painter Bel Canto – have been or will be forced to move, clearly because rents in the *quartier* have risen. A fly-poster represents a solitary voice of organized protest against this, but his credibility is perhaps undermined when he sticks a notice 'Béton Con Pas Bon' / 'Stupid Concrete No Good' right over one Chloé has just posted asking for news of her cat. As Elizabeth Ezra has pointed out, '[t]he idealized image of community, problematic throughout French history, is shown to be especially fragile in this film'.[22] Such an image recurs throughout in the form of the statue atop the July column, regularly glimpsed above the rooftops and the setting for a striking dream sequence involving Chloé, but it finds life at ground level markedly more difficult. The *beur* Djamel, unrequitedly attracted to Chloé, is a figure of fun for many locals because of his learning difficulties, while the only sub-Saharan Africans we see are three carpenters in a workshop – an intriguing fusion of the *quartier*'s artisanal past and its more multi-ethnic present – and a woman neighbour of Chloé's articulates overtly racist views of *beurs* and even more blacks. When we hear, along with Chloé, the news of Jacques Chirac's election to the presidency on the radio, we may recall that one of his major campaigning slogans was the fight against 'la fracture sociale' – an ironic sentiment in the light of the foregoing.

Yet the film presents a far less dismal view of life in the area than this may suggest, largely because Chloé's search for Gris-gris serves to distil a real *esprit de quartier* as it goes on. She develops affectionate feelings for her elderly neighbours – figures of fun for her workmates – retains her friendship with Djamel despite her lack of desire for him and experiences moments of happiness – mini-epiphanies – when walking through a market (which looks more like Aligre than Richard-Lenoir though the former is of course in the 12th) and watching a couple salsa-dancing in or near the rue de Lappe. The film's ending is revelatory here. The romantic attraction between Chloé and Bel Canto becomes obvious when he is moving out to the suburbs, and the film ends on her gazing wistfully after him, but they have exchanged telephone numbers and we get a strong sense that love is literally, as the removal-van drives off, around the corner. This may of course mean that Chloé will in her turn soon be leaving the *quartier;* neither a sense of neighbourhood nor *l'amour* is we suspect likely to get the better of the spiral of gentrification.

One of the film's strengths is that we meet no *bobos* or yuppies, which might have made it appear denunciatory rather than elegiac. Lucy Mazdon says that Klapisch 'criticises the impact of development on the traditional community and yet ultimately seems to embrace some aspects of it' – a

Janus-faced view which 'prevents the film from becoming little more than a rose-tinted vision of "traditional" Parisian life'.[23] The elderly population of Bastille figure importantly, above all in the person of Madame Renée, played by Renée Le Calm, whom Klapisch had discovered in 1992 and who has since appeared in five of his films and seventeen others. Madame Le Calm – born in 1918 and still alive as I write – had lived in the area for fifty-two years at the time of filming in a fifth-floor flat with no lift, working as a waitress and later a lavatory attendant until the age of seventy-three. It was there that Klapisch filmed her, allowing her like several other non-professional actors in the film to improvise her lines. A press interview with her plangently echoes, in more spontaneous vein, the nostalgia expressed by Tillinac, Dantzig and company; the rue de la Roquette dance-halls have become fashionable restaurants, she misses the old Auvergnat bistros and her favourite cinema (as in the film she misses her old music-shop, now a boutique) and the rue de Lappe is no longer what it was. The sense of social and political helplessness she expresses is all too poignant:

> Y a des choses pas mal d'ailleurs, mais tout ça, c'est construit pour les riches. On a pourtant fait des pétitions; j'ai signé dans tous les coins. Rien à faire. Ils détériorent.[24]

> There are some quite good things being built, but they're all for rich people. We've got up petitions, though; I've signed here, there and everywhere. But there's nothing to be done. It's getting worse.

Another article describes her daily routine in the *quartier*, in terms that echo the end of *Chacun cherche son chat* where a group in a café, including Madame Renée, sing Mistinguett's 1928 song 'Ça, c'est Paris!' at once to celebrate and to mourn a city that is disappearing:

> Un tour à Franprix pour acheter une tranche de pâté pour les chats. Avant de rentrer, Renée s'arrête souvent au bar des Taillandiers. Là, sous le regard complice du patron, Jean-Marie, sa petite voix éraillée aux accents d'Arletty vient égayer les après-midi tranquilles. 'Riquita, jolie fleur de java': Renée chante.[25]

> She stops by Franprix* to buy a slice of pâté for the cats. Before going

* A chain of generally small supermarkets, now as ubiquitous in Paris as Tesco in UK cities.

back home, Renée often calls in at the bar des Taillandiers. There, watched benignly by the *patron* Jean-Marie, her hoarse little voice like that of Arletty* brightens up quiet afternoons. 'Riquita, my pretty Javanese flower,' Renée sings.

Riquita is a 1920s song revived in 1968 by Georgette Plana, whose version sold 450 000 copies. I fondly imagine Madame Renée going on to sing Édith Piaf's 1962 *Le Diable de la Bastille* – about the 'devil' the singer met and fell in love with at a 14 July ball in the square – or even, at a perhaps wild stretch, Jacques Brel's *La Bastille*, a 1955 plea for peace and love which might seem to cut against the grain of the Faubourg's political reputation, though its final verse strikes a more optimistic note than Renée Le Calm's disabused observations on the development of her *quartier*:

> Hâtons-nous d'espérer
> Marchons aux lendemains
> Tendons une main
> Qui ne soit pas fermée
> On a détruit la Bastille
> Et ça n'a rien arrangé
> On a détruit la Bastille
> Ne pourrait-on pas s'aimer?[26]

> Let's make haste and hope
> Let's march towards tomorrow
> Let's stretch out an open hand
> We destroyed the Bastille
> And that didn't sort anything out
> We destroyed the Bastille
> Couldn't we love one another?

Madame Renée also makes a brief appearance in Klapisch's 2008 *Paris*, which centres on a dancer (Pierre / Romain Duris) with a serious heart condition. In the final sequence of *Paris*, Pierre is being driven to hospital in a taxi which avoids the rue du Faubourg Saint-Antoine because of a demonstration, and the film concludes on a shot of the July column.

Christophe Honoré's 2007 musical film *Les Chansons d'amour*, conversely,

---

* One of the greatest French cinema actresses of the 1930s and 1940s, renowned for her throaty and unmistakably Parisian accent.

opens with a shot of the column, though most of the action takes place in the 10th *arrondissement*. The film, which initially focuses on a bisexual *ménage à trois* between a man and two women (played by Louis Garrel, Ludivine Sagnier and Clotilde Hesme), includes a song entitled *Bastille*, like the fourteen others in the film written by Alex Beaupain – a singer / songwriter in the tradition of such figures as Jacques Brel and Serge Gainsbourg. *Bastille* paints a picture of a deserted, rain-sodden square overseen by 'l'ange ruisselant dans la nuit' / 'the angel streaming in the night' – a lugubrious tableau which Brel might well not have disowned, and one whose counter-vailing evocation of love ('On voudrait s'aimer à jamais'[27] / 'We'd like to love each other for ever') is undercut in the film by the abrupt death, in a concert-hall washroom, of Julie / Ludivine Sagnier.

The compilation-film *Paris, je t'aime* (2006) is made up of eighteen short episodes, each set in a different *arrondissement*. The two absentees are the 15th and, perhaps surprisingly, the 11th. Bastille is represented by an episode in the 12th shot by the Spanish director Isabel Coixet, in which a man is planning to leave his marriage for a younger woman – who in a homage to François Truffaut's *La Peau douce* is an air hostess – until he discovers that his wife is terminally ill with leukemia. Thereupon he rejects the younger woman and redoubles his attentions for his wife, so that 'à force de se comporter comme un homme amoureux, il devint de nouveau un homme amoureux' / 'through acting like a man in love, he once again became a man in love'. The episode ends with his falling into a terminal emotional coma when she dies in his arms.

Bastille opens with a crane-shot of the square from the Opéra side and a sequence in the Square Trousseau brasserie, where the husband (Sergio Castellitto) realizes that he no longer loves his wife (Miranda Richardson). *Le Figaro* (6 June 2010) ran a review of the restaurant headlined 'Quartier libre à Aligre', in an obvious reference to the Commune Libre that once characterized the area. The (unnamed) writer observes: 'On connaissait sa place, son marché, son ancienne mairie. On ne parle plus que de ses bars et bistrots, derniers repaires de la bobosphère' / 'We used to know its square, its market, its former town hall. Now all people talk about is its bars and bistros, the latest stronghold of the *bobo* world' – an assertion borne out when the article goes on to review a number of bars and restaurants in this part of the Faubourg while paying only the most cursory homage to the fact that: 'Aligre, c'est aussi les Puces sur la place, les vide-grenier et pique-nique annuels qui drainent tout le quartier'[28] / 'Aligre is also the flea-market on the square, the emptying of attics and the picnics that every year attract the whole neighbourhood.' Coixet's troubled couple clearly belong in the fashionable Belle Époque-style brasserie, but there is no suggestion that they are even aware of the existence of the market, let alone the Commune Libre. *Chacun cherche son chat* renders a *quartier* in transformation and upheaval; by the time Coixet shot *Bastille*, more than a decade later, that process had run its predictable course. It would have seemed anachronistic for her episode to have been entitled *Faubourg Saint-Antoine*.

Yet the walk through the *quartier* I propose in the next and final chapter will seek to show that the Faubourg, as *Le Figaro*'s grudging admission implies, is still there, albeit now the junior partner to its upstart and better-heeled successor. An endangered species it may well be, but attentive flânerie may play its modest part in combating that danger; and if for no other reason may this turn out to be a singularly productive way of whiling away space as well as time.

Chapter Eleven

Flânerie in the archive: the Faubourg/Bastille today

FLÂNERIE is a movement through space; the archive is a deposit in time. The flâneur follows his / her passing impulse; the archivist's avocation is a methodical and classificatory one. Flâneurs may or may not leave a trace of their own; archivists preserve and memorialize the traces of others. For Edmund White, following Walter Benjamin, 'the *flâneur* is in search of experience, not knowledge';[1] for Jacques Derrida, the archive 'ne sera jamais la mémoire ni l'anamnèse en leur expérience spontanée, vivante et intérieure'[2] / 'will never be memory nor anamnesis in their spontaneous, living, interior experience'. Flânerie, to reprise a distinction famously deconstructed by Derrida, might appear to correspond to the supposed spontaneity and immediacy of speech, while the archive is the quintessential domain of the written. This opposition, however, rests on a view of the archive as sedentary, as unproblematically 'there', which Derrida's deployment of the notion undercuts, notably when he speaks of the 'mal d'archive' / 'archive fever' as 'n'avoir de cesse, interminablement, de chercher l'archive là où elle se dérobe'[3] / 'endlessly and incessantly searching for the archive where it hides from sight'. That 'unsearching search' is what flânerie, for all its apparent disavowal of anything remotely task-orientated, may be described as doing, which is why it may be regarded not as the opposite of the archive but as its complement. Walter Benjamin implied as much in saying 'We know that, in the course of flânerie, far-off times and places interpenetrate the landscape and the present moment'[4] – a statement that will repeatedly be borne out by the walking-tour of the *quartier* which follows, and which has provided me with the basis for many happy hours' flânerie.

The 'built archive' through which the tour will make its sometimes digressive way is, as we saw in the Introduction, bounded by the *quartiers* of the Marais, Popincourt, Gare de Lyon and Nation. The bulk of it thus falls within the 11th *arrondissement*, with a strip in the 12th to the west of the

place d'Aligre and north of avenue Daumesnil / boulevard Voltaire. It is the
12th, however, that houses the Opéra, along with the July Column the area's
single most significant landmark, and given that building's immense impact
on the *quartier* it seems appropriate to begin our tour there.

For Jean-Paul Blais, 'la massivité et le quadrillage de la façade de cet
opéra restent l'objet de critiques esthétiques qui n'ouvrent guère la voie au
consensus'[5] / 'the massive four-square quality of this opera house's façade
is still the target of aesthetic criticisms which do not leave much room for
consensus'. My own view of the building is, given the constraints on its
design, a less censorious one (see Chapter Nine), not least because seen
from behind it blends in remarkably well with the older buildings in the rue
du Faubourg Saint-Antoine. The greyish-white colouring of these, which
the Opéra matches, is characteristic of the Paris cityscape – the result of
their being coated in plaster of Paris, a fireproofing material found in large
quantities near the city which Louis XIV decreed in 1667 should be used in
all buildings there.

The Opéra, which can be visited with a guided tour, houses two auditoria
– the main one with 2700 seats and the *salle modulable* – along with in-house
property and décor workshops and recording studios. Until Christmas
2009 the Opéra was complemented by a branch of the retailer FNAC (the
equivalent of HMV in the UK or Borders in the US) which specialized in
compact discs, but competition from online retailers and the popularity of
downloading led to its closure despite a petition with 15 000 signatures and
legal action – which was avoided thanks to an agreed settlement – by the
trade unions.

From the Opéra our steps, inevitably, take us down the rue du Faubourg-
Saint-Antoine. The proposed itinerary is in large part drawn from Denis
Michel and Dominique Renou's *Le Guide du promeneur: 11e arrondissement*,
published in 1993. There have obviously been many changes in the area
since then, partially overwriting Michel and Renou's guide much as for
Benjamin 'in the course of flânerie, far-off times and places interpenetrate
the landscape and the present moment'. These changes are not always, for
the flâneur at least, benign ones, for many of the courtyards described are
now behind locked doors and thus impossible to see unless one knows the
numerical code to get in – 'searching for the archive where it hides from
sight' indeed, in a considerably more mundane and frustrating sense than
anything imagined by Derrida.

The rue du Faubourg-Saint-Antoine as it curves through its 1.8 kilometres
forms the backbone of the *quartier* to which it gave its name, but many of
its most intriguing sights are in the passages and courtyards in which the

area abounds. We encounter the first of these at its junction with the rue de la Roquette – the passage du Cheval-Blanc, whose paved courtyards bear the names of months of the year. They have now been renovated to house such businesses as a radio station, an art dealer, a travel company and even, reviving the area's oldest artisanal tradition, a cabinet-makers in the last courtyard, the cour de Juin. Tagging on the walls – a widespread feature of the *quartier* – and a notice asking smokers not to throw their dog-ends into the nearby gas manhole stand in contrast to this otherwise wholesale *boboisation*.

Via the cité Parchappe we come back to the rue du Faubourg – I shall henceforth use this abbreviation – as we shall constantly do in the course of our flânerie. Number 25 is a splendid glass and metal construction from the 1870s, built for the manufacture and sale of furniture and now the major retail outlet for an extremely chic designer (manufacture goes on elsewhere). The upper floor, built of brick, initially housed two apartments. Number 33 – headquarters between 1979 and 1994 of the now defunct counter-cultural magazine *Actuel* – supposedly has a fine courtyard with a seventeenth-century wooden staircase, but like the cour du Nom-de-Jésus at number 47 with its cast-iron banister this is inaccessible without the numerical entry code.

The rue de Charonne, which runs virtually the whole width of the *arrondissement*, begins at number 61, where the Trogneux fountain is to be found. This, along with four others in the Faubourg, was built in 1719, before which date the inhabitants had no choice but to buy their water from itinerant carriers. The water gushes out of the mouths of two bronze lions, nowadays back into the mains through a grille in the pavement. The fountain was restored in 1963 and has been classed as a historic monument since 1995.

Walking north-east up the rue de Charonne we pass the cour Saint-Joseph at number 5, once the site of a china factory and still dedicated to craftsmanship. It houses the Académie Grandes-Terres – a school of textile, fashion and interior design – along with, more artisanally, a lute-makers. Just beyond this is the rue de Lappe, barely 300 yards long and despite its tumultuous nocturnal reputation now a species of urban theme-park. The Auvergnat metalworkers who once dominated the street are long gone, but their night-life heritage lives on, albeit in highly touristic form. The Balajo at number 9 is still decorated in its original candy-pink hues, though now it hosts rock music, disco and salsa; only on Sundays between 3 and 7 p.m. can one hear the strains of the *bal-musette*, sometimes with Jo Privat Junior. The street also houses the more than one hundred years old Produits d'Auvergne shop, specializing in ham and sausages, along with the up-market Auvergnat restaurant La Galoche d'Aurillac and, in a faint commercial echo of the *quartier*'s political traditions, a more modestly priced hotel-restaurant entitled Les Sans-Culottes. In the passage Louis-Philippe, off the rue de Lappe, the Café de la Danse, where Juliette Gréco once performed, was closed until the 1990s, but now hosts a variety of concerts, from rock to *chanson*, as well as helping to produce and distribute recordings, making it the rue de Lappe's most culturally alive establishment at least at the time of writing.

The rue de Lappe debouches into what is, along with the rue du Faubourg and the rue de Charonne, one of the *quartier*'s three major arteries, the rue de la Roquette – allegedly named after the herb (rocket) which used to grow nearby. Number 18 was occupied for more than a hundred years by a firm trading in café furniture, notably the zinc counters once characteristic of Parisian bars, but is now a branch of L'Univers de Léo, which sells artistic – sometimes kitschy – knick-knacks. Art-galleries and fashion shops, as elsewhere in today's Faubourg, are prominent in this street, which is linked to the rue de Charonne and the rue de Lappe by the passage Thiéré, once an important base of the Auvergnat trade. Back in the rue de la Roquette we see the church of Notre-Dame d'Espérance, whose demolition features in *Chacun cherche son chat* and which is now a contemporary glass-fronted building, briefly occupied in September 1998 by undocumented workers. In the rue des Taillandiers opposite I encountered the first of a number of graffiti spray-painted on the pavement detailing four possible lesbian role-models ('Gouine banale / fem (sic) fatale / butch brutal / dyke géniale – t'as le choix chaque jour' / 'Everyday lezzie / femme fatale / brutal butch / brilliant dyke – you've got the choice every day') – a reminder that until February 2008 the nearby rue Keller housed Paris's Gay and Lesbian Centre, now (and with the addition of 'Transsexual' to its title) based in the rue Beaubourg, on the other side of the Marais.

The rue des Taillandiers leads back to the rue de Charonne (Michel and Renou's itinerary, which I am following here, is an archetypal flânerie in that it constantly loops back as if by chance into the main streets of the *quartier*), at number 37 of which we find the pleasantly renovated cour Lépine, home to a picture-restorers and a photographic studio along with some older furniture workshops. The rue Keller on the left – once the centre of the coal-market, another Auvergnat trade – features a striking reinforced concrete school building from the late 1920s (at number 10). Back in the rue de la Roquette, beyond the 1846 fountain at number 70, we pass the Théâtre de la Bastille, opened in 1982 in the premises of the old cinema Cyrano. The *quartier*'s nine cinema-screens are now to be found within a hundred yards or so of one another – four at the MK2 Bastille in the boulevard Beaumarchais, three at La Bastille (5 rue du Faubourg) and two at the Majestic Bastille in the boulevard Richard-Lenoir, all showing for the most part art or independent films. We have seen that the two last-mentioned cinemas were far less up-market before *boboisation* set in, whereas the MK2 – named for its founder and owner, the former Maoist Marin Karmitz – began life in July 1974 as a politically committed venue 'dans un quartier très habité, populaire et sans vie culturelle'[6] / 'in a densely populated working-class neighbourhood with no cultural life' – a description that might seem to rest on a rather narrow view of what 'cultural life' is. It opened, housing three screens plus a left-wing bookshop, as Le 14 Juillet (a name initially borne by all Karmitz's cinemas), with a screening of a documentary about the revolt of Bolivian miners, but was to experience a variety of problems including the theft of books and a protest by hard-line Zionists against the showing of Godard and Miéville's pro-Palestinian film *Ici et ailleurs*. Of longer-term significance was the difficulty Karmitz experienced in getting distributors to make copies of their films for him; generally only two sub-titled prints would be struck, one for cinemas on the Champs-Élysées, the other for the Latin Quarter. The digital era of course put paid to such problems. In 1984 the bookshop became a fourth screen, placing Bastille along with the two areas just mentioned and Beaubourg / Les Halles among Paris's prime film-viewing *quartiers*.

The theatre, which has two auditoria, presents a programme of classic and modern plays along with workshops to discuss productions with the performers, in the best Jack Lang tradition. The building has long been devoted to entertainment in different guises – initially a theatre, then a Spanish dance-hall before becoming a cinema and then reverting to its original use. Further down the rue de la Roquette, at numbers 84–86, we find Bastille's only synagogue; the adjacent Marais, Paris's most traditionally Jewish area, by contrast has five. The Roquette synagogue, named after the fifteenth-century Portuguese philosopher and scriptural exegete Isaac Ababranel, was built in 1962, largely to cater for Jews who had fled northern Africa, and observes the Sephardic rite. The *quartier*'s proletarian traditions may come to mind if we turn town the passage Charles-Dallery, whose number 20 is a former working-class hostel dating from 1914, mostly built of brick but with rustic stone trimmings at ground-floor level. The nearby rue Sedaine, close to the boundary with Popincourt, is a centre of the 'rag trade', with more than 500 wholesale and retail outlets in the area, whose workforce, in large part Asian, are probably little less exploited nowadays than the *sans-culottes* were in their time, and alas far less likely, if only because many of them may be undeclared, to rebel against their wretched position.

By way of the rue Sedaine we make our way to the boulevard Richard-Lenoir – perhaps not quite the 'Champs-Élysées of Eastern Paris', as it has facetiously been dubbed, but on Thursdays and Sundays home to a wonderful street market with a vast range of foodstuffs along with cut-price clothing, CDs, DVDs and second-hand books. A slightly sad-seeming miniature funfair is also to be found close to the Place. Below the roadway runs the Canal Saint-Martin, almost three miles long, which connects the almost seventy-mile-long Canal de l'Ourcq to the Seine; we have seen that it was at Haussmann's instigation that the canal was covered over, giving a clear line of sight into the troublesome Faubourg. Walking down towards the Place we see the rue Saint-Sabin on our left, with its erstwhile furniture workshops transformed into art-galleries and fashion shops and at number 8 the headquarters of Médecins sans frontières – the charitable medical foundation for the developing world co-founded by Bernard Kouchner, a gastro-enterologist who served as a minister in several Socialist governments and between 2007 and 2010 Nicolas Sarkozy's foreign minister. Parallel to the boulevard Richard-Lenoir, just off the Place, is the cour Damoye, dating back to 1780 – once a hive of the metal industry, now gentrified after years of neglect and housing a film production company, a naturopathic centre and a coffee shop, renovated in 1999 and roasting its beans on the premises.

The boulevard Beaumarchais – the dividing-line between Bastille and the Marais – is named for the dramatist whose luxurious mansion formerly occupied the space between numbers 2 and 20. Number 28 is a richly decorated baker's shop whose ceramics and glass ceiling date back to 1900, while further north – almost into Popincourt / République – was the electrical shop featured by Claude Chabrol in his 1960 film *Les Bonnes Femmes*. Between 1963 and 1995 118 rue Amelot was the site of the Roullet-Decamps factory and showroom, specializing in mechanical toys and automata, and forced out of business by competition from Asia. Two museums, one in Souillac in south-west France, the other in Falaise (Normandy), preserve many of the factory's vintage artefacts.

The junction of the rue du Faubourg and the rue de Charonne is a key nodal point in the *quartier*, so it seems appropriate to follow Michel and Renou back there to explore the rue du Faubourg's eastern reaches. Number 75 gives on to the strikingly rural cour de l'Étoile-d'Or, mostly from the nineteenth century but featuring in the single-storey building that leads into the last of its courtyards a splendid seventeenth-century carved wooden interior staircase. 77 and 79 are the headquarters of the publishing-house Autrement, specializing in literature and social sciences and now part of the giant Flammarion group. Other nearby courtyards – Trois-Frères, Maison-Brûlée, L'Ours – still house furniture workshops cheek-by-jowl with modish latter-day activities such as textile and mosaic design. The intersection with the avenue Ledru-Rollin, a largely functional artery described we may recall by Alain Bellet in *Fausse commune* as 'sinistre', was once the site of the *trôle* market for cheap furniture (see Chapter Five).

Off number 115 we find the passage de la Bonne-Graine (literally, 'good seed'). This address figures in the first line of a favourite Édith Piaf song, 'Je m'en fous pas mal' / 'I couldn't give a damn', written by Michel Emer ('Je suis né passage de la Bonne-Graine / J'en ai pris de la graine et pour longtemps' / 'I was born in the passage de la Bonne-Graine / I learnt my lesson there for a long time to come'). Given that Piaf was born further north, in Belleville, I had always assumed that the address was a confected one to generate the (untranslatable) French pun in the opening couplet, so I was delighted to come across the real thing during my first wanderings in the area. Number 133 leads into the passage de la Main-d'Or, at number 15 of which we find the theatre of the same name, formerly a cabinet-makers, now hosting small-scale plays and variety shows. Its owner is the stand-up comedian Dieudonné, notorious for his association with Jean-Marie Le Pen and in particular his anti-semitism, which has led to a number of court convictions. If the *sans-culottes* and the Communards were alive they would surely be turning in their grave.

The rue de la Main-d'Or, which leads off the passage, features two bistrots, one formerly the base of one of Paris's last bonesetters, along with furniture-polishers and a lute-makers. Back in the rue du Faubourg we are reminded of the area's turbulent past by a plaque at number 151 in homage to the parliamentarian Baudin, killed during the 1851 protests against Napoleon III's coup d'état (see Chapter Three). By the junction with the rue de Montreuil the *quartier*'s second fountain, known as la fontaine de la Petite Halle, marks the point at which we could probably be said to be moving into the *quartier* of Nation, after the vast square half a mile or so to the east. Nearby, at 11 bis rue Faidherbe and 9 rue Chanzy, are two early twentieth-century Art Nouveau apartment blocks; another one, with a restaurant at street level, is at 1 rue Jules-Vallès, named for the Communard writer (see Chapter Four). In the rue de Charonne numbers 100 and 102 occupy the site of a convent and its grounds, founded in 1654 and closed after the Revolution. The buildings were bought in 1848 by the moderate Republican politician Ledru-Rollin; Vallès avers in *Le Tableau de Paris* that the workers who lived there were known, in what sounds like almost feudal fashion, as 'les Ledru-Rollin',[7] and that they were lodged in dormitories of poor quality – '[b]âtiments lugubres, enfer des pauvres!'[8] / 'mournful buildings, the poor people's hell!' The early twentieth-century building at number 102 is noteworthy for its large glass bay-windows.

At the junction of Faidherbe and Charonne is to be found, just north of the skilfully renovated 1926 building that houses offices of the Paris transport authority, the 1910 brick and stone Palais de la Femme – not an early architectural avatar of feminism but since 1926 a Salvation Army women's hostel, originally built to provide a healthy residential environment for working men who had on site a laundry, a tailors, a hairdressers and a cobblers. 'Le but était de sortir les célibataires de "leurs affreux garnis", et de leur permettre une vie sociale qui les éloigne du cabaret'[9] / 'The idea was to get unmarried workers out of their "dreadful furnished rooms", and to give them a social life which would keep them out of the bar' – an objective which for a different gender, and in a different guise, the building pursues to this day. Just off the rue de Charonne lies the square Raoul-Nordling, named for a diplomat who served as Swedish consul in Paris for fifty-four years, onto which gives a 1992 social-housing block designed by the Italian Massimiliano Fuksas in red brick and glass, an echo of the former workshops we have seen in the rue du Faubourg. Nearby, in the rue Saint-Bernard, we find the seventeenth-century Church of Sainte-Marguerite, with rich interior decoration which when I visited was undergoing restoration. Most noteworthy of its paintings is Briard's 1761 *trompe-l'oeil* depicting fortunate souls leaving Purgatory for Heaven. The church was used for meetings during the Revolution, unsurprisingly losing much of its artwork in the process, and was the centre of a scandal in 1792 when its curate got married. It was long rumoured to harbour the Faubourg's only royal relic – the remains of Louis XVII, son of Louis XVI and Marie-Antoinette, who died of tuberculosis in the Temple prison in 1795, sparking off a flurry of imposters and conspiracy theories. There is a memorial stone to 'L … XVII, 1785–1795' in the church, but excavation and scientific examination were to reveal that the remains were in fact of somebody much older. By way of a consolation prize, however, the church's graveyard can lay claim to sheltering the seventy-three victims of the guillotine that worked overtime in the place de la Bastille between 9 and 12 June 1794.

From the rue Saint-Bernard we walk back to the rue de Charonne, from whose junction with the rue Trousseau there is a particularly fine view of the July Column. 22 rue Trousseau boasts a 1904 Art Deco building richly adorned with carved sunflowers and daisies, while the rear elevation of 50 avenue Ledru-Rollin, backing onto the rue de Charonne, bears a fresco painted by Christian Zeimert in 1990 and depicting well-known characters and spots in the Faubourg. In large letters at the top is the word KUB – France's best-known make of stock-cube, an advertisement for which was covered over by Zeimert's now sadly faded mural. 116 avenue Ledru-Rollin

houses a 1902 Art Nouveau brasserie, Le Bistrot du Peintre, described as
the oldest in the *quartier*.

By way of the passage de la Bonne-Graine we return to the rue de
Charonne, where at number 26 we find one of the largest of Paris's *bande
dessinée* shops, close by the passage Lhomme, home to art-galleries and
craft workshops. This brings us back to the rue du Faubourg, crossing
over which we move from what Pinçon and Pinçon-Charlot have described
as the bourgeois 11th to the more popular 12th *arrondissement*, at least in
the latter's Bastille / Faubourg avatar. Both *arrondissements* currently have
Socialist mayors, though between 1983 and 1995 both were held by the right
and the 12th remained so until 2001. The mayor of the 11th between 1995
and 2008 was the veteran anti-Maastricht left-winger Georges Sarre, now a
deputy mayor of Paris with responsibility for law and order.

Much of the 12th *arrondissement*, notably towards the Bois de Vincennes
(the largest park in eastern Paris), is tranquilly residential, leafy and even
perhaps suburban. Pinçon and Pinçon-Charlot's description applies, as they
make clear, only to the fairly small part of the *arrondissement* – the second
largest in Paris – that falls within our *quartier*, particularly towards the
Aligre market. It was in the 12th that my interest in the area took flight,
for I frequently worked in the Bibliothèque du Film, the main Paris cinema
library, between 1996 and 2005, when it was housed at the archetypally
Haussmanian 100 rue du Faubourg, before moving to more modern but less
appealing premises in the new Bercy development, opposite the Bibliothèque
de France.

Administratively this part of the *quartier* is known as the Quinze-Vingts,
in reference to the eye hospital still located at 28 rue de Charenton, whither
it was transferred in 1780. An early urban myth had it that fog in Paris in
the late eighteenth century was so bad that inmates of the hospital hired
themselves out to guide carriages and pedestrians. The site is Paris's major
ophthalmic hospital, whose buildings were constructed in 1957; only the
entrance-gate and the chapel of the original buildings survive. Most of
the buildings of interest, however, are to be found in and near the rue
du Faubourg, such as number 28 – home of the art-gallery La Maison du
Faubourg – and number 30, which was at one time the headquarters of the
celebrated fashion designer Jean-Paul Gaultier. After Gaultier's relocation to
the more chic Avenue Georges V, just off the Champs-Élysées, the building,
with its mosaics and ceramic decoration, was taken over by the Paris
municipality, and now houses the Ateliers de Paris, providing an exhibition
space along with economic and legal advice and professional training facilities
for interior and fashion designers.

At number 50 we find the passage de la Boule-Blanche, constructed in 1700 to connect workshops in the rue du Faubourg with those in the rue de Charenton, into which it debouches hard by the Quinze-Vingts hospital. Number 9, as mentioned in Chapter Eight, has since 1974 housed the offices of the influential film journal *Cahiers du cinéma*, while also in the passage are the progressive Catholic publishing-house Desclée de Brouwer and two film production companies, Les Films du Rêve and Bodega Films. A few doors away, at number 62, is L'Arbre à Lettres, one of four bookstores of that name in Paris and the largest and best-stocked of those in the *quartier* – a type of business still flourishing in Paris, as elsewhere in France, despite the growth of on-line shopping (which L'Arbre à Lettres also offers), and as good a refutation as any of the claim that the capital now lags culturally behind its 'competitors'.

Number 66 leads into the passage du Chantier, whose name 'évoque les anciens chantiers de bois où étaient stockés les matériaux nécessaires aux menuisiers'[10] / 'reminds us of the old wood-yards used to store materials needed by carpenters'. This passage, much more than la Boule-Blanche, remains a temple to the furniture industry – a survival of the Faubourg as opposed to its near-neighbour's emphatic Bastille identity. Next door is a former industrial building now occupied by Jean-Michel Wilmotte, the architect responsible inter alia for the viaduc des Arts beneath the 'promenade plantée'. Wilmotte's premises, replete with large windows, are the centre of what is now a considerable architectural empire, with branches on the Riviera and in London and a Foundation offering an annual prize for the best projected renovation of an older building (in 2010, the old Bibliothèque Nationale archives in Versailles).

Number 74 is a stone-fronted building, built in 1850 to house workers' dwellings – the widest building in the entire street and, despite its sobriety of design, also the most opulent, 'Industrial Revolution' architecture at its apogee. The cour des Bourguignons behind houses perhaps the most striking, and certainly the most vividly industrial, building in the entire street – a vast former furniture factory dating from the mid-1850s, though the site had been used for similar purposes since the seventeenth century. Two five-storey wings flank a courtyard dominated by a hundred-foot brick chimney, behind which, at 59–61 rue de Charenton, is a handsome red-brick building of 1886 vintage, built to house former workers' dwellings. The courtyard is now occupied by a mixture of small businesses and residential units.

There is little to detain the flâneur in this part of the avenue Ledru-Rollin, though the late nineteenth-century church of Saint-Antoine-des-Quinze-Vingt, with its amalgam of modern materials (concrete, bricks, cast metal) and Romanesque style, may be worth a glance. The post-Haussmanian Square Trousseau, occupying the site of a former hospital, contains some of the area's most decorative architecture, including the brasserie mentioned in Chapter Ten, and allegedly a sometime haunt of the great actor Jean Gabin. To quote Maréchal:

> Chaque façade est ornée d'une floraison décorative unique composée de lucarnes, de mosaïques, ou de sculptures figurées ou décoratives qui rompent avec la monotonie des immeubles haussmanniens.[11]

> Each façade is adorned with a different decorative flourish including dormer-windows, mosaics or figurative or decorative sculptures – a sharp contrast with the monotony of Haussmannian buildings.

There could be no sharper contrast to the Square Trousseau's opulence than the quotidian bustle around the Marché Beauveau and the place d'Aligre, far more cosmopolitan than Richard-Lenoir with its nineteenth-century central building surrounded by blocks dating from 1968. Beyond here the gravitational pull of Nation begins to make itself felt; the fountain de la Petite Halle, on a traffic island in the middle of the rue du Faubourg and actually included in the 11th *arrondissement*, might as we have already seen be thought to mark a boundary between the two areas. This fountain, like its Trogneux counterpart, was designed by Jean Beausire, but dates from slightly earlier (1710). Opposite it, at 184 rue du Faubourg, is the Hôpital Saint-Antoine, founded on the site of the former abbey in 1795 and at the last count offering 780 beds. The old cloister remains, a historic monument since 1962, but most of the buildings are of recent date, designed as we have seen by Le Corbusier's close associate André Wogenscky. Of the new(er) hospital Anne-Gaëlle Moalic says: 'Témoin de l'architecture des Trente Glorieuses, elle mérite d'être redécouverte'[12] / 'A witness to the architecture of the *trente glorieuses*, it is worth rediscovering.'

And so, perhaps with a detour via the neo-classical 1885 barracks at the corner of the boulevard Diderot and the rue de Chaligny, or more ambitiously by way of the 'promenade plantée' with its view over the avenue Daumesnil police-station adorned with fourteen replica Michelangelo statues, back to where it all began – the place de la Bastille and its central column. This is a shrine rather than a tomb, since a fire in 1871 destroyed the bodies buried in its base, and despite Chloé's dream in *Chacun cherche son chat* or the implausible chase sequence in Pierre Tchernia's *Le Viager* (1972) its summit has long been inaccessible for safety reasons. Yet it is an emblem of the Faubourg as much as the neighbouring Opéra is of Bastille, a potent reminder of the radical political heritage of this most multifarious of Parisian *quartiers*. Attenuated by globalization and gentrification that may be, but it remains the area's major distinguishing mark. I hope that the preceding pages have given some indication of why this is so.

Notes

Introduction: The Place de la Bastille

1   Pierre Nora, (ed.), *Les Lieux de mémoire* (Gallimard, 1997), p. xxiv.

2   Georges Touchard-Lafosse, in Louis Lurine (ed.), *Les Rues de Paris* (Slatkine, Geneva/Paris, 1844/1982), p. 129.

3   Louis Chevalier, *Les Parisiens* (Hachette, 1967/1985), p. 168.

4   Éric Hazan, *L'invention de Paris: il n'y pas de pas perdus* (Seuil, 2002), p. 13.

5   Daniel Stern, *Histoire de la Révolution française* (Balland, 1850–53/1985), pp. 670–1.

6   Jean-Paul Blais, *A la Bastille … voyage autour d'une place* (L'Harmattan, 2004), p. 10.

7   Michel Pinçon and Monique Pinçon-Charlot, *Paris mosaïque* (Calmann-Lévy, 2001), p. 176.

8   Ibid., p. 190.

9   Andrew Webber, *Berlin in the Twentieth Century: A Cultural Topography* (Cambridge University Press, Cambridge, 2008), p. 1.

10 Andrew Hussey, *Paris: The Secret History* (Penguin, London, 2006), p. xvi.

11 Louis-Sébastien Mercier, 'Le Tableau de Paris', in *Paris le jour, Paris la nuit* (Robert Laffont/Bouquins, 1788/1990), p. 255.

12 Gregory Shaya, 'The Flaneur, the Badaud, and the Making of a Mass Public in France, circa 1860–1910', *The American Historical Review* 109.1 (2004), <http://www.historycooperative.org/journals/ahr/109.1/shaya.html> (accessed 17 February 2010).

13 Walter Benjamin (trans. Howard Elland and Kevin McLaughlin), *The Arcades Project* (Harvard University Press, Cambridge, MA, 1999), p. 416.

14 Ibid., p. 124.

15 Ibid., p. 521.

16 Louis Aragon, *Le Paysan de Paris* (Folio, 1926/1953), p. 22.

17 Léon-Paul Fargue, *Le Piéton de Paris* (Gallimard, 1939/1993), p. 11.

18 Ibid., p. 144.

19 Roger Caillois, 'Paris, mythe moderne', in *Le Mythe et l'homme* (Flammarion, 1938/1987), p. 154.

20 Ibid., p. 156.

21 Ibid., p. 157.

22 Ibid., p. 162.

23 Guy Debord, 'Théorie de la dérive' (first published in *Les Lèvres nues* no. 9, 1956), http://www.larevuedesressources.org/spip.php?article38 (accessed 17 February 2010).

24 Jacques Réda, *Les ruines de Paris* (Gallimard, 1993), p. 39.

25 Marc Augé, *Un ethnologue dans le métro* (Hachette, 2001), p. 53.

26 Ibid., p. 70.

27 Edmund White, *The Flâneur* (Bloomsbury, London, 2001), p. 156.

28 Ibid., p. 17.

29 Michael Sheringham, *Everyday Life: Theories and Practices from Surrealism to the Present* (Oxford University Press, Oxford, 2006), p. 304.

30 Ibid., p. 277.

31 Andrew Hussey, *Paris: The Secret History* (Bloomsbury, London, 2006), p. xvii.

32 Ibid.

33 Ibid., p. 432.

34 Louis Chevalier, *Classes laborieuses et classes dangereuses* (Perrin, 1958/2002), p. iv.

35 Christopher Prendergast, *For the People by the People. Eugène Sue's Les Mystères de Paris: A Hypothesis in the Sociology of Literature* (Legenda, Oxford, 2003), p. 123.

36 Chevalier, *Classes laborieuses*, p. 173.

37 Ibid., p. 319.

38 Ibid., p. 249.

39 Jean-Louis Robert and Danielle Tartakowsky (eds.), *Paris le peuple: XVIIIe–XXe siècle* (Sorbonne, 1999), p. 9.

40 Ibid., p. 47.

41 Karlheinz Stierle, *La Capitale des signes: Paris et son discours* (Maison des sciences de l'homme, 2001), p. 121.

42 Hussey, *Paris: The Secret History*, p. xvi.

Chapter 1: *'What's that poor creature doing here?': the area and the fortress before the Revolution of 1789*

1 Jean Diwo, *Le Génie de la Bastille* (Denoël, Paris, 1984/1999), p. 17.

2 Ibid., p. 21.

3 Ibid., p. 33.

4 Ibid., p. 57.

5 Ibid., p. 285.

6 Quoted in Claude Quétel, *La Bastille: histoire vraie d'une prison légendaire* (Robert Laffont, 1989), p. 10.

7 Mercier, 'Le Tableau de Paris', p. 265.

8 Simon-Nicholas Henri de Linguet, *Mémoires sur la Bastille, et sur la détention de Monsieur Linguet, écrits par lui-même* (Spilsbury, London, 1783), p. 52.

9 Frantz Funck-Brentano, *Légendes et archives de la Bastille* (Hachette, 1904), p. 155.

10 Restif de la Bretonne, 'Les Nuits de Paris', in *Paris le jour, Paris la nuit*, p. 865.

11 Alain Thillay, 'La Rue et le faubourg Saint-Antoine', in Gilles-Antoine Langlois (ed.), *Le douzième arrondissement: traditions et actualités* (Action artistique de la ville de Paris, 1996), p. 65.

12 Alain Thillay, *Le Faubourg-Saint-Antoine et ses «faux ouvriers»: la liberté du travail à Paris aux XVIIe et XVIIIe siècles* (Champ Vallon, 2002), p. 15.

13 Ibid., p. 366.

14 Ibid., p. 131.

Chapter 2: 'Thought blew the Bastille apart': the fall of the Fortress and the Revolutionary years, 1789–1815

1 Mercier, 'Le Tableau de Paris', p. 253.

2 From *Paris ridicule*; quoted in Claude Dubois, *Je me souviens de Paris* (Parigramme, 2007), p. 44.

3 Quétel, *La Bastille*, p. 382.

4 Jules Michelet, *Histoire de la Révolution française* (Éditions Saint-Clair, 1967), p. 208.

5 Christopher Prendergast, *Paris in the Nineteenth Century* (Blackwell, Oxford/Cambridge, MA, 1992), p. 108.

6 Quoted in Pierre Citron, *La Poésie de Paris dans la littérature française de Rousseau à Baudelaire* (Minuit, 1961/Paris Musées, 2006), p. 205.

7 Pierre-Mathieu Parein, *La Prise de la Bastille* (Girardin, 1791), p. 5.

8 Georges Lecocq, *La Prise de la Bastille et ses anniversaires d'après des documents inédits* (Craravray Frères, 1881), p. 29.

9 Alexandre Dumas, *Ange Pitou* (Complexe, 1989), vol. 1, p. 228.

10 Ibid., p. 274.

11 Romain Rolland, *Le 14 Juillet: action populaire* (Cahiers de la Quinzaine, 1902).

12 Funck-Brentano, *Bastille et Faubourg Saint-Antoine* (Hachette, 1925), p. 47.

13 Louis Madelin, *La Révolution* (Jules Taillandier, 1911/1979), p. 81.

14 Louis Chevalier, *La Formation de la population parisienne au dix-neuvième siècle* (PUF, 1950), p. 17.

15 Jean Diwo, *Le Lit d'acajou* (Denoël, 1984), p. 140.

16 Ibid., p. 92.

17 Ibid., p.360.

18 Tony Révillon, *Le Faubourg Saint-Antoine* (J. Rouff, 1881), p. 60.

19 Marcel Poëte, *Paris: une vie de cité* (Picard, 1925), p.303.

20 Paul-Georges Sansonetti, 'La Prise de la Bastille', unpublished thesis, École du Louvre, n.d.), p. 24.

21 Patrick Colias and Hadji Temglit, *Il y a deux cents ans la Révolution française* (Vents d'Ouest, 1989), pp. 46—7.

22 Quoted in Robert Brécy, *Florilège de la chanson révolutionnaire de 1789 au Front Populaire* (Hier et Demain, 1978), pp. 28—9.

23 Hélène Delanoë, *'Le Souverain Faubourg': le Faubourg Saint-Antoine et les métiers du meuble* (Maison des Sciences de l'Homme, 1987), p. 53.

24 Sophie Fagay, 'Bourgeois du faubourg Saint-Antoine, 1791—1792', in Michel Vovelle (ed.), *Paris et la Révolution* (Sorbonne, 1989), p. 95.

25 Gérard Moreau, introduction to Jean-François Vilar, *La Grande Ronde du Père Duchesne* (Épigramme, 1989): page not numbered.

26 Raymond Monnier, *Le Faubourg Saint-Antoine (1789—1815)* (Société des Études Robespierristes, 1981), p. 165.

27 Edward Said, *Orientalism* (Penguin, London, 1978/2003), p. 83.

28 Ibid., p. 88.

29 Jules Michelet, *Journal* (Gallimard, 1959), vol. I, p. 116.

30 Quoted in Funck-Brentano, *Bastille et Faubourg Saint-Antoine*, p. 52.

Chapter 3; 'The strategy of the generals of Africa shattered': the Restoration, Orleanist and Second Republic Years, 1815—1851

1 Blais, *A la Bastille*, p. 44.

2 Quoted in Bernard Champigneulle, *Paris, architecture, sites et jardins* (Seuil, 1973), p. 126.

3 Armand Lanoux, *Paris en forme de coeur; physiologie de Paris* (Fayard, 1954), p. 112.

4 Ibid., p. 48.

5 Patrice Higonnet, *Paris capitale du monde* (Tallandier, 2005), p. 66.

6 Jean Diwo, *Le Génie de la Bastille* (Denoël, 1984), p. 101.

7 Ibid., p. 133.

8 Antoine-François-Marius Rey-Dussueil, *Le Faubourg Saint-Merri* (Ambroise Dupont, 1832), pp. 1—2.

9 Frédéric Sayer, 'L'enfer parisien', in Crystel Pinçonnat and Chantal Liaroutzos, *Paris, cartographies littéraires* (Le Manuscrit, 2007), p. 70.

10 Victor Hugo, *Les Misérables* (Garnier-Flammarion, 1862/1967), vol. II, p. 372.

11 See ibid., vol. III, pp. 77—83.

12 Ibid., p. 90.

13 Ibid., vol. II, p. 484.

14 Jacques Seebacher, *Victor Hugo ou la calcul des profondeurs* (PUF, 1993), p. 227.

15 Ibid. p. 226.

16 Ibid., p. 194.

17 Ibid., p. 98.

18 Stierle, *La Capitale des signes*, p. 338.

19 Claudette Combes, *Paris dans 'Les Misérables'* (Centre Interculturel de Documentation, Nantes, 1981), p. 276.

20 Émile Tersen, 'Le Paris des *Misérables*', in special issue of *Europe* on *Les Misérables*, Fenruary–March 1962, p. 109.

21 Hugo, *Les Misérables*, vol. II, p. 198.

22 Ibid., p. 199.

23 Éric Hazan, *L'Invention de Paris: il n'y pas de pas perdus* (Seuil, 2002), p. 396.

24 Hugo, *Les Misérables*, vol. II, p. 199.

25 Ibid., p. 200.

26 Karen Masters-Wicks, *Victor Hugo's 'Les Misérables' and The Novels of the Grotesque* (Peter Lang, New York, 1994), p. 103.

27 Ibid., p. 202.

28 Hazan, *L'Invention de Paris*, p. 425.

29 Balzac, *Facino Cane*, in *Nouvelles* (GF Flammarion, 1836/2005), p. 485.

30 Ibid., p. 486.

31 Ibid., p. 487.

32 Balzac, *Le Père Goriot* (Gallimard, 1835/1971), p. 22.

33 Balzac, *Facino Cane*, p. 500.

34 Ibid., p. 489.

35 From a copy of *Le Faubourg Saint-Antoine* in the Bibliothèque nationale de France; the pages appear not to be numbered.

36 Roger V. Gould, *Insurgent Identities: Class, Community and Protest in Paris from 1848 to the Commune* (University of Chicago Press, Chicago/London, 1995), p. 39.

37 Jean Bruhat, Jean Dautry and Émile Tersen (eds.), *La Commune de 1871* (Éditions Sociales, 1960), p. 9.

38 Hazan, *L'Invention de Paris*, p. 380.

39 Stern, *Histoire de la Révolution*, p. 671.

40 Ibid., p. 680.

41 Ibid., p. 683.

42 Ibid., p. 672.

43 Ibid., p. 676.

44 Diwo, *Le Génie de la Bastille*, p. 286.

45 Graham Robb, *Victor Hugo: A Biography* (W.W. Norton, New York, 1997), p. 307.

46 Victor Hugo, *Histoire d'un crime* (Éditeurs Français Réunis, 1877–78/1958), p. 71.

47 Ibid., p. 141.

48 Ibid., p. 148.

49 Ibid., p. 149.

50 Ibid., p. 156.

51 Karl Marx, *The Eighteenth Brumaire of Louis Bonaparte*. (Available online at http://www.marxists.org/archive/marx/works/1852/18th-brumaire/ch01. htm, accessed 12 March 2010.)

52 Diwo, *Le Génie de la Bastille*, pp. 267–8.

53 Hazan, *L'Invention de Paris*, p. 403.

Chapter 4: 'Where is the noise of the storm that I love?': The Second Empire from Haussmann to the Commune

1 Edmond Texier, *Tableau de Paris* (Chevalier, 1852), vol. II, p. 328.

2 Ibid., p. 245.

3 Hazan, *L'Invention de Paris*, p. 176.

4 Georges-Eugène Haussmann, *Mémoires du Baron Haussmann* (Victor-Havard, 1890), vol. II, p. 318.

5 David Harvey, *Consciousness and the Urban Experience: Studies in the History and Theory of Capitalist Urbanization* (Johns Hopkins, Baltimore, 1985), p. 76.

6 Bernard Marchand, *Paris, histoire d'une ville: XIXe–XXe siècle* (Points, 1993), p. 101.

7 From Joseph Charlemont, *La Boxe française historique et biographique, souvenirs, notes, impressions, anecdotes*, quoted in Dubois, *Je me souviens de Paris*, p. 45.

8 Colin Jones, *Paris: Biography of a City* (Penguin, London, 2004/2006), p. 376.

9 Diwo, *Le Génie de la Bastille*, p. 444.

10 Prosper-Olivier Lissagaray, *Histoire de la Commune de 1871* (La Découverte, 1996/1876), p. 346.

11 Bertrand Tillier, http://www.histoire-image.org/site/etude_comp/etude_ comp_detail.php?i=71&d=31&c=propagande, accessed 22 March 2010.

12 Taken from the back cover of Jules Vallès, *L'Insurgé* (GF-Flammarion, 1886/1970).

13 Vallès, *Le Tableau de Paris*, p. 91.

14 Ibid., p. 129.

15 Ibid., p. 300.

16 Alphonse Daudet, *Les Contes du lundi* (Nelson, 1873/1957), pp. 132–3.

17 Ibid.

Chapter 5: 'Satan's bagpipes': La Belle Époque's forty-three years of peace

1 Quoted in Nora, *Les Lieux de mémoire*, vol. 1, p. 472.

2 Quoted in Rosamonde Sanson, *Les 14 Juillet (1789–1975): fête et conscience nationale* (Flammarion, 1976), p. 58.

3 Nora, *Les Lieux de mémoire*, p. 436.

4 Ibid., p. 453.

5 Daniel Halévy, *Pays parisiens* (Grasset, 1932), p.177.

6 Quoted in Geneviève Poujol, *L'Éducation populaire, histoires et pouvoirs* (Éditions Ouvrières, 1981), p. 96.

7 Christophe Charle, *Paris fin de siècle: culture et politique* (Seuil, 1998), p. 13.

8 Ibid., p. 50.

9 Pierre Pinon, in *Sous les pavés, la Bastille: archéologie d'un mythe révolutionnaire* (Caisse nationale des monuments et des sites, 1989), p. 150.

10 Géraldine Rideau, 'Une place, des percées', in Jean-Baptiste Minnaert (ed.), *Le Faubourg Saint-Antoine: architecture et métiers d'art* (Action artistique de la ville de Paris, 1998), p. 144.

11 Blais, *A la Bastille*, p. 63.

12 In Claude Eveno, *Les Cours du 11ème arrondissement* (Archipress, 1997), p. 8.

13 Ibid., p. 5.

14 Marie-Claire Bancquart, *Images littéraires de Paris 'fin-de-siècle'* (La Différence, 1979), p. 45.

15 Jules Vallès, *Le Tableau de Paris* (Éditeurs Français Réunis, 1882–83/1971), p. 241.

16 Ibid., p. 232.

17 Ibid., p. 238.

18 Ibid., p. 239.

19 Roger Girard, *Quand les Auvergnats partaient conquérir Paris* (Fayard, 1979), p. 167.

20 Marie-Claude Blanc-Chaléard, 'Les trois temps du bal-musette ou la place des étrangers (1880–1960)', in Jean-Louis Robert and Danièle Tartakowsky, *Paris le peuple: XVIIIe–XXe siècle* (Publications de la Sorbonne, 1999), p. 77.

21 Vallès, *Le Tableau de Paris*, p. 242.

22 Alfred Fierro, *Vie et histoire du XIIe arrondissement* (Harvas, 1988), p. 119.

23 Louis Péguri, *Du bouge au conservatoire* (1950), quoted at http://mondomix. com/blogs/accordeon.php/2009/06/07/la-photo-du-lundi-le-beau-bal-de-bouscat (accessed 14 May 2010).

24 See Régis Revenin, *Homosexualité et prostitution masculines à Paris, 1870–1918* (L'Harmattan, 2005).

25 Alain Corbin, *Les Filles de noce: misère sexuelle et prostitution aux 19e et 20e siècles* (Aubier Montaigne, 1978), p. 293.

26 Jules de Neuville, *Encore un livre rose: Rigolboch's question* (Les Libraires, 1860), p. 72.

27 See Dominique Kalifa, *Crime et culture au XIXe siècle* (Perrin, 2005), Chapter 2.

28 *Crime et châtiment* (L'Express/Musée d'Orsay, 2010), p. 31.

29 Dominique Kalifa, *Les Crimes de Paris: lieux et non-lieux du crime à Paris au XIXe siècle* (BILIPO, 2001), pp. 29–32.

30 Kalifa, *Crime et culture au XIXe siècle*, p. 248.

31 For further information see Sarah Leahy, *Casque d'or* (I.B. Tauris, London/New York, 2007), pp. 9–14.

32 Leahy, *Casque d'or*, p. 11.

33 Diana Holmes and Carrie Tarr, in Holmes and Tarr (eds), *A 'Belle Époque'?: Women in French Society and Culture, 1890–1914* (Berghahn, New York/Oxford, 2006), p. 17.

34 Adrian Rifkin, *Street Noises: Parisian Pleasure, 1900–1940* (Manchester University Press, Manchester/New York, 1993), p. 4.

35 Jean-Marc Berlière, *Le Crime de Soleilland (1907): les journalistes et l'assassin* (Tallandier, 2003), p. 30.

36 André Billy, *Le Badaud de Paris et d'ailleurs* (Arthème Fayard, 1907/1959), pp. 86–7.

Chapter 6: *'Villains, stars and everybody in between': The First War and the entre-deux-guerres*

1 Laurent Azzano, *Mes joyeuses années au Faubourg* (France-Empire, 1985), p. 41.

2 Ibid., p. 47.

3 Ibid., p. 216.

4 Jean Diwo, *249, faubourg Saint-Antoine* (Flammarion, 2006), back jacket cover.

5 Diwo, *249, faubourg Saint-Antoine*, p. 143.

6 Marc Dumas, *Voie royale: le faubourg Saint-Antoine* (MMI Éditions, 2001), p. 2.

7 Ibid., p. 77.

8 Alain Bellet, *Les Mutins du faubourg* (Magnard Jeunesse, 1999), p. 127.

9 Ibid., p. 140.

10 Jean Follain, *Paris* (Phébus, 1935/2006), p. 78.

11 Jules Romains, *Françoise* (Flammarion, 1958), p. 512.

12 Léon Daudet, *Paris vécu* (Gallimard, 1928/1969), p. 29.

13 Ibid., p. 36.

14 Jacques Valdour, *Le Faubourg* (Éditions Spes, 1925). pp. 114–15.

15 Ibid., p. 188.

16 Ibid., p. 187.

17 See http://fr.wikipedia.org/wiki/Prix_du_roman_populiste#cite_note-0 (accessed 22 May 2010).

18 François Raynal, *Faubourg* (Dumas, 1950), p. 17.

19 Ibid., p. 308.

20 Ibid., p. 322.

21 Claude Dubois, *Apaches, voyous et gonzes poilus: le milieu parisien du début du siècle aux années 60* (Parigramme, 1996), p. 18.

22 Lucien Lariche, *Les Jetons de bal, 1830–1940* (ACJM, Neuilly-sur-Seine, 2006), p. 25.

23 Dubois, *Apaches, voyous et gonzes poilus*, p. 53.

24 Ibid., p. 130.

25 Francis Carco, *De Montmartre au Quartier Latin* (Sauret, Monaco, 1927/1993), pp. 91–2.

26 See Jean-Jacques Bedu, *Francis Carco au coeur de la bohème* (Rocher, 2001), p. 207.

27 André Picard and Francis Carco, *Mon homme* (Ferenczi, 1921), p. 81.

28 Ibid., p. 189.

29 Robert Lageat, *Des Halles au Balajo* (Les Éditions de Paris, 1993), p. 190.

30 Diwo, *249, faubourg Saint-Antoine*, p. 207.

31 http://mondomix.com/blogs/accordeon.php/2010/03/22/a-la-decouverte-des-bals-musette-de-pari (accessed 10 July 2010).

32 Lageat, *Des Halles au Balajo*, p. 193.

33 Claude Dubois, *Je me souviens de Paris* (Parigramme, 20070, pp. 403–4.

34 Follain, *Paris*, p. 136.

35 Dubois, *Je me souviens de Paris*, p. 194.

36 http://swingjo.apinc.org/articles.php?id=29 (accessed 23 July 2010).

37 Clément Lepidis, *Les Bals à Jo* (Le Sémaphore, 1998), p. 62.

38 Bedu, *Francis Carco*, p. 142.

39 Dudley Andrew and Steven Ungar, *Popular Front Paris and the Poetics of Culture* (Belknap/Harvard University Press, Cambridge, MA/London, 2005), p. 249.

40 Ibid., p. 251.

41 For reproductions of nine of the photographs the Séebergers took, see Gilbert Salachas, *Le Paris d'Hollywood: sur un air de réalité* (Caisse nationale des monuments historiques et des sites, 1994), pp. 76–83.

42 See Andrew and Ungar, *Popular Front Paris*, p. 251.

43 Ibid., p. 252.

44 Jacques Borel, *L'Adoration* (Gallimard, 1965), p. 50.

45 Ibid., p. 426.

46 Quoted in Christian Amalvi, 'Le 14-juillet: du *Dies irae* à *Jour de fête*', in Nora, *Les Lieux de mémoire*, p. 458.

47 Nora, *Les Lieux de mémoire*, p. 439.

48 Ibid., p. 440.

49 Jacques Borel, *L'Aveu différé* (Gallimard, 1997), p. 129.

50 Ibid., p. 225.

Chapter 7: 'Slicked hair and splendid sideburns': Occupation and Liberation

1 See http://philippepoisson-hotmail.com.over-blog.com/ext/http://prisons-cherche-midi-mauzac.com/des-prisons/lexode-de-36-detenues-de-la-

petite-roquette-transferees-a-libourne-en-juin-1940-1438 (accessed 25 July 210).

2 France Hamelin, *Femmes dans la nuit: 1939–1944* (Renaudot et Cᶦᵉ, 1988), pp. 137–247.

3 Hélène Cuénat, *La Porte verte* (Éditions Bouchène, 2001), notably pp. 144–53.

4 See http://www.lyricspond.com/artist-edith-piaf/lyrics-de-lautre-cote-de-la-rue (accessed 10 June 2010).

5 Claude Blanchard, *Le Parisien de Paris* (La Jeune Parque, 1946), p. 99.

6 Ibid., p. 101.

7 Ibid., p. 103.

8 Francis Lemarque, *J'ai la mémoire qui chante* (Presses de la Cité, 1992), p. 14.

9 See http://mondomix.com/blogs/accordeon.php/2010/03/22/a-la-decouverte-des-bals-musette-de-pari (accessed 10 July 2010).

10 See http://paroles.abazada.com/chanson,rue-de-lappe,21419.htm (accessed 9 June 2010).

11 Claude Garric, in Jules Romains (ed.), *Le Peuple de Paris* (Perrin, 1951), p. 159.

12 See in particular the photographs of strongmen and a man swallowing frogs – the latter evocative of Agnès Varda's 1962 film *Cléo de 5 à 7* – in Lionel Mouraux, *Je me souviens du 11e arroidnssement* (Pargiramme, 1998), pp. 114–15.

13 *Le Gavroche d'Aligre*, July/August/September 1959 (pages not numbered).

14 *Le Gavroche d'Aligre*, July/August/September 1960 (pages not numbered).

15 See http://forum.muzika.fr/read.php?1,657615,722958,quote=1 (accessed 10 July 2010).

16 Cyrille Fleischman, *Riverains rêveurs du métro Bastille* (Le Dilettante, 2007), p. 14.

17 Ibid., p.27.

18 Ibid., p.39.

19 Ibid., p.46.

20 Léo Malet, *Casse-pipe à la Nation*, in *Les Nouveaux Mystères de Paris*, vol. 1, p. 359,

21 See http://www.trussel.com/maig (accessed 13 July 2010).

22 Pierre Bourgeade, *Les Immortelles* (Gallimard, 1966), p. 36.

23 Ibid., p. 35.

24 Ibid., p. 37.

25 For more detailed information and analysis see Keith A. Reader, *The May 1968 Events in France* (Macmillan/St Martin's Press, London/New York, 1993).

Chapter 8: 'Let's have some sun!': post-Gaullism and the Mitterrand years

1 Hervé Hamon and Patrick Rotman, *Génération 2: les années de poudre* (Seuil, 1988), p. 122.

2 Rosemonde Sanson, *Les 14 Juillet (1789–1975): fête et conscience nationale* (Flammarion, 1976), p. 165.

3 This can be viewed at http://www.ina.fr/economie-et-societe/justice-et-faits-divers/video/CPF07006187/marguerite-duras-a-la-petite-roquette.fr.html (accessed 5 July 2010).

4 Lageat, *Des Halles au Balajo*, p. 190.

5 Isabelle Chipault, in Isabelle Chipault and Alfred Fierro, *Paris XIIe* (Éditions Bonneton, 1992), p. 80.

6 Véronique de Rudder with Michelle Guillon, *Autochtones et immigrés en quartier populaire: du marché d'Aligre à l'Îlot Chalon* (L'Harmattan, 1987), p. 111.

7 Chipault in Chipault and Fierro, *Paris XIIe*, p. 81.

8 Chevalier, *Les Parisiens*, p. 446.

9 Ibid., p. 449.

10 Blais, *A la Bastille*, p. 81.

Chapter 9: 'A building, not a monument': the construction of the Bastille Opéra

1 Maryvonne de Saint-Pulgent, *Le Syndrome de l'Opéra* (Robert Laffont, 1991), p. 123.

2 Frédérique Jourda, *A l'Opéra aujourd'hui: de Garnier à la Bastille* (Hachette, 2004), p. 167.

3 François Chaslin, *Les Paris de François Mitterrand* (Gallimard, 1985), p. 187.

4 Pierre-Jean Rémy, *Bastille: Rêver un Opéra* (Plon, 1989), p. 61.

5 Ibid., p. 99.

6 Chaslin, *Les Paris de François Mitterrand*, p. 195.

7 Ibid., p. 199.

8 Ibid., p. 203.

9 Marie Delarue, *Un pharaon républicain: Les Grands Travaux de Mitterrand* (Jacques Grancher, 1999), p. 103.

10 Sébastien Maréchal, *Le 12e Arrondissement: itinéraires d'histoire et d'architecture* (Action Artistique de la Ville de Paris, 2000), p. 121.

11 David Looseley, *The Politics of Fun: Cultural Policy and Debate in Contemporary France* (Berg, Oxford/New York, 1995), p. 122.

12 Saint-Pulgent, *Le Syndrome de l'Opéra*, p. 291.

13 Looseley, *The Politics of Fun*, p. 184.

14 Delarue, *Un pharaon républicain*, p. 141.

15 Michèle Leloup in *L'Express* – http://www.lexpress.fr/informations/opera-bastille-vous-avez-dit-populaire_642368.html (accessed 6 August 2010).

16 http://cgttefsas.wordpress.com/2010/06/06/greve-des-travailleurs-sans-papiers-a-lopera-bastile-le-piquet-des-piquets-tient-toujours/ accessed 6 August 2010).

Chapter 10: 'A real earthquake': the impact of the Opéra on the quartier
1 In *Figaroscope*, 16 July 1998.
2 Pinçon and Pinçon-Charlot, *Paris mosaïque*, p. 183.
3 Philippe Mathieux, in Langlois, *Le douzième arrondissement*, p. 222.
4 Maréchal, *Le 12e arrondissement*, p. 108.
5 Denis Tillinac, *Je me souviens de Paris* (Flammarion, 1998), p. 16.
6 Charles Dantzig, *Le Style cinquième (iconoclastes)* (Les Belles Lettres, 1992), pp. 31–2.
7 Jean-Claude Gautrand (ed.) *A la Bastille!* (PICTO, 1998), in the preface (pages not numbered).
8 Michel Pinçon and Monique Pinçon-Charlot, *Sociologie de Paris* (La Découverte, 2004), p. 70.
9 http://www.parisbalades.com/Cadres/cadres11bastille.htm (accessed 9 August 2010).
10 Guy Lesève, quoted in *Figaroscope*, 17 June 1998.
11 Jean-François Vilar, *Bastille Tango* (Actes Sud, Arles, 1986/1998), p. 244.
12 Ibid., p. 257.
13 Ibid., p. 101.
14 Ibid., p. 322.
15 Ibid., p. 247.
16 Ibid., p. 130.
17 José-Louis Bocquet, *Sur la ligne blanche* (NRF/Gallimard, 1993), p. 19.
18 Alain Bellet, *Fausse commune* (Le Passage, Paris/new York, 2003), p. 65.
19 Ibid., p. 130.
20 Ibid., p. 142.
21 Alain Maury and Thierry Robberecht, *Beluga 1: Du rififi à la Bastille* (Casterman, 2001), p. 46.
22 Elizabeth Ezra, 'Cats in the 'Hood: The Unspeakable Truth about *Chacun cherche son chat*', in Phil Powrie (ed.), *French Cinema in the 1990s: Continuity and Difference* (Oxford University Press, Oxford/New York, 1999), p. 218.
23 Lucy Mazdon, 'Space, place and community in *Chacun cherche son chat*', in Lucy Mazdon (ed.), *France on Film: reflections on popular French cinema* (Wallflower Press, London, 2001), p. 104.
24 Interview with Philippe Piazzo in *Télérama*, no 2412, 3 April 1996. (This and the following endnote refer to electronically stored documents in the Bibliothèque du Film, which do not bear page numbers.)

25 Nathalie Journo, 'C'est madame Renée qui a perdu son chat', *Libération*, 6 April 1996.

26 http://www.mp3lyrics.org/j/jacques-brel/la-bastille/ (accessed 3 September 2010).

27 http://www.lyricstime.com/alex-beaupain-la-bastille-lyrics.html (accessed 3 September 2010).

28 http://www.lefigaro.fr/sortir-paris/2010/06/01/03013-20100601ARTFIG00577-quartier-libre-a-aligre.php (accessed 4 October 2010).

Chapter 11: *Flânerie in the archive: the Faubourg/Bastille today*

1 White, *The Flâneur*, p. 47.

2 Jacques Derrida, *Mal d'archive* (Galilée, 1995), p. 26.

3 Ibid., p. 142.

4 Benjamin, *The Arcades Project*, p. 419.

5 Blais, *A la Bastille*, p. 94.

6 Virginie Champion, Bertrand Lemoine and Claude Terreaux, *Les Cinémas de Paris, 1945–1995* (Direction d'Action Artistique de la Ville de Paris, 1995), p. 51.

7 Vallès, *Le Tableau de Paris*, p. 235.

8 Ibid., p. 236.

9 Denis Michel and Dominique Renou, *Le Guide du promeneur: 11e arrondissement* (Parigramme, 1993), p. 131.

10 Sebastien Maréchal, *Le 12e arrondissement: itinéraires d'histoire et d'architecture* (Action Artistique de la Ville de Paris, 2000), p. 125. I am indebted to this book for much of the information contained in this section.

11 Ibid., p. 130

12 Anne-Gaëlle Moalic, in Jean-Baptiste Minnaert (ed.), *Le Faubourg Saint-Antoine: architecture et métiers d'art* (Action artistique de la ville de Paris, 1998), p. 182.

Bibliography

Unless otherwise stated, the place of publication is Paris

Andrew, Dudley, and Steven Ungar, *Popular Front Paris and the Poetics of Culture* (Belknap/ Harvard University Press, Cambridge, MA/London, 2005)

Aragon, Louis, *Le Paysan de Paris* (Folio, 1926/1953)

Augé, Marc, *Un ethnologue dans le métro* (Hachette, 2001)

Azzano, Laurent, *Mes joyeuses années au Faubourg* (France-Empire, 1985)

Balzac, Honoré de, *Le Père Goriot* (Gallimard, 1835/1971)

Balzac, Honoré de, *Facino Cane*, in *Nouvelles* (GF Flammarion, 1836/2005)

Bancquart, Marie-Claire, *Images littéraires de Paris 'fin-de-siècle'* (La Différence, 1979)

Bedu, Jean-Jacques, *Francis Carco au coeur de la bohème* (Rocher, 2001)

Bellet, Alain, *Les Mutins du faubourg* (Magnard Jeunesse, 1999)

Bellet, Alain, *Fausse commune* (Le Passage, Paris/New York, 2003)

Benjamin, Walter (trans. Howard Elland and Kevin McLaughlin), *The Arcades Project* (Harvard University Press, Cambridge, MA, 1999)

Berlière, Jean-Marc, *Le Crime de Soleilland (1907): les journalistes et l'assassin* (Tallandier, 2003)

Billy, André, *Le Badaud de Paris et d'ailleurs* (Arthème Fayard, 1907/1959)

Blais, Jean-Paul, *A la Bastille … voyage autour d'une place* (L'Harmattan, 2004)

Blanchard, Claude, *Le Parisien de Paris* (La Jeune Parque, 1946)

Bocquet, José-Louis, *Sur la ligne blanche* (NRF/Gallimard, 1993)

Borel, Jacques, *L'Adoration* (Gallimard, 1965)

Borel, Jacques, *L'Aveu différé* (Gallimard, 1997)

Bourgeade, Pierre, *Les Immortelles* (Gallimard, 1966)

Brécy, Robert, *Florilège de la chanson révolutionnaire de 1789 au Front Populaire* (Hier et Demain, 1978)

de la Bretonne, Restif, *Les Nuits de Paris*, in *Paris le jour, Paris la nuit* (Robert Laffont/ Bouquins, 1788–94/1990)

Bruhat, Jean, Jean Dautry and Émile Tersen (eds), *La Commune de 1871* (Éditions Sociales, 1960)

Caillois, Roger, 'Paris, mythe moderne,' in *Le Mythe et l'homme* (Flammarion, 1938/1987)

Carco, Francis, *De Montmartre au Quartier Latin* (Sauret, Monaco, 1927/1993)

Champigneulle, Bernard, *Paris, architecture, sites et jardins* (Seuil, 1973)

Champion, Virginie, Bertrand Lemoine and Claude Terreaux, *Les Cinémas de Paris, 1945–1995* (Direction d'Action Artistique de la Ville de Paris, 1995)

Charle, Christophe, *Paris fin de siècle: culture et politique* (Seuil, 1998)

Chaslin, François, *Les Paris de François Mitterrand* (Gallimard, 1985)

Chevalier, Louis, *La Formation de la population parisienne au dix-neuvième siècle* (PUF, 1950)

Chevalier, Louis, *Classes laborieuses et classes dangereuses* (Perrin, 1958/2002)

Chevalier, Louis, *Les Parisiens* (Hachette, 1967/1985)

Chipault, Isabelle, and Alfred Fierro, *Paris XIIe* (Éditions Bonneton, 1992)

Citron, Pierre, *La Poésie de Paris dans la littérature française de Rousseau à Baudelaire* (Minuit, 1961/Paris Musées, 2006)

Colias, Patrick, and Hadji Temglit, *Il y a deux cents ans la Révolution française* (Vents d'Ouest, 1989)

Combes, Claudette, *Paris dans 'Les Misérables'* (Centre Interculturel de Documentation, Nantes, 1981)

Corbin, Alain, *Les Filles de noce: misère sexuelle et prostitution aux 19e et 20e siècles* (Aubier Montaigne, 1978)

Crime et châtiment (L'Express/Musée d'Orsay, 2010)

Cuénat, Hélène, *La Porte verte* (Éditions Bouchène, 2001)

Dantzig, Charles, *Le Style cinquième (iconoclastes)* (Les Belles Lettres, 1992)

Daudet, Alphonse, *Les Contes du lundi* (Nelson, 1873/1957). (Available online at http://www.evene.fr/livres/livre/alphonse-daudet-les-contes-du-lundi-9246.php, accessed 14 April 2010.)

Daudet, Léon, *Paris vécu* (Gallimard, 1928/1969)

Debord, Guy, 'Théorie de la dérive' (first published in *Les Lèvres nues* no. 9, 1956). (Available online at http://www.larevuedesressources.org/spip.php?article38, accessed 17 February 2010.)

Delanoë, Hélène, *'Le Souverain Faubourg' : le Faubourg Saint-Antoine et les métiers du meuble* (Maison des Sciences de l'Homme, 1987)

Delarue, Marie, *Un pharaon républicain: Les Grands Travaux de Mitterrand* (Jacques Grancher, 1999)

Derrida, Jacques, *Mal d'archive* (Galilée, 1995)

Diwo, Jean, *Les Dames du faubourg* (Denoël, 1984)

Diwo, Jean, *Le Génie de la Bastille* (Denoël, 1984/1999)

Diwo, Jean, *Le Lit d'acajou* (Denoël, 1984)

Diwo, Jean, *249, faubourg Saint-Antoine* (Flammarion, 2006)

Dubois, Claude, *Apaches, voyous et gonzes poilus: le milieu parisien du début du siècle aux années 60* (Parigramme, 1996)

Dubois, Claude, *Je me souviens de Paris* (Parigramme, 2007)

Dumas, Alexandre, *Ange Pitou* (Complexe, 1853–1989)

Dumas, Marc, *Voie royale: le faubourg Saint-Antoine* (MMI Éditions, 2001)

Eveno, Claude, *Les Cours du 11ème arrondissement* (Archipress, 1997)

Fargue, Léon-Paul, *Le Piéton de Paris* (Gallimard, 1939/1993)

Fierro, Alfred, *Vie et histoire du XIIe arrondissement* (Harvas, 1988)

Fleischman, Cyrille, *Riverains rêveurs du métro Bastille* (Le Dilettante, 2007)

Follain, Jean, *Paris* (Phébus, 1935/2006)

Funck-Brentano, Frantz, *Légendes et archives de la Bastille* (Hachette, 1904)

Funck-Brentano, Frantz, *Bastille et Faubourg Saint-Antoine* (Hachette, 1925)

Gautrand, Jean-Claude (ed.), *A la Bastille!* (PICTO, 1998)

Girard, Roger, *Quand les Auvergnats partaient conquérir Paris* (Fayard, 1979)

Gould, Roger V., *Insurgent Identities: Class, Community and Protest in Paris from 1848 to the Commune* (University of Chicago Press, Chicago/London, 1995)

Halévy, Daniel, *Pays parisiens* (Grasset, 1932)

Hamelin, France, *Femmes dans la nuit: 1939–1944* (Renaudot et Cie, 1988)

Hamon, Hervé, and Patrick Rotman, *Génération 2: les années de poudre* (Seuil, 1987)

Harvey, David, *Consciousness and the Urban Experience: Studies in the History and Theory of Capitalist Urbanization* (Johns Hopkins, Baltimore, 1985)

Haussmann, Georges-Eugène, *Mémoires du Baron Haussmann* (Victor-Havard, 1890)

Hazan, Éric, *L'Invention de Paris: il n'y pas de pas perdus* (Seuil, 2002)

Higonnet, Patrice, *Paris capitale du monde* (Tallandier, 2005)

Holmes, Diana, and Carrie Tarr (eds), *A 'Belle Époque'?: Women in French Society and Culture, 1890–1914* (Berghahn, New York/Oxford, 2006)

Hugo, Victor, *Les Misérables* (Garnier-Flammarion, 1862/1967)

Hugo, Victor, *Histoire d'un crime* (Éditeurs Français Réunis, 1877–78/1958)

Hussey, Andrew, *Paris; The Secret History* (Bloomsbury, London, 2006)

Jones, Colin, *Paris: Biography of a City* (Penguin, London, 2004/2006)

Jourda, Frédérique, *A l'Opéra aujourd'hui: de Garnier à la Bastille* (Hachette, 2004)

Journo, Nathalie, 'C'est madame Renée qui a perdu son chat,' *Libération*, 6 April 1996

Kalifa, Dominique, *Les Crimes de Paris: lieux et non-lieux du crime à Paris au XIXe siècle* (BILIPO, 2001)

Kalifa, Dominique, *Crime et culture au XIXe siècle* (Perrin, 2005)

Lageat, Robert, *Des Halles au Balajo* (Les Éditions de Paris, 1993)

Langlois, Gilles-Antoine (ed.), *Le Douzième arrondissement: traditions et actualités* (Action artistique de la ville de Paris, 1996)

Lanoux, Armand, *Paris en forme de coeur; physiologie de Paris* (Fayard, 1954)

Lariche, Lucien, *Les Jetons de bal, 1830–1940* (ACJM, Neuilly-sur-Seine, 2006)

Leahy, Sarah, *Casque d'or* (I.B. Tauris, London/New York, 2007)

Lecocq, Georges, *La Prise de la Bastille et ses anniversaires d'après des documents inédits* (Craravray Frères, 1881)

Lemarque, Francis, *J'ai la mémoire qui chante* (Presses de la Cité, 1992)

Lepidis, Clément, *Les Bals à Jo* (Le Sémaphore, 1998)

de Linguet, Simon-Nicholas Henri, *Mémoires sur la Bastille, et sur la détention de Monsieur Linguet, écrits par lui-même* (Spilsbury, London, 1783)

Lissagaray, Prosper-Olivier, *Histoire de la Commune de 1871* (La Découverte, 1876/1996)

Looseley, David, *The Politics of Fun: Cultural Policy and Debate in Contemporary France* (Berg, Oxford/New York, 1995)

Lurine, Louis (ed.), *Les Rues de Paris* (Slatkine, Geneva/Paris, 1844/1982)

Madelin, Louis, *La Révolution* (Jules Taillandier, 1911/1979)

Malet, Léo, *Casse-pipe à la Nation*, in *Les Nouveaux Mystères de Paris* (Robert Laffont, 1957/2006)

Marchand, Bernard, *Paris, histoire d'une ville: XIXe–XXe siècle* (Points, 1993)

Maréchal, Sebastien, *Le 12e arrondissement: itinéraires d'histoire et d'architecture* (Action Artistique de la Ville de Paris, 2000)

Marx, Karl, *The Eighteenth Brumaire of Louis Bonaparte*. (Available online at http://www.marxists.org/archive/marx/works/1852/18th-brumaire/ch01.htm, accessed 12 March 2010.)

Masters-Wicks, Karen, *Victor Hugo's 'Les Misérables' and The Novels of the Grotesque* (Peter Lang, New York, 1994)

Maury, Alain, and Thierry Robberecht, *Beluga 1: Du rififi à la Bastille* (Casterman, 2001)

Mazdon, Lucy (ed.), *France on Film: reflections on popular French cinema* (Wallflower Press, London, 2001)

Mercier, Louis-Sébastien, 'Le Tableau de Paris', in *Paris le jour, Paris la nuit* (Robert Laffont/Bouquins, 1788/1990)

Michel, Denis, and Dominique Renou, *Le Guide du promeneur: 11e arrondissement* (Parigramme, 1993)

Michelet, Jules, *Journal* (Gallimard, 1828–1960/1959)

Michelet, Jules, *Histoire de la Révolution française* (Éditions Saint-Clair, 1967)

Minnaert, Jean-Baptiste (ed.), *Le Faubourg Saint-Antoine: architecture et métiers d'art* (Action artistique de la ville de Paris, 1998)

Monnier, Raymond, *Le Faubourg Saint-Antoine (1789–1815)* (Société des Études Robespierristes, 1981)

Mouraux, Lionel, *Je me souviens du 11e arroidnssement* (Pargiramme, 1998)

Nora, Pierre (ed.), *Les Lieux de mémoire* (Gallimard, 1997)

de Neuville, Jules, *Encore un livre rose: Rigolboch's question* (Les Libraires, 1860)

Parein, Pierre-Mathieu, *La Prise de la Bastille* (Girardin, 1791)

Péguri, Louis, *Du bouge au conservatoire* (1950): quoted at http://mondomix.com/blogs/accordeon.php/2009/06/07/la-photo-du-lundi-le-beau-bal-de-bouscat (accessed 14 May 2010)

Piazzo, Philippe, interview in *Télérama*, no 2412, 3 April 1996

Picard, André, and Francis Carco, *Mon homme* (Ferenczi, 1921)

Pinçon, Michel, and Monique Pinçon-Charlot, *Paris mosaïque* (Calmann-Lévy, 2001)

Pinçon, Michel, and Monique Pinçon-Charlot, *Sociologie de Paris* (La Découverte, 2004)

Pinçonnat, Crystel, and Chantal Liaroutzos, *Paris, cartographies littéraires* (Le Manuscrit, 2007)

Poëte, Marcel, *Paris: une vie de cité* (Picard, 1925)

Poujol, Geneviève, *L'Éducation populaire, histoires et pouvoirs* (Éditions Ouvrières, 1981)

Powrie, Phil (ed.), *French Cinema in the 1990s: Continuity and Difference* (Oxford University Press, Oxford/New York, 1999)

Prendergast, Christopher, *Paris in the Nineteenth Century* (Blackwell, Oxford, UK/Cambridge, MA, 1992)

Prendergast, Christopher, *For the People by the People. Eugène Sue's Les Mystères de Paris: A Hypothesis in the Sociology of Literature* (Legenda, Oxford, 2003)

Quétel, Claude, *La Bastille: histoire vraie d'une prison légendaire* (Robert Laffont, 1989)

Raynal, François, *Faubourg* (Dumas, 1950)

Reader, Keith A., *The May 1968 Events in France* (Macmillan/St Martin's Press, London/ New York, 1993)

Réda, Jacques, *Les Ruines de Paris* (Gallimard, 1993)

Rémy, Pierre-Jean, *Bastille: Rêver un Opéra* (Plon, 1989)

Revenin, Régis, *Homosexualité et prostitution masculines à Paris, 1870–1918* (L'Harmattan, 2005)

Révillon, Tony, *Le Faubourg Saint-Antoine* (J. Rouff, 1881)

Rey-Dussueil, Antoine-François-Marius, *Le Faubourg Saint-Merri* (Ambroise Dupont, 1832)

Rifkin, Adrian, *Street Noises: Parisian Pleasure, 1900–1940* (Manchester University Press, Manchester/New York, 1993)

Robb, Graham, *Victor Hugo: A Biography* (W.W. Norton, New York, 1997)

Robert, Jean-Louis, and Danièle Tartakowsky, *Paris le peuple: XVIIIe–XXe siècle* (Publications de la Sorbonne, 1999)

Rolland, Romain, *Le 14 Juillet: action populaire* (Cahiers de la Quinzaine, 1902)

Romains, Jules (ed.), *Le Peuple de Paris* (Perrin, 1951)

Romains, Jules, *Françoise* (Flammarion, 1958)

de Rudder, Véronique, with Michelle Guillon, *Autochtones et immigrés en quartier populaire: du marché d'Aligre à l'Îlot Chalon* (L'Harmattan,1987)

Said, Edward, *Orientalism* (Penguin, London, 1978/2003)

de Saint-Pulgent, Maryvonne, *Le Syndrome de l'Opéra* (Robert Laffont, 1991)

Salachas, Gilbert, *Le Paris d'Hollywood: sur un air de réalité* (Caisse nationale des monuments historiques et des sites, 1994)

Sanson, Rosamonde, *Les 14 Juillet (1789–1975): fête et conscience nationale* (Flammarion, 1976)

Sansonetti, Paul-Georges, 'La Prise de la Bastille' unpublished thesis, École du Louvre, n.d.)

Seebacher, Jacques, *Victor Hugo ou le calcul des profondeurs* (PUF, 1993)

Shaya, Gregory, 'The Flaneur, the Badaud, and the Making of a Mass Public in France, circa 1860–1910,' in *The American Historical Review* 109.1 (2004). (Available online at <http://www.historycooperative.org/journals/ahr/109.1/shaya.html, (accessed 17 February 2010.)

Sheringham, Michael, *Everyday Life: Theories and Practices from Surrealism to the Present* (Oxford University Press, Oxford, 2006)

Sous les pavés, la Bastille: archéologie d'un mythe révolutionnaire (Caisse nationale des monuments et des sites, 1989)

Stern, Daniel, *Histoire de la Révolution française* (Balland, 1850–53/1985)

Stierle, Karlheinz, *La Capitale des signes: Paris et son discours* (Maison des sciences de l'homme, 2001)

Tersen, Émile, 'Le Paris des *Misérables*,' in special issue of *Europe* on *Les Misérables*, February–March 1962

Texier, Edmond, *Tableau de Paris* (Chevalier, 1852)

Thillay, Alain, *Le Faubourg-Saint-Antoine et ses « faux ouvriers » : la liberté du travail à Paris aux XVIIe et XVIIIe siècles* (Champ Vallon, 2002)

Tillinac, Denis, *Je me souviens de Paris* (Flammarion, 1998)

Valdour, Jacques, *Le Faubourg* (Éditions Spes, 1925)

Vallès, Jules, *L'Insurgé* (GF-Flammarion, 1886/1970)

Vallès, Jules, *Le Tableau de Paris* (Éditeurs Français Réunis, 1882–83/1971)

Vilar, Jean-François, *Bastille Tango* (Actes Sud, Arles, 1986/1998)

Vilar, Jean-François, *La Grande Ronde du Père Duchesne* (Épigramme, 1989)

Vovelle, Michel (ed.), *Paris et la Révolution* (Sorbonne, 1989)

Webber, Andrew, *Berlin in the Twentieth Century: A Cultural Topography* (Cambridge University Press, Cambridge, 2008)

White, Edmund, *The Flâneur* (Bloomsbury, London, 2001)

Websites

http://cgttefsas.wordpress.com/2010/06/06/greve-des-travailleurs-sans-papiers-a-lopera-bastille-le-piquet-des-piquets-tient-toujours/ (accessed 6 August 2010)

http://forum.muzika.fr/read.php?1,657615,722958,quote=1 (accessed 10 July 2010)

http://fr.wikipedia.org/wiki/Prix_du_roman_populiste#cite_note-0 (accessed 22 May 2010)

http://www.histoire-image.org/site/etude_comp/etude_comp_detail. php?i=71&d=31&c=propagande (accessed 22 March 2010)

http://mondomix.com/blogs/accordeon.php/2010/03/22/a-la-decouverte-des-bals-musette-de-pari (accessed 10 July 2010)

http://mondomix.com/blogs/accordeon.php/2010/03/22/a-la-decouverte-des-bals-musette-de-pari (accessed 10 July 2010)

http://paroles.abazada.com/chanson,rue-de-lappe,21419.htm (accessed 9 June 2010)

http://philippepoisson-hotmail.com.over-blog.com/ext/http:// prisons-cherche-midi-mauzac.com/des-prisons/lexode-de-36-detenues-de-la-petite-roquette-transferees-a-libourne-en-juin-1940-1438 (accessed 25 July 2010)

http://swingjo.apinc.org/articles.php?id=29 (accessed 23 July 2010)

http://www.ina.fr/economie-et-societe/justice-et-faits-divers/video/CPF07006187/ marguerite-duras-a-la-petite-roquette.fr.html (accessed 5 July 2010)

http://www.lefigaro.fr/sortir-paris/2010/06/01/03013-20100601ARTFIG00577-quartier-libre-a-aligre.php (accessed 4 October 2010)

http://www.lexpress.fr/informations/opera-bastille-vous-avez-dit-populaire_642368. html (accessed 6 August 2010)

http://www.lyricspond.com/artist-edith-piaf/lyrics-de-lautre-cote-de-la-rue (accessed 10 June 2010)

http://www.lyricstime.com/alex-beaupain-la-bastille-lyrics.html (accessed 3 September 2010)

http://www.mp3lyrics.org/j/jacques-brel/la-bastille/ (accessed 3 September 2010)

http://www.parisbalades.com/Cadres/cadres11bastille.htm (accessed 9 August 2010)

http://www.trussel.com/maig (accessed 13 July 2010)

Index